HOUSE
IN
DAMASCUS

Before the Fall

Brian Stoddart

BISAC: BIO019000 Biography & Autobiography /Educators, TRV015000 Travel/Middle East/General

Cover and Book design by eBook Prep www.ebookprep.com

December, 2015
ISBN: 978-1-61417-585-8

ePublishing Works!
www.epublishingworks.com

DEDICATION

For My Friends In Damascus:
May You Prevail.

TABLE OF CONTENTS

6 *Brian Stoddart*

PREFACE

While there were some issues along the way and later, I am extremely grateful to the companies that commissioned me to work in Damascus and Syria, and so finally gave me the excuse to be somewhere I had always wanted to be. The European Union's aid and development arm provided the funding for the project that, sadly, was suspended at the onset of the 2011 troubles. Those organisations, then, very kindly made it possible for me to *live* in Damascus which, as always, is significantly different from *visiting*.

My project colleagues, local and international, may or may not recognise some of this. I learned much from them directly and indirectly and, unknowingly, they were wonderful sounding boards as I went about Damascus in search of understanding, ideas, inspiration and insight. Given what has transpired in the past year or so I am not naming them here, most especially not those Syrian colleagues who were all fabulous to work for, and whose loyalty to Syria deserves far more than they have received recently. They will all know who they are, and I hope they will know also just how much I am in their debt.

I am very grateful, too, to Joshua Landis and Matthew Gray, wonderful Syrian specialists who supported and indulged the enthusiasm of a curious newcomer to their field. Joshua generously posted to his excellent *Syria Comment* website anything I wrote on Syria through my blogsite, or through other website outlets like *The Conversation.* It has been enriching to exchange thoughts and ideas with people like Joshua and Matthew. Their on-going work reaffirms just how important it is that we continue to support and fund adequately all those universities around the world whose staff, at crucial moments, provide us with the deeper insight we so desperately need.

This venture into the new world of e-publishing has been facilitated by Nina Paules and her great team at ebookprep.com. Their production and design skills have turned an idea into an attractive reality for which I am extremely grateful. Numerous friends and acquaintances helped keep me going when it all seemed too hard, so thanks to them as well. Lynne McDonald, a friend from schooldays, kindly proofread an earlier version, as did an again unnamed friend in Damascus—any mistakes that remain are mine alone.

As always I owe the greatest thanks to my family who forever put up with me going off to do exotic things, and who have to rely on a usually unreliable Skype connection, text or email to keep up with what I am doing. Sandi was able to spend time with me in the House in Damascus, and came very quickly to love the place and the city as much as I did and still do. For the most part, though, she held everything together back home while I lived this latest dream. I can never thank her enough for allowing me all my adventures while she sacrifices many of her own interests. Our daughters Kirsten and Laura, film producer/writer and international relations specialist respectively, themselves global citizens and travellers, were also great supporters of what became one of the best experiences I have had anywhere in the world.

For that very reason and memory, it has been both difficult and sad to complete this book against the backdrop of the unfolding Syrian horrors of 2011 into 2012. Those events themselves have been bad enough, but made all the worse because of the personal connections I have back in Damascus and Syria. My colleagues, friends and acquaintances have gone through hell, and it has been hard to sit by and just watch, think and write. May they all survive, and know that at least one foreigner come to Damascus had them in his thoughts throughout.

PRELUDE

Even before the present troubles began in Syria early in 2011, Damascus was regarded generally as a fabled city now tainted by allegations of links to terrorism. Despite that, it remained and still remains one of the world's great destinations. Perhaps the longest inhabited capital anywhere, and still strategically significant if now for political as opposed to the commercial reasons of earlier times, "Old Damascus" still retains a romantic ring. Following Edward Said's most famous work, some might say much of the attraction for outsiders is "Orientalist" in sway and, therefore, irrelevant.[1] There might be something to that, but it would be wrong to accept such a reading as the whole version. Damascus

---

[1]Edward Said, *Orientalism* (Harmondsworth, Penguin, 1978)

has welcomed and accepted people now for two
millennia and, during that time, some have come to
conquer and be tolerated rather than welcomed.

In the modern world Damascus maintains an allure,
especially for those in the West. By definition, much
of that comes from its place in the Christian history
that preceded its significance as a major intellectual
influence on the Muslim world. After all, it was on the
way here that Saul is said to have had his personal
epiphany to become Paul and eventually St Paul.
Once in the city, he had to escape pursuers wanting to
rid themselves of a Christian nuisance, and there is
still a symbolic basket at Bab Kissan where he was
allegedly lowered over the wall. Almost two thousand
years later, a generation in the British world saw
either themselves or their family or friends in and
around Damascus and Arabia as soldiers in two world
wars, first against the Turks then, later, against the
Germans but with the complication of the Vichy
French. In between those odd polarities the world
interacted with Damascus, Syria and its region in
trade, diplomacy, politics and religious war.

Yet nowadays Syria remains an enigma, especially so
after the events of 2011 that still continue. Under-
reported and poorly reported, the country's reputation
rather than its reality shaped perceptions everywhere.
The complexities of its place in the Arab and Islamic
world, its nuanced relationships with Iran and
Lebanon, its intransigence on Israel, and the nature of
its government under the al-Assad father and son
succession at the head of the Baath Party, all
combined to blur the picture of what Syria was really
like.

For that reason, anyone venturing to Damascus and
Syria on the eve of the troubles encountered a host of

questions and expressions of concern. "Will you be safe?" was a too-common query from those whose knowledge came from a media fixated by anything that might be or potentially labelled or carry potential to as terrorism. In the general mind, there was little if any distinction between either the different segments of the Arab world or of the broader Islamic one. The great tragedy of the past twenty years is the approximation of Islam with what has too easily and readily been identified as "fundamentalism". The easy elision, consequently, is to see the whole of the former Arabia as a hotbed of pernicious paranoia leading to unprincipled attacks on a non-offensive West. Samuel Huntington's *Clash of Civilizations* will come to be seen as having had a very large hand in that, but he was not alone.[2]

Granted, a first time visitor to Damascus or elsewhere in the region could find it affronting when young boys run about neighbourhoods armed with replica pistols and AK-47s, reflecting in some ways the media images that led to all the disillusions in the first place. Granted, Syria plays an obvious and aggressive role against Israel within the Arab coalition. Granted, Syria's opposition to the allied invasion of Iraq and subsequent siding with Ahmajinedad's Shia-dominated Iran did not help improve its reputation.

Despite all that, anyone with a sense of history should welcome an opportunity to spend time in and learn about Damascus and Syria, especially if living there and working with a major government department as well as the university sector, trying to build future capacity. For a trained historian, that chance was also

---

[2]Samuel P. Huntington, *The Clash of Civilizations and the Remaking of World Order* (New York, Simon & Schuster, 1996)

daunting, because the trade builds respect for accumulating detailed knowledge of a place and people over a long period. It doubts, even derides observations not based on masses of factual evidence, dismissing the idea that an intelligent observer might have useful and interesting things to say about such an experience.

Perhaps, then, it was an historian who reckoned that anyone visiting a new place and culture should write a book about it either within twenty four hours or after twenty four years, because everything in between lacked value. This book ignores that dictum and draws on the historical training, but ignores many of its rules in order to produce a sense of a place that deserves to be far better understood and, indeed, needs to be far better understood. It proceeds from a love of Damascus and its people, and of Syria, and is written from a perspective of sadness over what has happened in such a very short time.

Perhaps, in some ways, it is a memoir of a Damascus that may well take some time to reappear if, indeed, it ever does. If so, it will also be a memoir for what might have been.

BOUTIQUE DAYS

A couple of weeks let alone months or even years later, the first days in a new place, especially a "foreign" one, seem far off. The elapse of time can eradicate memories of three days survived without bags in the middle of a major Muslim festival because no-one was looking for them. More significantly, what initially seems a remote and bewildering maze later takes on ordered familiarity. It is important all the more, then, to remember those early points, because they mark the beginning of growth and learning.

During the thirty minute drive into Damascus from its airport, it is hard to imagine what the city might look like. It will not reflect those mid-nineteenth century W.H. Bartlett prints, obviously, and there is not a camel in sight. Yet all the guidebooks still refer to Damascus essentially as a magical place. To reach that magic now, you must cross flat, dry, whitish plains with little greenery or sign of life apart from people on building sites. This is not the view marvelled at by all the old time travellers, the one from the passes coming through from Beirut. Plastic bags bowl across the landscape, driven by the strong, hot winds of the dry season. The freeway eventually reaches the outskirts of the city and Mount Qassioun rears up in the background, suburbs now half way up its slopes.

At this point Damascus resembles many other cities in the region, strewn over now subjugated hills that host cement blocked apartment buildings sprouting forests of television and radio antennae. The outskirts are dusty, rubbishy, undistinguished. Sporadic stalls and markets appear in spaces and along streets, carrying everything from vegetables to toys. The elaborate freeway system funnels towards the centre, and tailored parks appear along with more substantial buildings and grander houses. Mosques stand out, but so do churches. Traffic thickens and the usual global brands appear: Toyota, Mazda, Citroen, BMW, Mercedes. Motor cycles are rare, a shock for anyone used to being in Asia. Bicycles are an endangered species. There are pedestrians, but not in that sense: they are more like free range people who just happen to be crossing roads. In short, there is little about Damascus that is different from most other places in the world, apart from the expectation.

Depending on the approach, coming into the Old City may or not be a surprise. The driver pulled up at the bottom of a one-way street that later revealed itself as Al Amin, which separates the Southern Muslim and

Jewish Quarters and retains a strong Shia character. There was no gate or wall, and the area was surrounded by multi-storied apartment blocks fronted by fruit and vegetable stalls. But we were in the Old City, the driver said. A young man arrived with a two wheeled trolley in vain expectation of bags to carry, unaware of the non-services rendered by the airline that day. He took what there was, and led off up Al Amin.

The area was closed for the holidays, but kids were playing with toy guns, people were talking and surveying new passersby. After one hundred and fifty metres, the trolley boy swung left into what looked like a laneway to nowhere crammed with broken stuff. He swung right then left again, into an apparently dead-end alleyway. On one side, an open area hosted the remains of a collapsed house. Next to it stood another, looking like it would soon follow suit. At the end of the lane, the upper levels of buildings leaned in towards each other, almost touching. We were almost in a tunnel without windows. He stopped, reached up a wall, rang an unnoticed bell. What was this?

The brown wooden door in a lime washed lemon-coloured wall opened—into a serene, picturesque, elegant space with a fountain in the middle surrounded by wooden tables bearing plates of fruit and a breakfast out of *Gourmet Traveller*: olives, flat bread, *hommus,* yoghurt, several different cheeses that obviously included *haloumi,* pastries, and several other things yet to be identified. And there was the smell of coffee.

For once, the booking engine-identified boutique hotel outmatched its online promise. As it would turn out, most such establishments did in Damascus. This one had a small number of mostly small rooms apart from the one to which I was directed, up in the top corner looking out onto a little patio. Its interior was entirely Damascene with painted poles supporting the roof, with the cupboards and furniture done in similarly distinctive style. The stairs were steep, the absent bags an unexpected blessing.

Then the only hotel like it in the immediate area, but with several others planned, this gem was fashioned out of a house at least four hundred years old. The essential bones of its Arab design were maintained, giving the place a character not found in homogenised Hyatts and subjugated Sheratons. Among the guests were some Australian refugees in from Dubai looking for holiday freedom, a family from France, a small group of Scandinavians, and a Kuwaiti couple, all drawn to Damascus for different reasons. This hotel also had an interesting precedent, too.

In the first edition of Murray's *Handbook* to the region, published in 1858, travellers were advised of two hotels now available to them. The Hotel de Palmyre was on Straight Street, but reportedly "neither clean nor comfortable", and an owner with a reputation for "Arab tricks." The other was the Locanda Malluk. Originally one of the first fine houses in Damascus, it was now refurbished in the best Damascene architectural style. The Melluk family were also among the leading silk merchants in the city. It was clear where the author thought travellers should stay.[3]

Three days now stretched out ahead before the office opened, and this present hotel in the Melluk tradition had no map. Directions were simple. Out the door,

---

[3]*A Handbook for Travellers in Syria and Palestine* (London, Murray, 1858), pp. 468-9

turn left, and immediately hit a T junction. Turn right, and pass a lovely little local mosque with a delicate turret before hitting another T. You are in the southern section. Turn left—and come to another left, a right incline up a sloping alley, or a hard right, and there will be Straight Street. These lanes were tight, the walls anonymous, shafts of bright early autumn sun warming sections of the street and throwing shadows from the tiny Damascene "balconies" that appeared in all the books. There was almost nothing open, apart from a tiny hole in the wall that dispensed nothing but bags of chips, and there were few people about.

Thus began three days of wanderings that led all over the Old City, blurring direction as well as time and sense. Al Hamidiyeh was as towering a *souk* as promised and some of its outlets were open to catch the tourists, especially those in search of towels or stuffed eagles. The outside walls of the Umayyad Mosque were as impressive as promised. The alleyways went in all directions. "Lost in the Jewish Quarter" sounds more like the title of an oil painting by a minor later-nineteenth century British painter than a state of being. A coffee shop had men outside nursing the smallest cups imaginable, and negotiating the overwhelming *nargileh* from which emanated massive clouds of sweet smoke. Promising streets narrowed to blank walls. Inconspicuous alleys led to major walkways. Here and there an open door revealed a massive interior courtyard. Rows and rows of shuttered doors hinted at the size and scope of interconnected *souks*. A profusion of black-garbed women (in 1883 an acerbic Mrs Mackintosh described them as "very substantial ghosts") were entering a modern mosque that looked Iranian from its markings,

so must the Sayyida Ruqayya in the Shia Quarter.[4]
The mosque is named after the daughter of Hussein,
son of the first Shia *imam* and one of the great Shia
martyrs. (In mid-May 2012 came reports that the
mosque's *imam* had been assassinated as the Syrian
unrest took on distinctly sectarian tones). An
inadvertent venture outside the wall led eventually
back into the Old City, at Bab Touma in the Christian
Quarter with its profusion of churches. That led down
to the bottom of Straight Street at Bab Sharqi, from
where a walk back up Straight Street led to the
covered *Souk* Medhat Pasha (*Pasha* is the Turkish
rather than Arabic spelling, but is used commonly to
identify the *souk*).

Almost two hundred years earlier, another traveller
expressed disappointment as he turned off Straight
Street into yet another lane:

A narrow street lined with houses built of unburnt
brick on each hand, and we were so much
disappointed by their mean, and even ruinous
appearance, that we began to suspect that travellers, in
calling this a terrestrial paradise, really meant to pun
on the material of which it is built.[5]

All this time later, it was hard to see why because this
really was magical, a walk with history ending each
day in a house with a past now masquerading as a
hotel. Regrettably, though, the holiday combined with
high season meant a limited booking, but that
prompted relocation to an even more marvellous
boutique hotel over in the Christian Quarter, an early

---

[4]Mrs Mackintosh, *Damascus and its People: Sketches of Modern Life in Syria* (London, Seeley Jackson Halliday, 1883), p.6

[5]Robert Richardson, *Travels Along the Mediterranean* (London, Cadell Blackwood, 1822), p. 461

lesson in how a very small distance could mark a very large cultural shift.

By the time that holiday period ended, I had walked most inches of the Old City in this strangely deserted mode that, in some ways, provided the best possible introduction. Gawking at roofs was possible, so was walking up the tiniest of alleyways to see where they went. The geography began falling into place (apart from the Jewish Quarter that would take a bit longer). Landmarks began appearing. The calls from the different mosques began distinguishing themselves one from another. People now appeared to come from very different places and groups. The "knowledge" began, about where best to find taxis, a SIM card, basic supplies, bakeries, restaurants, the tourist traps to avoid (but only after falling in a couple of times), where might constitute off-the-beaten track, when best to go to the Mosque, where to buy a shirt in Bab Touma on a public holiday.

The overriding sensation about the Old City was the depth of its history and who might have passed by this very spot previously at, for example, the remains of the Roman temple wall just along from the *souk* on the way to the ATM in Hariqa. Who else had walked around the back of the mosque on the way through the Shia section? Who else had visited the *khans* built around the twelfth and thirteenth centuries to serve the caravans along their trade routes? Looking out from the roof terrace of the Al Khawali restaurant, it was easy to recall to that some of the most famous figures of earlier times had lingered beneath the domes of the nearby Khan Ahmed Pasha. This was, indeed, a magical place, and would become more so.

NOT A PALACE

The agent described the first place as a "palace". It was tucked up a side street near the Shia Quarter, the enticing suggestion being that a neighbour was one of the Jumblatt political bosses from Lebanon who had spent a fortune restoring his house to original condition. That seemed unlikely. Walid Jumblatt, although married to the daughter of a former Syrian Defence Minister, was by now reckoned an opponent of Bashar al-Assad. The veracity of the claim was impossible to confirm by visual sighting, because by definition Damascene houses, like all Arabic ones, turn in rather than out. A door in a wall opens into an open courtyard around which the house is built, usually on two or three levels. In the middle of the courtyard larger houses will have a fountain, but smaller places frequently do not.

The "palace" proved less than that. It had a nice courtyard with a bright fountain, but was a poor house: a couple of sitting rooms downstairs, a tiny kitchen, dim light. Up off a landing was the bathroom, again tiny, and on the final level two bedrooms renovated in uninspiring fashion. It was a quick fix to hit the market—at a price. The owner was asking SYP 125,000, about $2,800 per month at that stage, so almost $100 per day. Given that a boutique hotel would match that rate long term, it was no deal. Moreover, it prompted unsettling concerns about what other properties might be like, and just how much this enterprise was really going to cost.

Next morning's offering was even better, said the agent—presumably a grand palace—but at lower price. A much lower price. It was near the agent's own house off Quemariye, the main walking and car route from Bab Touma to the Umayyad Mosque, and really in the middle of the Old City. The location was good. So was the door in the anonymous wall. The courtyard was big but the fountain gone. Maybe that was why the price was lower. This house was renovated, too, but botched. A gloomy sitting room adjoined an even gloomier tiny kitchen. A sitting room had an unpainted, thin plywood sliding door shoved across it to make a second bedroom. Upstairs lay a bathroom and another bedroom that was alright, but just. This was SYP 75,000 a month so better, but no bargain.

The hotel checkout date was looming now, and the pressure to find somewhere growing in an unknown city. Being in the Old City was mandatory, why come to Damascus otherwise? The diplomatic and upmarket suburbs of Abou Roumaneh and Shaalan were all very well and closer to the office, but hardly unique. This was the oldest inhabited city in the world, so why be anywhere other than the Old City? The guidebooks and websites all claimed that finding apartments and houses was simple, almost a matter of simply standing on a corner and announcing your need. Announce it and they will come. It was not working like that, however, and time was pressing.

The hotel manager had feelers out, too, so the next inspection was of a set of rooms overlooking Straight Street in the Christian Quarter. The anonymous door off the street led down into a huge courtyard with a substantial fountain. Up on a landing were the three bedrooms, a bathroom, and a kitchen-sitting area that looked down into the courtyard and ran across the front of all three bedrooms. Normally it was leased to three female foreigners at a time, Arabic language students come to Damascus. There were hundreds of these then in the city at any given time. However, the woman head of the house was persuaded that the professor from Australia was old and harmless— thanks for that—so set aside her normal policy, reasoning that one person producing the same amount of income as three was a better and more cost effective deal for her. That would be $1,000 a month, all laundry included.

It was a nice place, they were nice people, and it was tempting. If Damascus is the oldest inhabited city then, surely, Straight Street must be one of the oldest inhabited streets. Via Recta was laid in Roman times and effectively runs through the middle of the entire Old City. It starts at *Souk* Medhat Pasha, some of which is under cover and, through the day, closed to traffic. The road then heads towards the Roman Arch that now marks the divide between the Muslim and Christian Quarters. Through here nut sellers mix with watchmakers, key cutters, carpet shops and the all-encompassing "Orientals" providers whose goods range from antiques to Bashar al-Assad key rings. From there the street becomes Bab Sharqi, for the gate of the same name that leaves the Old City at its other end. Some higher quality artisans have shops along here and in nearby feeder streets.

The rooms were just into the Christian Quarter, but not quite right. While there is a lot of genuine Damascus along Straight Street it is really a tourist haunt, and frequently there were far more foreigners than locals present. Ironically enough, most of the foreign language students reside in the Christian Quarter, and Straight Street especially has become almost neutralised. Was there any point in coming to the Old City then escaping from it? There were practicalities to consider, too. At night and especially at the weekends—Thursday night to Saturday night in the Arab world—Straight Street was also "car display" street for people heading to the restaurants and bars, because the Christian Quarter has the most alcohol outlets in Damascus. That meant noise, and the rooms literally hung over Straight Street. Reluctantly, it was a "no".

By now there was one choice left, and one day left to decide. The agent set out from his shop, near where Quemariye takes a small shimmy down towards the back of the Mosque, and set off up the gentle slope heading towards Straight Street. He turned right into a narrower lane down past Jabri House, the most famous of Old City restaurants. On the left were some antique shops. By now heading towards the *souk*, he turned sharply into a very narrow laneway with steps leading up, the walls of the houses on either side leaning towards each other. It was unquestionably exotic, confirmed weeks later by a European couple taking photographs of "mysterious laneways in Old Damascus" up the steps towards the house. Stopping at an innocuous and weather-beaten door, the agent discovered he had the wrong key. We were opposite a small landing space with a bicycle left over from the 1920s that stood under a window covered with cardboard. A few minutes later his brother arrived with the right key, the door opened.

Immediately inside the door, on the left of a dark alley roofed by the second level of the house, was a toilet, an Arabic toilet, a squattie in traveller language. This was the only house I had ever seen where the toilet was the first feature encountered inside the front door. A couple of further steps up on the left came a disused wash-house, and what looked like a broom cupboard containing a washing machine obviously used last in the previous millennium. That broom cupboard looked onto a small, tiled courtyard with one corner covered in pot plants. No fountain. Above the courtyard the sky was clear blue, the early autumn sun shining warmly. The kitchen, apparently unused for some time, stood opposite the alley and contained a gas stove with attached cylinder, a fridge stood up on blocks, cupboards stuffed with enormous jars of olives in brine, and several layers of dust. Two other rooms were on this level. One was in an L shape, formed from two previously separate rooms. This was a big sitting room with a bed at one end, and two doors at each end accessing the courtyard. The other was a second sitting room done in Muslim style with framed quotations from the Quran on the walls, some sitting cushions on the floor, and little else apart from a small side table supporting two vases of dried flowers.

Next to the kitchen, a set of stairs wound upwards in three sections. At the bottom of the second section a handmade but sturdy wooden ladder was propped against the wall to provide access to the clothesline on top of the kitchen roof. At the top, the stairs opened to a big landing. On one side were two bedrooms, on the other a further unused storage room which featured an unplumbed "French" (or western) toilet. Next to that came a large bathroom, for want of a more accurate word.

The place was old, original (meaning not renovated), dusty, and full of the owners stuff. I loved it. It had character. It was a house in Damascus in the best sense of those words. It was truly in the Old City. Just one hundred metres from the Umayyad Mosque and only slightly further to the *Souk* Hamidiyeh complex, it was also just ten minutes walk from the Christian Quarter. There was a deliberation about the squattie, though. It was a long time back to postgraduate days in India and elsewhere in Asia, and some of those memories were unpleasant. The I-phone conversation with Australia, though, determined that this was a small matter in the broader cosmos and would, indeed, be a necessary part of the experience. Besides, the thighs would become stronger and, after all, it was a flush squattie.

So it became the House in Damascus. But only after several ATM trips to acquire the requisite cash because no credit cards or cheques were involved—as a Kiwi colleague at another project place and time was told, "better to have no record!" Predictably, shifting in was eventful. The place was to have been cleared and cleaned, but was not. The owner ended up shoving spare timber from behind the door of one of the upstairs rooms into the nearby storage room, joining the unplumbed toilet. Clothes and belongings were flung into plastic bags but, by agreement, some were crammed into other spaces. Buckets of water were thrown about to disperse the dust of several vacant weeks, and there was much huffing and puffing about whether or not it was acceptable. It was, even if behind a bedroom door there still remained a magnificently rescued old Damascene door. That was very welcome to stay.

The owner and the agent left, and it was now dark. A ladder, not the wooden one, gave access to the roof, a dusty patio featuring the water tank. It was clear, the stars were out, and the backdrop was the slope of Mount Qassioun with the lights of its suburbs and mosques standing out clearly. And squarely in the foreground ran the south wall of the great Umayyad Mosque with the Minaret of Qait Bey at the far end, the Dome of the Eagles in the middle and, closest, the Jesus Minaret, all three lit and glimmering. It seemed touchable. This house came with a presence.

THE JESUS MINARET

Out the door and down to the bottom of the steps, turn left then right while walking about 130 metres, and there is the massive southern wall of the Great Umayyad Mosque, generally ranked number four in the Islamic pantheon behind Mecca, Medina, and the Dome of the Rock. In 708, just a century or so on from the Prophet's work and the taking of Damascus in 636 by the Caliphs, the Christians were persuaded to turn over their church in return for gaining control over other church sites in the Christian quarter, and the transformation began. The work was long and expensive, and there may have been as many as 12,000 workers involved in creating this magnificent mosque out of a church on a site that formerly hosted pagan then Greek and Roman temples. In the walls now may be seen huge

Roman blocks and traces of all the precedent cultures. Despite trials and tribulations and fires, the Umayyad Mosque now essentially is that which emerged in the 7th century, although some of the mosaic work has long disappeared.

It is huge, one hundred and twenty two metres by fifty in the courtyard which is paved with shimmering pink marble that shows up subtly in photographs. The walls under the covered ways are filled with elaborate mosaics, and the roof arches tower what seem like hundreds of feet above. The Dome of the Clocks and the Treasury building are exquisite, the latter perched on four perfect marble pillars, and decorated in the green and gold mosaics that characterise the whole space. All this is dominated by the enormous façade that frames the Dome of the Eagles, focusing attention towards the interior and the site of the *mihrab,* the main prayer spot marking the way towards Mecca.

Along the eastern wall stands the hall that contains the shrine for Hussein, the son of Ali, grandson of the Prophet and great martyr for the Shia. Many Shiites believe his head is buried here, others that it was displayed here by his conquerers to humiliate his followers. It is a tiny area and, in truth, worn from the constant attention it gets daily from the Shia faithful who flock there before moving on to the nearby Ruqayya Mosque.

The Umayyad Mosque prayer hall is a massive, vaulted space well over one hundred metres long and splendidly wide, carpeted and sparsely furnished apart from the formal prayer sites. The Dome itself sails high, decorated in splendid mosaics. The focal points are the *mihrab,* and what is said to be the tomb of John the Baptist. That is in a beautiful domed and latticed tower, marking where his head is supposed to have been brought after his execution in Palestine. Whether that happened or not is a moot point, but everyday people still come to venerate the marble tomb that dates only from the 1890s—the original was replaced after a massive fire swept through the mosque.

In many respects this is just a vast, empty space sprawling behind its high walls and heavy gates. Yet it carries the full gravitas of its thirteen hundred years and seems surprisingly modern. In some sections it is modern, restoration and rebuilding recurring after crises throughout its history. One of its many great secrets is that even on a crowded day, the individual can still find enough seclusion for either prayer and/or contemplation within the throng. And the throng, it should be said, was just like the one that buys indulgences at Sacre Coeur or begrudgingly places coins in the "gift" boxes at places like Winchester or Durham. People were on their cellphones: "I am just at the Umayyad Mosque". Others contorted around those phones to somehow get a photograph of themselves entering the Mosque, standing in front of the *mihrab,* or the *finbar* from whence *imams* dispense wisdom and exhortation. Some visitors slept in a corner, exhausted by it all, undeterred by the whirring of fans and heaters trying to disperse moisture after rainfall or snow has sprung leaks. Kids raced around excitedly. Other people were off in the distance, quietly praying to their God, seeking serenity and guidance. Tour groups of black garbed figures traipsed around after guides holding aloft those signs that aid the directionless.

This is not only the heartbeat of faith for Damascenes and Syrians, but for people from around the Islamic world. Every day, differently and brightly clothed devotees from Africa and Asia appeared, mixing with immaculately dressed *imams* who had brought their people up from the country on a day trip. Many of these groups spent their time outside singing in prayer while waiting for the huge iron main gates to swing back and allow them a great life moment. Non-Muslim tourists walked about in awe, but in winter glad that they thought to wear two pairs of socks in which to walk about, because that marble is cold on shoeless feet, especially after the courtyard has been washed down in the cool chill of dawn.

It is a place to soak up rather than explore because, to the surprise of many, there is not that much to see. Most devotees raced through the "sights", then simply sprawled in the prayer hall pleased to be a close part of one of the great Islamic experiences, refreshed and re-committed from having been there. That is probably what all great spiritual places do: create a space in which revision can occur, reworking the individual faith that goes to make up a far greater collective. There is an unfathomability to it—it looks too simple. It cannot be that simple. Islam, as portrayed in the West, all too often has a hard edge that is impossible to find in a monument like the Umayyad Mosque. Once more there is a gap between image and reality to be explored and explained, not ignored in favour of an easier branding that serves other purposes.

From the main bedroom upstairs in the house, the view out its flyscreen-covered windows behind the lattice shutters was of the Jesus Minaret at the southeast corner of the Mosque. The ladder up to its peak was almost in touching distance so that the *muezzin,* if he ever climbed up there again (he would now only do so to check if the loudspeaker was working), would be clearly visible. Not too far away, in the Shaghour district, there is said to lie the grave of Bilal, the Ethiopian who was the prophet's first *muezzin* in Mecca, but come to Damascus after the leader's death. At night, the Minaret was lit brightly, shining through the bedroom door and window as a constant reminder of just how long the Mosque had been there and, intriguingly, just how long people must have been living on the house site. From the little balcony outside that bedroom, I could see the Dome of the Eagles. A scramble up onto the bathroom roof near the water tank revealed the Minaret of Qait Bey on the south western corner of the Mosque, and through to the Minaret of the Bride in the middle of the northern wall, just down from the tomb of Salah ah-Din (better known in the West as Saladin). This house site has long had a presence with the Mosque and especially, then, with the Jesus Minaret.

The idea of the Jesus Minaret being in the Mosque surprises those who believe Islam and Christianity to be so far apart as to have nothing whatsoever in common. There are, in fact, points of commonality along with the differences. This minaret dates from the 13th century, and was probably built in stages, because it has a classic Umayyad base topped by a distinctly Ottoman upper section. In many ways it captures the syncretic, synthesising nature of the Mosque incorporating those pre-Greek pagan foundations as well as the Greek, Roman other formations that preceded it.

One interesting sidebar reveals a little of this Christian-Muslim paradox. In the mid-nineteenth century, the author of Murray's guide pointed out a particular inscription that readers should inspect in the Umayyad Mosque:

Thy Kingdom, O Christ, is an everlasting Kingdom,and Thy dominion endureth throughout all generations.[6]

The writer reflected on how strange it was to discover that here—was it to be interpreted as a rebuke, or as an encouragement from Islam for closer engagement between the faiths? More the former than the latter, it seems, because this followed:

God grant the time may soon come when it will be an appropriate motto for this noble structure.

The other major nineteenth century guide books picked up on both the inscription and, in different ways, the wishful thinking: the Umayyad Mosque had something of a Christian heritage, so the demise of Islam would return the building to its rightful state. The Reverend W.M. Teape wrote: "the Mahommedan has dealt harshly with the magnificence of the church." He had hope, though, because the cup and leaves etching on the doors, he thought, could mean only the Eucharist.[7]

However, in retrospect, the Murray guide sentiment was not surprising. Although unacknowledged, the author was the Reverend Josias Leslie Porter, resident in Damascus between 1849 and 1859 when he served as a missionary to the Jews on behalf of the Irish Presbyterians.[8] That admixture could scarcely be stranger. Born in 1823, the son of a wealthy Donegal loyalist farmer, Porter trained initially in Glasgow

---

[6]*A Handbook for Travellers in Syria and Palestine,* p. 483

[7]W.M. Teape, *In Tents and on Horseback Through the Holy Land* (Stockton, Harrison, nd), pp. 50-1

[8]W.B.C. Lister, *A Bibliography of Murrays Handbooks for Travellers* (Dereham, Dereham Books, 1993)

before being appointed to a parish in Newcastle. From there he went to the Levant to begin his mission, but also to begin writing what would be a string of books on the region and on religion. He married the daughter of his Church's Moderator whom he later succeeded, before coming President of Queens College in Belfast where he died in 1889.

Writing the guide was lucrative, reflecting the popularity of Syria amongst the well off travelling public. For the first edition Porter was paid the substantial sum of £382/4/0. In 1868 he received a further £101/5/0 for producing the second edition. In 1875 he earned another £210. The book was clearly popular because after Porter's death another religious man, the Reverend Haskett Smith, was commissioned to take it over and he produced the fourth edition. Haskett Smith, however, turned out to be more troublesome writer for Murray.

He was born the son of a London cleric and graduated from Cambridge before taking holy orders. A teacher and a cleric before going to the Levant, he lived for a time on Mount Carmel, then bought land in the Druze country. Like Porter he wrote several books but, unlike his predecessor, Haskett Smith turned that into an industry, embarking on magic lantern lecture tours all over the world, including Australia and New Zealand. Some of his writings were controversial, such as a suggested link between Druze social practices and those of the Masonic orders, of which he was a member. One acid reviewer of his work remarked that "It would not be strange if Mr. Smith has been hoaxed by some astute Oriental."[9] He was

---

[9]See the review in *The Old and New Testament Student,* 12, 3 (March, 1891), p. 188

also a controversialist, some of his suggestions about the history of Jerusalem causing considerable discussion. It seems he became too exciting for Murray, because in 1905 he was quietly replaced on the Palestine and Syria volume by Mary Brodrick.

She was born the daughter of a London solicitor in 1858, and showed great perseverance in becoming one of the first women students of Egyptology at the Sorbonne in Paris, prior to joining the University of London in 1888 where she had a long tenure before her death in 1933. For several years around the turn of the twentieth century she was based in Cairo, working with all the leading names in archaeology while living on one of the great Nile houseboats that became something of a *salon.* There is still a lecture in her name at University College London. She obviously had safer hands than Haskett Smith so far as Murray was concerned, because they gave her charge of the guidebook even though she knew relatively little of Syria.

What seems to have escaped all these august writers, however, was that the Mosque's minders obviously saw value in their visits. Somewhere between 1858 (when the Murray guide appeared) and 1876 (when the Thomas Cook variation was published), this great Islamic centre was opened to foreign tour groups. No more than twenty people could visit at a time, and the price per group was twenty French francs.[10] The authorities were charging the tourists to come and see the slogan at which they could then rail once back outside.

According to the Islamic tradition, the Jesus Minaret

---

[10]*Cook's Tourists' Handbook for Palestine and Syria* (London, Cook, 1876).

marks the spot where Jesus will descend on the Day of Judgment, prepared to fight the anti-Christ. The symbolism of anti-Bashar al-Assad demonstrations staged near the Mosque a few months later had powerful resonance.

A MANAGER FROM
MELBOURNE

He awaited the first morning after I checked into his excellent hotel in Bab Touma. Two years in the making, an old Damascene house was now a boutique hotel visible from the square and accessible up Al Hammam Bakri.

His English was excellent and he was a short, neat, trim bundle of energy.

"You are from Australia? Where abouts?

Melbourne.

"I worked in Fitzroy for six years, in restaurants. I am

an Australian citizen and so are my kids, and I have a sister there and another in Sydney."

People like him had been coming from Syria to Australia for a very long time. In 1891, the census recorded 142 Syrians living in Victoria, while Sydney already had an identified "Syrian Quarter." That was slightly misleading, because for a long time all Lebanese migrants (who began coming to Australia in the 1850s) were identified as Syrians. With the onset of the 1901 White Australia policy the Syrian/Lebanese inflow slowed, but by 1921 there were still over 400 identified Syrians in Victoria, and the figure stuck around that level until the 1960s. A steady growth from then meant that by 2011 there were approximately 7,000 clearly identified Syrians living in Australia, primarily in Melbourne and Sydney. Of the contemporary community about 60% identify as Christian and 33% as Muslim, with a significant number nominating no religious affiliation. Statistically the community shows up strongly in retail and manufacturing occupations but, significantly, underscores the general migrant community and the Australian non-migrant sectors on most significant measures such as educational qualifications and income. Their most obvious presence comes in the form of organisations like the Syrian Orthodox Church with its distinctive buildings, patriarchs and rituals.

Over the years Australia has maintained a fleeting connection with Syria, in two major forms: either as part of regional parliamentary delegations such as the one in 2003 that visited Israel and Lebanon as well as Syria; or more latterly as concern arose about the activities of Hamas and Hezbollah that came to have their headquarters in Syria. That last issue became the subject of constant reference in the Australian Parliament as Department of Foreign Affairs and Attorney-General representatives announced the latest sanctions. In among that came things like representatives from the travel industry protesting the levels of "travel advisories" to places like Damascus where, industry figures suggested, they were as safe and perhaps even safer as they were anywhere—a comment echoed by most travellers to Damascus before the troubles of 2011 began.

My manager friend, then, was part of a long line of Syrians who had developed Australian connections, and I soon met others. Several taxi drivers said they had family members or relatives in Perth, Sydney or Melbourne. The man in the *souk* who sold me sheets and pillows asked from whence I came. He had a sister in Melbourne and a brother in Sydney whom he hoped to visit soon because he missed them. I wonder if he has achieved that yet? While staying at a hotel in a very small village looking up to the ramparts of the mighty Krak Des Chevaliers out past Homs, I went down the street to one of two restaurants. When it came time to order, the young man asked, inevitably, was I Australian?

Well, yes, Australian and a New Zealander.

"Where do you live?"

Near Melbourne.

"I have a sister studying in Melbourne and I am saving money so that I can go and study, too."

He got a good tip.

A TAXI TO WORK

Yellow taxis in various states of disrepair almost swamp Damascus with their numbers. They are everywhere, all the time, and are as likely encountered in an impossibly narrow Old City laneway as outside the wall on the main roads.

They keep the city moving. The microbuses are cheaper for people coming in from the outskirts or even from around the country, but have a fearsome reputation for being overcrowded and driven by daredevils. For SYP 10 you can reach the Old City from the farthest flung new concrete suburbs mushrooming all over the hills. And the newer big buses do a good job of transporting people about the country. But taxis reign supreme in the city proper. They are cheap, too. A ride from Hariqa to, say,

Umawiyeen Square (which is really a traffic circle and one of the major vehicle circuses) might cost SYP 25 on the meter and 50 with a tip, about $US1 at that point. While car ownership was booming, most people still travelled by taxi because it was affordable, and avoided parking dramas.

There were fewer more entertaining moments than watching Citroen, Peugeot and even Chevrolet vintage enthusiasts parking in the Old City, or navigating the corners. Enthusiasm definitely replaced common sense for these people as it does, let's face it, for anyone keen on cars. Many Syrians are no different in this respect, otherwise why would Hummers appear on the streets of Damascus? Given the potential for serious wear and tear, why would anyone here run an Audi Q7, a BMW 740IL, a Mercedes 500 or any similar vehicle? The Landrover Discovery makes some sense in that the driver can see over everything else and it is handy once out of town, which is why many of them have Kingdom of Saudi Arabia plates having swept their owners up through the desert, the modern replacement for the camel.

The taxi, then, was cheap transport and even cheaper entertainment, if sometimes producing more adrenalin flow than normally contemplated.

The first decision was really about what sort of ride was contemplated. If the answer to that question was "calm", then a ready rule of thumb was to look for a taxi that seemed well cared for, shiny, polished and free of scrapes and dents. The driver might be old or young (but always male), but the car was the giveaway. Unless it was brand new out of the showroom, then that car likely had a careful driver.

By definition, the reverse was also true. If "adventure"

was desired, the battered car with dust and tape its covering holes was the answer. The more battered the better, and the jackpot had been hit if the seatbelt in the front did not work, the seat itself rocked uncontrollably, and all its springs had apparently been dropped somewhere near Homs.

The careful driver would almost certainly provide a steady ride to the destination, little or no commentary on the behaviour of fellow road users, and the meter would invariably go on. You would be asked to put on the seatbelt if sitting in the front. Belts were not then mandatory in the backseat, that law was apparently in the offing.

Of all Syria's interesting reforms before the disturbances of 2011-12, the one most foreigners prized was that governing speed on the roads. The Government imposed a strict speed of 110kph on the open road, 80 in other areas and 50 around town. The consequent reduction in the road toll was dramatic in a country where President Bashar al-Assad only came to office because his elder brother Basel died in a car crash. For anyone who had travelled the roads elsewhere through the Arab world, like neighbouring Jordan, this new regime was a blessing. No 180kph races on the highways, no 110 rides around the city, no racing to beat the oncoming car now heading directly at you at 130 kph. A trip to Homs, Lattakia or Aleppo, or even out in the desert was now relatively benign, traffic-wise at least, so that the emphasis was on watching the sights rather than cramping up from clutching the emergency grip too tightly.

That did not mean the taxis were dull, though, especially if "Battered For Adventure" was the vehicle selected. One day, the drive to work came courtesy of a very nice man with a "sensible driver" vehicle. We set off from behind the Hamidiyeh at dignified pace, swung around in front of the Citadel and down past *Souk* Sarouja on the inside lane, back under the flyover and out onto Shukri Al Qwatli. While calmly waiting for the traffic lights to change there, the driver pointed out a traffic policeman renowned across the city, apparently, as "the nice one" who had been on duty there for years. It was all very peaceful.

Somewhere around the Four Seasons hotel, however, a boy racer cut across in front of us, spurted forward then back out again in front of another car. His Kia had a throaty roar. For some reason Mr Sensible took immediate offence. He floored the accelerator, also slipped between two cars and set off in pursuit. Follow that car. He caught the racer near what was then still called the Dedeman Hotel but the boy spotted him in the mirror. We were jammed in on all sides, panels close to panels on either side, noses to tails front and back. That closeness made the speeds seem so much greater. Could we possibly escape this unscathed? The Kia held position across a couple of lines of traffic and the sensible one got frustrated, so cut back right to the edge of the inside lane, muscled up inside then in front of another car, this all at about 80kph in packed traffic. The racer held his nerve, and his line. My guy swung to the outside across about five lanes of traffic, then back across to position himself for the swing into the off ramp to Umawiyeen and round past the huge military centre patrolled by red-bereted soldiers carrying machine guns.

The pair were nip and tuck, trying to out-manoeuvre each other. That was interesting here because on the roundabout six major roads fed in with a nominal "in turns" sequence sort-of commanded by the traffic police, many of whom were on national service and not exactly career or "best practice" minded. "In turns" would never satisfy this pair, both barging their way through the six streams of traffic coming from down past the bottom of the office. At least the end was in sight and I might just survive. We raced up the hill, the Damascus Opera flashing by on the left, the National TV and Tadio buildings on the right. Respite came at the top. The boy racer went left, we turned right towards the front of the office. Mr Sensible immediately reverted to type, dropped me at the office, accepted the tip gracefully, wished me a good day, and took off in search of more clients.

This man had considered himself provoked, but others came more naturally to the aggressive approach. Late one afternoon a "Battered For Adventure" taxi lurched to a halt outside the office, and we set off for Hamidiyeh. On that road late afternoon traffic is gridlocked but, never fear, we cut straight out across four lines to get pole position leading to the lights so we could then swing down past the Opera then back onto the "freeway", a misleading term at this time of day. The lights were with us. All the way around and down, we were a cigarette paper thickness from the cars in front and to each side as Fangio sought maximum advantage. It was warm, and all windows were open in all cars. I could have reached into the next car and taken a sip of the coffee the driver had in a holder in front of him. He looked at me, I looked at him, we exchanged smiles and quizzical looks. Then came the green light and Fangio took off, weaving in out of seemingly non-existent spaces. He certainly knew where his panels were because, on half a dozen occasions, impact seemed inevitable at 90kph and I was looking for somewhere, anywhere to go—but we missed everything.

To be fair, technically everything missed us, evasive action taken by other drivers on all sides putting us in what NASCAR devotees know as "the bubble". We thus travelled all the way back into town threading through and across traffic, simply because others gave us space. The variation is this—what is the best way to go when there are cars either side and two in front? Easy. Simply drive right in between all adjoining vehicles and snuggle up to the two in front, at 80 kph, and especially the battered utility vehicle with all the pipes sticking out the back at about eye level on the passenger's side.

All this and more was mostly done with great grace, favour and equable spirit, but not always. Mr Grumpy came along one day, in a not-bad car. The first victims were a couple of the inevitable pedestrians who believe that, by waving, they become bullet proof while crossing five lanes of traffic travelling at 70kph. Most drivers avoid them by slowing or going wide. Mr Grumpy went straight at them, hitting the brake at precisely the moment he began delivering them a speech out his window. The journey resumed. A couple of minutes later, as we sailed along in the outside lane, there came from behind the preliminary "I am here, might you move over?" toot. There is a delightful moment in Agatha Christie's autobiography where she describes her driver on an expedition to an archaeological dig: "Aristotle honks his horn ceaselessly in the Syrian fashion".[11] This practice clearly began as soon as vehicles arrived in the Levant.

My man looked around, even though the car in front

---

[11] Agatha Christie Mallowan, *Tell Me How You Live* (London, Collins, 1975 edn), p.33

was only two metres away. He resumed the speech delivered to the pedestrians, and did not move. That provoked the "Fuck, I am trying to be reasonable but get out of the way" horn blast from behind. In turn, that intensified the speech. By now, the in-pursuit vehicle was about twenty centimetres from the boot of the taxi. Grumpy decided the pursuer might just be serious so swung in, only to be savaged by a horn blast from the guy in the vehicle a metre to my right. He got a speech, too. Grumpy then moved fractionally so Pursuer could edge past, just, without scraping paint on the concrete divider wall. As Pursuer passed, the pair of them slowed, exchanging pleasantries accompanied by wild hand gestures through the open windows. Not to be outdone, the guy on the right pulled level with the window on my side and he, too, began contributing to the discussion. This went on for two hundred metres before we all went our ways, and I got the benefit of Grumpy's final version of affairs. That was an exciting start to the day of planning and policy-making.

Adventurous or sedate, most drivers were straightforward, turning on the meter and taking the most direct route to the stated destination. Of course, some do not. And some did not learn—one tried the same trick on two different occasions, but I guess we all looked the same to him. It emerged in the office that some consultants, conspicuously the Americans, paid up to SYP 650 for a SYP 50 max trip, and one was even asked for 1,650, so the gougers were about.

The classic dodger, though, arrived at peak time outside the office on a day just before a public holiday when taxis were rarer than a Middle East peace accord. He raced past but, figuring I was not from around there, backed up into the protesting traffic and beckoned me in.

"Hariqa" I said, figuring a walk back to the house through the *souk.*

"Uh?"

OK. "Hamidiyeh."

Off we went. He then grabbed my hand, and looked at my ring. "Give me the ring" he said, with a smirk. This would be a long ride. And the meter off.

"Adaysh?"

He indicated three hundred pounds, and it was a fifty ride normally. Still, I had a cab so we plea bargained it back to one hundred which was what I would normally pay, fare plus tip that delighted most drivers.

"Give me your watch, too."

This was getting weird, and then my phone rang so I got it out. Call over, he gives me his phone and wants mine. It all looked like it was an attempt at entertainment because, by then, he was also singing along with Fairuz (the legendary Lebanese *diva* revered in the Levant), waving to passersby to whom he also flexed his muscles.

By now we were taking the familiar taxi cut through Damascus' version of Car City to get a run down to Hamidiyeh. A woman driver wearing a *hijab* and with her child in the back, unrestrained, ranged up on my side, so the clown prince began obviously to chat her up, the two of them chatting across me. Interestingly, she clearly did not mind and drove off with a smile, at which my man naturally considered himself the logical successor to and swashbuckler in the *Thousand And One Nights.* His chest puffed, he continued the performance, lecturing other motorists, haranguing pedestrians, singing new tunes, and waving wildly to all and sundry.

We finally arrived across from Hamidiyeh and I escaped light one hundred pounds but still in possession of watch, phone and wedding ring, along with another cultural experience.

AIDING AND ABETTING

The office was in an elegantly shaped building out towards Mezze, sitting atop a slope overlooking on one side Umawiyeen "Square" and its ever-present traffic entertainment, and on the other a major artery that leads down to Yarmouk Square near Al Midan to the south of the Old City. The traffic snarl in the latter was spectacular for most of the day, the noise and associated smog pervading offices which, on that side of the building, were already constantly hotter than those on the other side because of the building's alignment.

From the men's *pissoir* on the northern side there was a spectacular view out towards Mt Qassioun and Abu Roumaneh, taking in the Sheraton and its swimming pool. It was disconcerting initially, because while standing there looking out, matter in hand as it were, it occurred that the reverse might be true from other buildings, with just as spectacular results. Well, maybe not that spectacular because this was the fifth floor, after all, so unless they had binoculars and knew where to look....

The project was a sprawling, ambitious one aimed at aiding Syrian development by improving the impact of its higher education system. In 2012, the eminent Arab scholar but heavily anti-regime Fouad Ajami described the Syrian university system at that time as a "shambles".[12] In the arcane world of international aid and development, though, this was just a small exercise to fix that state of affairs. It was funded by the European Union, now one of the major world "donor agencies" along with the World Bank and the Asian Development Bank, joined by a myriad of smaller players like AusAID from Australia, DfID from the United Kingdom, JICA from Japan and now increasingly, especially in Africa, the Chinese who play the game very differently.

These agencies are served by a phalanx of contracting agents who tender for projects as a whole, then in turn engage an army of "consultants", individuals from around the world who do things like advise on approaches to strategic planning in higher education. Word-of-mouth is a powerful weapon in determining employment, but most contractors advertise via major websites like Devex, DevelopmentAid, and JobsForDevelopment. It is one of the world's great multinational systems, and has attracted its fair share

---

[12]Fouad Ajami, *The Syrian Rebellion* (Washington DC, Hoover, 2012), ch. 4

of critics.

The criticism of aid has produced a large literature, but ranges from the view that all such efforts are mere bandaids plastered over gaping wounds, right through to conspiracy theories that see all aid as a postcolonial means by which former imperial powers maintain covert exploitation rights over impoverished, enchained "third world" countries. This latter view was particularly apparent in anti-globalisation debates attendant upon recent World Trade Organisation and G-8/G-20 meetings around the world. In between those stark polarities fall a range of emphases, such as the idea that aid simply entrenches already corrupt regimes, ignores local context, subjugates rather than liberates women, enshrines extant power and social structures, and enriches a few individuals rather than large populations.

Early in 2010, Oxfam produced a thoughtful if partisan view, responding to more trenchant critics seeking abolition of aid.[13] The paper divided aid into two categories: politically-driven or ineffective aid; and twenty first century aid channelled more directly into recipient government budgets to help develop vital infrastructure and services. That is, under the latter system aid funds would go into general revenue for application as thought fit by the host government, but in negotiation with donors. Being Oxfam there was a predictably strong focus on grass roots issues like infant health and basic education, but the twenty first century vision imagined more of a capacity-building emphasis with stronger performance protocols exercised over recipients. The issue of

---

[13]*21st Century Aid: Recognising Success and Tackling Failure.* Oxfam Briefing Paper 137, (London, Oxfam, 2010)

corruption, notorious in some companies, was dealt with simply by saying that not all aid was lost to corruption, a novel defence for any contractors familiar with some of the more rampantly rapacious regimes. In fact, Oxfam considered the bribe-giver to be more at fault than the taker. There was also a swipe at aid considered to be "too often squandered on expensive consultants" and, so, unlikely to succeed. All consultants might either shake or bristle at this point. However, the Oxfam paper's ultimate suggestion was that far too little money was going into aid. In 1970 the United Nations set a minimum figure of contribution at 0.7% of Gross National Income, but by 2010 only five countries had met or exceeded those levels, the Scandinavians plus Luxembourg and the Netherlands.

This was all thought provoking for those involved in projects around the world, and particularly for those headed each day towards Mezze on what was then a harbinger for other programs that Syria might attract. The project fitted the capacity-building model, as do many programs emanating from the major agencies these days. Yet the challenge is always to connect that work directly to national benefits and "outcomes", as the jargon dictates, in systems that might take years to evolve. The "expensive consultants"" might well have a far bigger cumulative and national impact than the heroic, at-the-coalface volunteers whose contributions often go unnoticed. However, there is at least an argument for saying that both "inputs" should be valued equally, so long as there is clear return on the investment.

Syria is an interesting case from the Oxfam angle. A pariah state politically in the minds of many, it became the focus for aid givers in the years just prior to 2011, including the World Bank normally thought of as American-dominated. That is, the "Axis of Evil" thinking might have still be in vogue, but the World Bank was cautiously beginning a support program, perhaps another sign of changes in American thinking. Syria was not abjectly poor by global standards though the inevitable decline of its oil revenues, the rise of climate change-related problems like water scarcity, and persistent graduate unemployment created an increasing range of problems for its essentially undemocratic government. In many conversations, locals mumbled quietly about the absence of "democracy", all the while appreciating that the term could have nuanced meaning, even if people like George Bush did not think so.

The motives for this rising interest from donors was varied: genuine interest in the rights of people thought under-supported and marginalised in health and education; a desire to help significant minorities like the Kurds; sympathy for causes like Palestine because, like its neighbours, Syria has had a resident Palestinian refugee population since 1948; and the powerful if fragile idea that aid might somehow be a useful lever in the struggle to keep Syria "onside" geopolitically. Against the background of these varying ideas, projects struggled to deliver results on the ground while navigating local ways of doing things, and dealing with funding agencies increasingly pressed by "accountability" regimes demanding value for investment, but with apparently little idea what that might really mean.

Being big in scope, this specific project had a range of consultants providing a snapshot of people typically involved in such work all over the world at any given time. Of the two long-term experts, one was South

African-born, raised in England, now based in Italy after having worked all over the world. Such is the dwindling world—I had once worked with his brother at a university in Australia. The other was born in America to British parents but, after a long international career, now based in Vietnam with kids at school in England. This industry is the true face of the modern global world, almost the modern continuation of the travels of people like Ibn Battuta and Marco Polo. There is at once a mix of curiosity, restlessness, good intentions and professional pride at work here.

That was reflected in the rest. One Scot was based in Brussels, another in Tallin, Estonia. Two Brits were based in Cambridge having worked and lived all over the world, one resident in Singapore for a long time. A Dutchman had once worked for Shell but escaped to his own space and now worked all over Europe, the Middle East, Africa, and Mongolia. One German had an IT background and a solid EU experience. There were odd Australians and Americans. A German woman met her Kiwi husband while working in the Pacific, and now commuted to the project from Auckland. An Irishman had partnered another Kiwi, so was now based in Wellington having lived previously in Strasbourg. Then, adding further to the mix, a range of regional experts drawn from Egypt and elsewhere made up the full team. During one especially frenzied week, something like twenty two international consultants hit the office at once.

This eclectic bunch had development experience ranging from extensive to very little, and were senior to junior in an institutional sense. They were employed by a range of different companies in a complex consortium as now mandated by the EU in order to reflect "Europe", and a constant source of discussion was the bureaucratic dance required to get anything done, including being paid. That latter question continued to be discussed long after the life of the project. Many of the international consultants come in for very short periods, so stayed in hotels like the Four Seasons, the Dedeman, the Sheraton, with a few unwary ending up at the Carlton which soon developed a reputation for being expensively hopeless. The group, as on projects elsewhere, developed a local knowledge that becomes useful in a surviving comfortably sense, as the great anthropologist Clifford Geertz pointed out several years ago.[14] In some respects, aid game players become a sort of ennobled version of the 60s hippie trail, moving from places like the Day Inn in Vientiane to the Goldiana in Phnom Penh, soon learning that it is cheaper to live in those places than in cities like Amman and elsewhere.

For those players "in-country" for longer periods, the choice of where to live became interesting and complex. This project's consultants plumped largely for apartments in Shaalan, the nearby middle-class area in the so-called 'central city'. That term implied the more modern elements of Damascus stretching out from the Old City, up the lower slopes of Mount Qassioun and towards the older, cooler slopes of Salihiye where once lived interesting expats like Sir Richard Burton the nineteenth century linguist, traveller, anthropologist and, for some at that time, pornographer, because of his translations of some of the "East's" raunchier texts. That included the full version of *One Thousand and One Nights* that

---

[14]Clifford Geertz, Local Knowledge: Further essays in Interpretive Anthropology (New York, Basic, 1985)

shocked many of his contemporaries in England. This area, then, was a sensible location close to work, amidst ready food and necessities supplies, and near a range of modern shops and amenities. Even though this is modern Damascus its streets, curiously, are sometimes as narrow as major ones in the Old City so that traffic in and around many of the apartments was a nightmare. Nevertheless, the Shaalan gang quickly developed a Geertzian local knowledge as to the best sources of *falafel* (deep fried chick pea paste) and *shawarma* (shaved meat in flat bread), fruit and nuts, restaurants, DVD and book shops, and even where to find musical instrument shops. Some began walking to the office, learning how to navigate the major traffic circles.

There was a constant group debate about the relative merits of living in Shaalan or the Old City. For most people coming in for 2-4 weeks at a time it was a simple matter of availability. The network could lay on a Shaalan abode at a phone call, and it would await a person straight off the plane. That apartment was close to work. The Old City was less straightforward, partly because the knowledge network about it had not evolved, and partly because of a perception that the Old City was "far". The only obvious and easy choice was to stay in the burgeoning Old City boutique hotels, but even though the negotiated rate for those came in below the per diem paid by the project, most self-employed consultants with commitments like anyone else looked towards conserving money.

On top of that, though, sat the element of the unknown and, for many, the prospect of an Arab toilet became a squat too far, as it were. Some consultants investigated living in the Old City because of all its obvious attractions and experiences, but the predominantly traditional design of houses and apartments with outside bathrooms (even if they had "French" toilets) was finally too much. And that was fair enough because people had work to do, and needed to be comfortable in order to do that work. For most, then, the Old City became a visiting site, a home away from Shaalan.

This polyglot group worked with a range of national professionals from the Minister down and, as always on these projects, the first step was to understand how it all worked—sometimes that understanding never really arrives, particularly when one major bureaucracy intersects with another. At Ministerial and Deputy Ministerial level some really impressive and talented people worked with limited resources, endeavouring to find a way ahead for a country moving uncertainly from a directed and post-Soviet style development model, towards a more deregulated and market economy-driven one. That meant dealing with issues not previously encountered, like how to match massive higher education participation growth with labour market needs. Some of those senior people spoke excellent English, German or French.

The next level was as impressive. The Director was a seriously bright young Syrian, with a PhD in English and linguistics from Edinburgh University, and with perfect English modulated by a wonderful Scottish burr. The senior translator had an undergraduate degree in English completed in Damascus and the United States, a Masters in International Relations from the United Kingdom, and another Masters in simultaneous translation and interpreting from Damascus. Her English was better than anyone's, including all the international consultants. These two stood out as a new breed of Syrian women, but obviously faced career choice decisions in an environment where women still could not easily if ever reach the very senior ranks. The same went for the very talented, capable, under-utilised and underpaid women who staffed the project office.

The objects of all this work were the Syrian universities. The five publicly funded ones were all huge in numbers by world standards: over 160,000 at Damascus, about 140, 000 in Aleppo, upwards of 80,000 at the university in Homs and another 60,000 plus at Lattakia on the Mediterranean coast, a short distance from Cyprus. Those cities, of course, all became far more familiar around the world as 2011 dragged into 2012. The exception in size was Al Furat out on the Tigris-Euphrates, five hours on the road away from Damascus: it was much smaller because of its catchment area, but had been established to help develop the area with higher education serving as a social and economic driver. Its location would also become far more widely known later: Deir ez-Zor, which became a major Syrian "revolution" centre. These massive numbers of students everywhere overwhelmed the too-low numbers of talented staff who managed and taught in the institutions, so the main project aim was to try and alleviate that pressure.

The question central to the aid and development debate looms large here. What is the best way to introduce so-called "international best practice" into a specific local context? Syrian university staff, for example, taught long hours for very little pay. Was it possible or even fair to demand they undergo professional development in order to provide better learning and teaching for students, if they saw relatively little return for themselves? Then, was it reasonable to ask an entire government to change the way it funded higher education so that it might better meet international "best practice"? The theoretical answer was probably "yes", but perhaps not the practical one. The prime objective, obviously, would be to improve the student experience so that graduates gained stronger and more applicable skills, but amidst a huge and complex project that goal sometimes slipped from sight in face of the daily struggle with systems, logistics, paperwork, and changes in direction.

In doing this work the international consultants and their national counterparts travelled all over Syria, experiencing the magnificently varied landscape, meeting fascinating people, trying hard to understand local nuances that might produce better insight for their work. There were delights—like driving past and underneath the looming Marqab Castle on the main coastal road between Tartous and Lattakia. It just sits there, a natural part of the landscape, as it has done for over 1,000 years. Originally an Arab stronghold, it was taken over by the Crusaders who built it up during the twelfth and thirteenth centuries. It was bigger than the more famous Krak Des Chevaliers and was, in fact, the last of the great castles to fall. Then there were disappointments—like driving for four hours to find that the expected work had not been begun let alone completed, and that the anticipated meeting had not been scheduled let alone cancelled.

Yet in all that driving and all that experience outside Damascus the prevailing thought remained—how could the university system best help improve national life and productivity? That question helped remove all the frustrations of the aid system, focused the work, and helped unite what was otherwise a bewildering collection of very different people.

HOUSES AROUND
THE CORNER

The House in Damascus was almost literally over the wall from a much grander dwelling. On the morning walk route towards a taxi, five metre high rendered walls topped with barbed wire flanked the first third of the journey towards the spice *souk*. In the far left of the *souk*'s tiny square, next to a small mosque, stood a heavy, studded wooden door. When that was open so, too, was the Azem Palace. An innocuous entry to a ticket office preceded a turn to the left then right, into an astonishing space.

Built during the eighteenth century, the house was home to the powerful Azem family that rose to power during the early stages of the Ottoman Empire. Remarkably, that one family produced several

Governors of Damascus as well as important leaders
in other provinces and localities. As a signifier of the
family's position and wealth, the house was much
more spread out than was normally the case, built
around enormous courtyards replete with fountains
and pools, groves of trees and shrubs. Several public
reception areas surround this central space, with all
the family quarters much more removed and divided
into male and female sections. The whole place was
lined with elaborate timber decorations said to have
consumed at least four hundred trees. Throughout, the
decoration was and remains Arab/Ottoman design,
based around elaborate mosaics and subdued colour.

This style and interior has been well recognised in the
West. During the 1930s, for example, the collector
Hagop Kevorkian bought and packed up two entire
stately rooms in Damascus, shipped them to the
United States and put them into storage. One, at least,
came from a very prominent Damascene family, and
the other one most likely did as well. Both were from
the eighteenth century. Kevorkian shipped everything:
walls, ceilings, roof, and floor including the
Damascene tiles. All of this was richly embellished
with intricate woodwork, design and styling, and
included engraved poetry. In 1970, the rooms
emerged from storage and were donated to the
Metropolitan Museum of Art and to New York
University's Kevorkian Center of Near Eastern
Studies, where they were reassembled in all their
splendour.[15]

The Azem Palace now doubles as a showcase of this

---

[15]Annie-Christine Daskalakis Mathews, "A Room of 'Splendour
and Generosity' from Ottoman Damascus," *Metropolitan
Museum Journal*, 32, (1997)

architectural style and as a museum of popular arts, crafts and traditions, with a relaxed approach to its work. Ladders may be found leaning against walls along with spare bits and pieces. The interior rooms are supposed to be photography-free but, as at least one warden indicated sheepishly, that rule really meant "no tip, no photography". I took some photographs.

The Palace was regarded as a prime residence from the time of its construction, so when his country assumed control of Syria at the end of World War I the new French political controller promptly set up house there, right near the Mosque and the *souk*. When the 1925 Arab revolt erupted, the crowds came right to the Palace door, with sections of the building badly damaged by fires resulting from the French bombing used to quell the uprising. Power comes at a cost, as 2011-12 would reaffirm.

From time immemorial, the Arab house has followed central design features that emerge directly from matters of the mind and body, Islam and climate. As Khaled Azad, amongst others, points out, Arab houses are effectively built from the inside out in the design sense, because they are based on the principle of privacy rather than display.[16] Because the sanctity and strength of the family lies at the heart of Islam, by definition the buildings that house those families reflect their needs and their unity. For that reason, even in modern design few if any Arab houses will reflect outwardly anywhere near the elements of conspicuous consumption seen in the West. Any display of wealth will be well on the inside for the

---

[16]Kahaled Azad, "Residential Architecture in Islamic Civilization", Journal Islam Today, 25, 1429H/2008

benefit of the family and those others privileged to enter. A doorway in a wall opens to a passageway that invariably stands at ninety degrees to the main layout of the house. That is so passing strangers will see little of the house if the door happens to be open.

Walking around the Old City, there were constant and tantalising glimpses down passageways to the corners of courtyards that were clearly large, interesting spaces at the heart of large and interesting houses, or even small and interesting ones. This was best demonstrated by the several major renovations of notable old houses then going on, particularly in the southern Muslim quarter and increasingly in the Jewish one. *Beit* Nizam (Nizam House) and some nearby former mansions were being developed into a heritage hotel by the Aga Khan Development Network. Very small doorways in very large walls lay open to reveal massive, soaring walls and roofs, with interesting mosaic tiles on floors and walls in every direction. The design principle was obvious, with living areas built around the courtyard on at least two and often more levels depending on the size of the house.

The courtyard is essentially the living heart of the house, because it provides social interaction space to counterbalance the privacy otherwise dominant. In this, the Islamic world took over the principles begun in hot regions during Greco-Roman times, then refined them in line with Islamic needs and philosophy. Consequently, the courtyard has an important climatic role, and provides tranquillity away from the outside world. That is why the main door in the house opens onto the courtyard and not the street—the street door is merely an access way. The courtyard essentially captures the family's private piece of the sky.[17]

Most courtyards have a fountain. While there is an obvious suggestion that this evokes the importance of water in the Arab world and perhaps a reminder of the oasis, it also has a distinct climate function. Running water acts as a humidifier in hot climates, helping lower temperatures. That function is aided by the presence of a small garden, small trees and shrubs, like jasmine. These also help reduce temperature, so that the courtyard maintains temperature balance. Given the traditionally thick walls used to construct the houses, that means the courtyard helps reduce temperature in summer but maintain warmth in winter.

Unlike the grandeur of the Azem Palace, the House in Damascus garden was tiny but followed the same principles. It occupied the three sides of the small alcove in the courtyard between what was once the "public" sitting room and the now-standalone kitchen with clothesline atop. This small area was covered by a plastic sheet suspended on an incline from the top of the balcony outside the main bedroom upstairs, down to the top of the kitchen. This was mainly to provide shade in the hot summer, and block the winter rain when it arrived. The three walls were also sheathed in plastic to prevent further water getting into the walls, because the house definitely had a nascent rising damp problem. Around these three sides, a series of pots and tubs filled with essentially hardy plants, but including things like rubber plants, were arranged on racks. Above them, plants flowed out and over the

---

[17]Abdel-moniem El-Shorbagy, "Traditional Islamic-Arab House: Vocabulary and Syntax", International Journal of Civil and Environmental Engineering, Vol 10 No 4

baskets slung from hooks under the cover. More shrubs lurked at the end of the entrance way, too, having assumed triffid-like proportions as a result of heading towards the light. In late summer and early autumn many of these plants and shrubs flowered, including one variety with burgundy leaves that produced constantly reappearing small purple flowers.

The landlord was lackadaisical about most things, but very anxious about the garden. There were great mime displays of how to water plants, how to stand on a stool to make sure the hanging baskets were well soaked, and several clear indications that this watering and caring had to be done daily even though the hot weather was now on the wane. This small garden meant a great deal to him, as it does to most Arab homeowners. So, every day before breakfast I spent several minutes bucketing water onto the plants, then sweeping excess water across the courtyard into the drains, washing away the previous day's dust. It was a peaceful and serene setting into which to arise. The watering was therapeutic, as was the subsequent sitting out among the plants while sipping a coffee and having breakfast under a clear sky, before heading through the *souk* in search of the day's taxi adventure.

That serenity has long been an important consideration in the social function of all these houses, large or small. Because the design swings around privacy, the courtyard provides the central place where family members meet, guests arrive to be directed to the appropriate place and where, in summer especially, food might be served. The privacy is structured away from this central meeting zone. Traditionally there would be an immediate space where male visitors might be received. In the grander old houses that could have been an entire wing, but even now in the most modest of homes will be at least a room. There was then a semi-private space for family purposes, with an even more strictly private area that was and still is the domain of women.

Furthermore, that all created a peaceful environment. In Old Damascus, still, houses front right onto the narrow lanes and alleyways so that there is a constant ebb and flow of people along with, these days, vehicles. The noise factor is considerable, but those ancient design principles mean much of that noise is eliminated in the courtyard behind thick walls. These principles were visible in another magnificent building close to the house but in the opposite direction, up past Jabri House then right into the laneway leading to Straight Street. Fittingly, the street is now largely an art and artefacts one dominated by Maktab Anbar, another beautifully restored house that, appropriately, now hosts the main heritage conservation group. This organisation was overseeing restoration of several major buildings in the southern Muslim section, just down from the notably inconspicuous Al Khawali restaurant at the end of the Medhat Pasha covered *souk*.

In seeing all these wonderful buildings, my appreciation was heightened by the experience of actually living in and experiencing such a house, albeit on a much more modest scale. That only further sharpened the senses as to what might really be just around the corner at the end of that drab looking corridor seen in every laneway in the Old City. That was part of the allure.

THE *SOUK* LIFE

At some point, most guide books for most places anywhere in the world build you up for a letdown. That might just be the case with the *souk* Hamidiyeh, surprisingly enough, at least in the beginning. Many of the books insist you get a first glimpse at the Citadel end, in order to get the best impact of the soaring roof and its bullet-riddled iron sheets that, in the right light, create a planetarium-like atmosphere. Once on the ground, though, that is not an entirely convincing argument. There is a broad enough walkway outside it, coming on one side from the Hariqa end and, on the other, from the Salah ah-Din statue and the *souk* Sarouja beyond. That is fine in itself, but there is also a solid iron rail fencing along that expansive walkway to prevent all but the criminally inane attempting to cross the always-busy several lane freeway. It is scarcely less inviting to get to the Hamidiyeh via the underground walkway at that end—the escalators rarely worked. No, this is not the best introduction to what is widely regarded as among the "best" *souks* left anywhere—the various guides to these things usually rate Hamidiyeh right at or near the top, with real purists suggesting that only the Aleppo labyrinth might outdo it anywhere in the region.

Coming from the other end is much more evocative. The entrance is off from the square outside the Umayyad Mosque, and reached by walking through from the old Muslim Quarter, or from the Shia section, or down Quemariye and around the Mosque itself. It is impossible to think other than about the length of time this trading practice has been here in some form or other, the lives and destinies shaped by this enterprise, and the *souk*'s centrality to the entire Damascene story. In the early twelfth century a group of Damascene merchants, their business concluded and anxious to get home, set sail from Cairo at a time when the danger from marauding parties was high. Sure enough, they were taken by the Franks who confiscated all their money and belongings (a considerable sum on money, as it turned out) and ransomed them to boot. Ibn Al-Qalanisi records that the merchants "pledged all that remained of their deposits in Damascus and elsewhere".[18] Even at this early point, these traders might have been based in Damascus, but had global minds appropriate to the time.

When he encountered the "bazaars" in the 1840s,

---

[18]Ibn Al-Qalanisi, *The Damascus Chronicle of the Crusades* (translated by H.A.R. Gibb) (New York, Dover, 2002 edn), p. 108.

A.A.Paton thought them more like a fair than anything else: he was overwhelmed by the array of "naked mad men", people grinding coffee, sherbert and ice cream makers, the profusion of goods like pomegranate sauce and honeyed pastries. He also noted the intense trading knowledge. There were piles of tobacco everywhere for sale, mainly for the *nargileh*. One old Baghdad merchant (note the cosmopolitan trading environment) commented to Paton on the imbalance of trade with Great Britain, arguing that there were a large numbers of British goods available in Damascus, but that Britain would not take Syrian ones. The old merchant opined that nearly every lady in the city now needed some sort of British product, so the trade should be reciprocal, with tobacco an obvious target.[19] This was a very simple reflection of the central role played by trading in the Damascene culture, and the way that trading impulse gave it a world view well beyond its immediate geographical boundaries. It was for that reason the *souks* in Damascus were never the "mongrel affairs" to be found elsewhere, like Cairo, according to one guide, at least.[20]

While little of that original atmosphere remains in Hamidiyeh or the other *souks* these days, the impulse persists. What the Orientalist view of the markets always missed was the fact that they were and remain simply shops, most of which sold common or garden variety goods, the basic necessities of life. These days in the Hamidiyeh, a swathe of outlets sell items like toothpaste and toilet paper. (That was one of the old

---

[19]An Oriental Student [A.A. Paton], *The Modern Syrians* (London, Longman Green, pp.12-14

[20]Murray *Handbook,* p. 469

Baghdad merchant's implications: people need things so traders should be able to supply them). The only real difference from the West here now is that unlike in the supermarket, it is possible both to "comparison shop" in neighbouring outlets, and to have some fun trying to shave the price. The point here is the principle of the bargain, rather than the necessary achievement of a great financial gain. These sorts of common goods are found everywhere: basic clothes, household mops and brooms, plastic ware (the earlier traders would have loved that durability), sheets and towels, ladders, glassware, shoes and all the rest. While the vision of the exotic is powerful, then, the practical slant of the *souk* can be underwhelming.

Whatever happened to all those exotic things with which the *souks* were replete in earlier times? In truth, they were only ever a small part of the great trading enterprise: the rugs, the Damascene steel, the frankincense and myrrh. Frankincense was a good case in point. Known under various names, this aromatic resin had been traded throughout the Levant and further for thousands of years. It was used widely in aromatherapy, traditional medicine and as an essential oil. The Frankincense name followed the Crusaders (the Franks) who took it back to Europe with them. In many respects, this was a very early example of the Swiss "added value" principle, the product standing out among a more TESCO-dominated range of options.

Luckily, some of the Swiss end still survives, but not in the main arcade of the Hamidiyeh. When the initial awe wears off ("I am in the Hamidiyeh *souk!*"), it can be replaced by a disenchantment, especially in that main lane. As rental and sale prices rose before the troubles of early 2011, the unique and the unusual bowed to the mainstream and the guaranteed selling item. That is no different to what has happened in the UK High Street or the American strip malls or major shopping thoroughfares elsewhere around the world. Here, though, it has changed the character of an environment that has had a reputation and an atmosphere for centuries. As tourism grew in Damascus so did the provision of tourist items, so all the "Orientals" sellers could stock (replica) swords, helmets, chain mail, statues or whatever else was required. Those were supplemented by the *keffiye* (the head scarves popularised by Yassar Arafat and now often bearing the pro-Palestinian insignia), the winter cloaks when appropriate, or even the obligatory symbolic item, like *harem* pants.

At one point there were a lot of German groups in town (or "come from German" as one of my shopkeeper friends put it). One of these was trudging through the *souk* one day, and riding shotgun at the back was a very large German man. He was very tall, extremely broad, and considerably, well, fat. He trailed his colleagues in a way suggesting that rather being tail gunner, like the good ship *Queen Mary* he might take some time to change course. The obligatory camera at shoulder and interested in all the stalls, he was just like any other traveller/tourist/other—except for the attire. He had been in town long enough to buy a black and white *keffiye,* now employed as a bandana, Rambo-style. The aviator-style dark glasses came under that, even though the light in the *souk* was subdued. His T shirt was stretched to capacity, barely holding together. The footwear was the *de rigueur* Velcro-strapped sandals. That left the highlight. Somewhere on his Arabian travels he had contrived to both find and buy a pair of black, transparent Aladdin-type pants, drawn at the ankles. At least he did not go commando—the pantaloons were paired with white boxer undershorts that made a wonderful contrast, along with the visibly hairy legs. Like the *Queen Mary,* he drew much attention to which he feigned oblivion. The most remarkable feature of this extravaganza was that his minders allowed him out looking like this. What were they thinking? Perhaps he did not have any. Perhaps he was an individualist.

Many such individualists have visited Damascus over the centuries. As Colin Thubron recounts lyrically, the Greeks and the Romans were followed by waves of other invaders leading down to the Crusaders from Europe, before eventually the Ottomans took over for 400 years of rule ended by World War I, after which followed the brief French Mandate, then the independence of Syria through to the Baathists and the Assads. Through all that time, Damascus was visited and reported upon by some marvellously different people.

Crassus, of Julius Caesar fame, was once the ruler here. The great traveller Ibn Jubayr visited the Umayyad Mosque not that long after it was completed, and declared it one of the finest in the whole of Islam. He also declared Damascus itself "the Paradise of the Orient". A little under two hundred years later the even greater traveller, Ibn Battuta, thought that Damascus' only rival was Shiraz. By 1331 Venice had a consulate in Damascus, such was the city's international significance. In the 1480s, there were at least forty Venetians resident in the city, those numbers swelled again by more itinerant merchants in from *La Serenissima.* As Deborah Howard points out, a good many of these adapted their lifestyle and living quarters *alla moresca* (in the

Moorish style), and frequently took houses outside the Christian Quarter.[21] There was good precedent, then, for the House in Damascus. Thubron, again, points out that in 1499 Arnold von Harff, a knight from Cologne, produced possibly the first-ever guide book to the area and the city. In 1614 William Lithgow, a Scot, became the latest to describe Damascus as the "most beautiful place" in Asia, the definition of that region being broader then than now. By the nineteenth century, the flow of travellers had become a flood and included a bevy of bewilderingly different names: Mark Twain, Edward Lear, and the extraordinary Richard Burton, while into the twentieth came Gertrude Bell, Freya Stark, Wilfred Thesiger and, of course, Agatha Christie along with T.E. Lawrence.

Since that heyday, however, Syria and Damascus had rather fallen from view, mainly of late because of global politics that saw it placed high on the "travel advisory" warnings, posted by global governments more interested in constraining their insurance and legal liabilities than in giving a true picture about the local conditions. For many people, Syria became a "no go" zone, aggravated by the sanctions imposed following the George Bush "Axis of Evil" declaration in 2002, and it's even more pernicious derivative, "Beyond the Axis of Evil" produced by the acid-tongued John Bolton, the Bush hardliner at the United Nations.

One immediate nonsense proceeding from those sanctions, for example, concerned PayPal, supposedly the panacea for secure international financial transfer. Before coming to Damascus I booked a hotel online,

---

[21]Deborah Howard, "Death in Damascus: Venetians in Syria in the Mid-Fifteenth Century," *Murqanas,* 20 (2003)

and paid straightforwardly by PayPal as requested. So money was transferred into the pariah Syria. Once in Damascus, though, when I tried to book another hotel by the same method, that was blocked by PayPal on the grounds I was in a sanctioned country. So I could transfer funds *into* a sanctioned country from outside, but not *within* that same country. The logic of that remains elusive.

An American colleague captured another part of the paradox. Anxious about his reception, he braced himself for a response when first asked where he was from. When he replied, his questioner did not break stride or warmth of gaze: "You are welcome in Syria". In order to achieve that welcome, however, my colleague was technically required by the American authorities to renounce all citizenship rights and privileges and protection for the time he was in Syria, because he was in a forbidden state.

The result of such difficulties was that traveller numbers declined until the few years immediately prior to 2011, when Syria was "re- found" by growing numbers of tourists who, on the surface anyway, seemed to think that no-one else had ever heard of the place. That would have amused Crassus and all those others in times when Damascus was a place *everybody* went.

Nowadays, the intrepid explorers of Straight Street come armed with the *Lonely Planet Guide,* the Bradt Guide, or the curiously outdated *Rough Guide,* each catering to a slightly different audience. There seems now to be an inverse relationship between the numbers of travel guides advocating cultural sensitivity, and the numbers of tourists displaying none. Either they missed those pages on the way to the shopping ones or, more likely, considered those cultural pages as not applying to them. That stands reflected in the numbers of people who seem to think that buying the airline ticket to X actually means they have bought X itself. This attitude creates spectacular moments, such as an Italian's performance in Luang Prabang in the Lao People's Democratic Republic. The monks' morning rounds for alms gathering there is now a colourful magnet for everyone with a camera. This guy was armed with both still and movie cameras, and managed to get right in front of and under the noses of the monks at every point on the walk, so that they had somehow to get around him to do their daily work. He even managed to get between the monks and their devoted givers, a particularly dreadful act. Not content with that he later invaded the pagoda, putting himself and cameras between the novice monks and breakfast. It was a breathtakingly crass display of ignorance.

Our *harem*-panted friend did not cause that sort of intrusion, at least. Nevertheless, it might well be argued that the shopkeepers of the main Hamidiyeh arcade now had his type more in mind as their customers than those travellers on the lookout for a genuine piece of craft, an artefact, or an antique. Most of the shops carried standard textile items (many of them imported from Asia), ceramic musical instruments shaped as maps of Syria, brass objects, chess sets with Crusader pieces, standard wood ware boxes, guide books and maps (most not very good) along with other assorted knickknacks. These outlets were interspersed with a small number of outlets still stubbornly selling to the locals, especially women's clothes, a couple of ice cream shops and the very odd speciality venue like the musical instrument centre up near the Citadel end.

The real interest is off in the side alleys where, with diligence, both the everyday and the unusual may be found. It was in one of those alleyways I first encountered my Aramaic friend. He was in the same spot almost every day, a strategic location where the spice *souk* winds into the jewellery one. He would be either standing in front of or sitting on his chair, watching for customers whom he might escort to his shop a few metres away. It was a nice shop, a peaceful place with some nice things in among the usual range of mosaics, fabrics, jewellery, ceramics and the odd sabre. There was no sales pitch, just his pleasant company on a tour of inspection before he returned to his vigil, ready to greet people in English or German or French or Italian or Spanish, and he had a good eye for nationality. We exchanged greetings on many days, his post on my normal route home.

Busy day?

"Yes, high season, a lot from German."

He knew a lot about the Germans, it emerged, because he had married one. This was another aspect of Damascus and Syria that continued to unfold, the number of foreigners who had married into the country, as it were, and seemed very happy with their lot. Somehow Syria seemed better at this than several other neighbouring countries, and much of that could then be put down to the fact that despite sanctions, there was strong Syrian interaction with and great knowledge about the rest of the world. It was one of the many promising features of Syrian life that suggested things might be returning to normal.

Busy day?

"Not so many now, low season. There will be more towards Xmas."

It is getting colder. Does that reduce the numbers of tourists?

"Not really, they still come, but in lower numbers."

This was the stock in trade of the stall holder. Many complained that business was slow no matter how many came, because tourists were leaving no money. They came, looked, touched, left. Sometimes they might even ask a price.

Early on in our discussions, he revealed he was an Aramaic speaker, the language of Christ, and so a Christian from Maaloula, a tiny place of about 2, 000 people in the mountains to the north of Damascus, and the last place on earth (including a couple of nearby small villages) to speak the language. The town is thus a literal connection with the Bible. That was yet another twist to the Damascus tale: here was a man from that unique background, working in Damascus surrounded by an inestimable number of variations on the faith scale, and doing so happily.

The day before I left Damascus, my last walk back through the *souk,* he was still there, if looking more tired than normal.

Are you ok, my friend?

"Yes", he replied, "the cold weather does not agree with me and there are not enough customers to take my mind off it. Would you like to come and visit my shop?"

Of course.

SOUK SAROUJA

Of course, part of Hamidiyeh's problem is that it has the name, so tour groups meander through daily, vainly trying to follow the fluttering flags held aloft by their harried leaders. Hamidiyeh has become as much a destination on the "tick off" list as an experience, and that by definition changes the place. Therein lies the irony that dogs many such places around the world: it is overwhelmed by popularity, so what made it great in the first place is now in danger of disappearing.

Right nearby, though, lies the antidote, a guide to something of what it was all like once. It takes a short walk to the right at the freeway end of Hamidiyeh, towards Salah ah-Din's statue outside the Citadel.

Cross the little road that runs around the side of the Citadel, and then a small bridge over what in the drier seasons is a fetid offshoot of the Barada river, itself almost unrecognisable from its former glories. Just along from the bridge a row of old houses hang over the stream, festooned with leather and craft works put together by a craft guild. Immediately over the bridge on the right comes what looks like a dead-end covered laneway.

This is the beginning of Souk Sarouja, the Saddlemaker's Market that covers a huge area, wending in and out of neighbourhoods, broken up by new developments and even split by the highway that runs past Hamidiyeh. It is complex and fascinating, take any alley and a new world awaits. The fact that Sarouja sits immediately outside the Old City walls is indication enough of its age. The area probably began its real development during the fourteenth century, a spill over from the bustle and business of Hamidiyeh, in much the same way that the Midan developed immediately outside the walls to the southwest. These two areas were necessary to the continuing prosperity of the city then, but not necessarily or automatically considered part of it. Visitors throughout the years always distinguished the different areas but, while giving due deference to the main *souk,* were always careful to emphasise just how important areas like Sarouja were. By the nineteenth century, Sarouja was nicknamed "Little Istanbul" because of its popularity as a residential site among the Ottoman official caste, which also spilled over into the nearby Qanawat quarter, as well.

Sarouja was where the Bedouin came to buy the horse gear that can still be found today, in that first little alley just over the bridge. Half a dozen vendors crammed into small alcoves stock a profusion of the distinctive saddles, bags, covers, rugs, bridles, halters, leads, decorations and other equipment all made in the instantly recognised colours, mostly black and red but also green and red as well as some others. This is an immediate connection with the famous Arab equestrian past and tradition that many people in Syria and elsewhere in the region are trying to revive. It is a more immediate evocation of the rich past than anything encountered in Hamidiyeh.

Sarouja is also home to many of the great craft traditions, notably brass making. There are a couple of blocks in the area where the old style huge brass trays, jugs, ewers and cooking implements are made, amidst a fury of sparks, noise, water and hammering. The workshops sit alongside or behind the display rooms: the means of production for any piece is on direct show, what you see is what you get. That is no longer automatically the case in Hamidiyeh. There was a lovely touch in one especially busy if small alley hosting some exquisite pieces. Amidst the cacophony, sitting free on the top of their cage, were two gray parrots, every now and then adding their voices to the Babel going on around them. There are not that many birds to be seen in Damascus, apart from the free range pigeons around the Mosque and the homing ones housed in a myriad of lofts, so this was a welcome sight.

Wandering through Sarouja now takes a lot longer than the same exercise through Hamidiyeh, because it is seemingly endless. Tightly packed rows of small shops give way to older, larger and now abandoned buildings. The facades of old, once grander residences mask the desolation behind. Lorries navigate through impossibly small tunnels. Little alleyways open up to reveal marvellously eclectic building styles. Elegant little mosques with their graveyards dot the area, and bath houses still ply their trade. Business is everywhere: fresh fish, vegetables, clothes, bags, hardware, electrical goods, musical instruments. The butcher shops are especially striking, at least to Westerners for whom meat now appears either in packaged form at the supermarket, or in neatly arrayed trays at the butcher's. Here the carcases hang in sight, mostly in the open air outside the shop so that prospective customers might inspect them, then are attacked with large knives for whatever slab is required. Just near the house, almost on Straight Street, a poultry shop followed the same principle. The birds were hooked on a rail outside, awaiting selection by customers. Feathers and feet then flew about in a flurry of knife work, to the inevitable consternation of passing foreign tour groups.

Sarouja, is a strong reminder of how life was and in many ways remains for large numbers of Damascenes. There are modernities in the *souk,* yes, mostly in the form of the phone shops with all their deals offered by franchises said to be dominated by relatives of President Bashar al-Assad. That discussion about "connections" was never far away, and would increase in volume as the conflicts developed during 2011, a far cry from days not that long ago. Siham Tergeman's delightful memoir, *Daughter of Damascus,* recalls the close-knit social unity of Sarouja as she grew up there in the last days of the French mandate and the early ones of the "new" Syria.[22] Something of the old conditions are remembered, too. Her "old" house, the one in which

---

[22]Siham Tergeman, *Daughter of Damascus* (Austin, University of Texas Press, 1994)

she grew up, had character along with snakes, scorpions, spiders, centipedes, lizards, rats, chameleons, mice, snails, ants and cockroaches.

We fled from the snakes in our beautiful Arabic house to a modern house where snakes don't come out of the walls, and neighbours also don't bother to greet each other. There in that old house lies my true essence which I can never relinquish for the sake of a smart, clean luxurious street in a new Damascus where houses rise high over the roofs of the city.[23]

Souk Sarouja still retains that atmosphere, as demonstrated in one particular trail. The walk through past the equestrian suppliers takes in some plumbing merchants, wholesale grocers and plastic goods providers before opening onto a little square where street vendors sell vegetables and second hand goods. The street here is busy because it is a major by-pass around the Old City, and its possible extension had become the subject of a major heritage debate. A walk along to the right encountered some of these butchers where pedestrians might occasionally have to duck under flying chunks. Then came a covered arcade leading off diagonally to the right, a formerly grand space now down at heel and peopled by metal merchants, building suppliers and electricians. This was still a tradesmen's area. Further in, though, the arcade changed. Handmade shoe suppliers appeared, alongside their more commercial counterparts. Craft shops popped up, along with small restaurants and teashops. *Nargileh* suppliers were numerous. By now the arcade had given way to a narrow winding alley. Off to the right came more of these treasures, while away to the left lay the Shia quarter. The alleys were

---

[23]*Ibid.,* p. 17

packed with people all impatient to be somewhere else, so leisurely browsing was a challenge. This entire, vast area is a working space rather than a tourist one, then, pockets of intensive trading interspersed with residential quarters. Traders might set up shop by simply laying a large cloth on the ground from which to sell their vegetables or fruit or second hand goods. Others pushed hand carts piled high with peanuts in the shell or other produce.

Then there was the weekend flea market. On Saturday mornings, especially, just near the bridle sellers and just back from the freeway, a couple of city blocks gave way to weekend trading. Cars and vans appeared from everywhere and disgorged all manner of unwanted goods that might produce a little ready cash. Packed crowds rummaged through piles of old clothes. There was the odd live bird sitting alongside battered old brass plates, ottoman-style brass lamps and long-disabled brownie box cameras. There were books, old radios, glassware, magazines, old record players and some vinyl discs, spectacles, footwear, foodstuffs, coffee beans, old prints and pictures. In a couple of the covered ways, groups of men drank short black Turkish coffees while crashing their backgammon pieces or playing cards in the local noisy fashion.

This was the weekend in Sarouja, a few short steps from Hamidiyeh but a big reminder that the real Syria was still present and, because of that, a place to visit constantly. There was always something new to learn.

Eid Al-Adhar (the Feast of the Sacrifice that recalls Abraham's willingness to sacrifice his own son) is one of the great Muslim holidays. One of its many features is that almost all barber shops remain open, because the practice is to visit them and pay extra for the privilege as a mark of thanks and respect. On Day Two of this Eid, in a little square on Al-Seikeh in *Souk* Sarouja, Hussam was one of the many barbers open that day when almost all other shops were closed.

Barbers have long traditions in most cultures, of course, and Islam is no exception in that there are connections between practice and belief, but with some Syrian twists. Clearly, men need to perform this task on other men because of rulings on contact with women (although in more modern days men do work as hairdressers for women). Then, it is supposedly forbidden for barbers to completely shave a beard, although these days clearly not all Muslim men maintain a beard. As Egypt went through its 2010-12 changes, there were reports of *Salafis* visiting barber shops to encourage more modernist proprietors against shaving beards. The *Salafis,* often paired with the *Wahhabis,* support the teachings of the original Islamic principles, and it is these groups that are generally labelled as "fundamentalists". Strictly speaking, they are "originalists" but, even so, have become identified with the use of violence— *Wahhabis* were allegedly behind the mid-May 2012 killing of the Sayyida Ruqayya mosque's *imam.* In much earlier times, barbers also bled people as part of medical treatment. Thankfully, that is no longer the case and definitely not on the agenda this day.

The Barber had a customer in the chair, and another talking companion, along with several fish in an immaculate aquarium, a parrot in one cage and several canaries in another. The conversation was fast and furious, but I was welcome to join the queue. People came and went, money changed hands, and the styling went on. There was sterilising equipment and Hussam washed his hands frequently. Scissors and razors flashed. One man had what looked like blue plasticine already applied to his beard when I arrived, and was still sporting it when I left. I hope the effect was worth the effort.

It turned out that the man in the chair was the barber's brother who, like all other Damascenes, was keen to welcome a stranger now found in Sarouja. He spoke English having, he said, been poor at it in school so he went to formal classes later, then taught himself. This is a common and impressive characteristic that many foreigners wish they could accomplish with Arabic.

Where are you from?

Australia.

Ah, a very long way. Which hotel you are staying in? So you are not a tourist. Welcome. Where are you living? The Old City is very expensive, but it is very beautiful. Please, you must ring me if you need any help. You are most welcome to Syria, we must be sure you enjoy your stay.

His brother was an excellent cutter and followed the style given to Ahmad. It was all scissor and razor cut, apart from the beard that got the customary Arab treatment (trimmed, not shaved) in designer stubble style, so far as designer stubble can be achieved with a blonde, greying, fine-haired beard. But he left the overall shape immaculate, obviously used to fussy owners of beards. The neck was razored, the edges trimmed, the final effects finalised and the whole thing gelled. It was the perfect job.

The whole experience cost $5, and that included a very generous tip for the Eid holiday.

THE CARRIERS

Early in the morning and late in the afternoon, the streets in and around the Old City *souk* complex are piled high with bags and packages in paper, cardboard and modern jute, ready for transport either to or from a trading destination. The small and under-powered Chinese Chang He vans that predominate in the city are then loaded to the gunwales, driving off with front wheels barely touching the road and engines protesting at being asked to carry so much.

All those bags and packages are delivered by a myriad of barrow men and boys who race in and out of crowds, somehow manoeuvring the handles of their metal framed, rubber wheeled trolleys so as to not maim passersby. The loads carried by some, including very young boys, are phenomenal, and they may be seen pulling or pushing these vast bulks through traffic from inside the *souk*, or going ever deeper into the labyrinthine inner recesses of the markets, emerging sometime later for their next deliveries.

For someone brought up in the west, this is pre-industrial. It is the modern manifestation of the trading impulse that has propelled Damascus from the time of its founding.

The city was blessed geographically from the outset. It was and to some extent remains an oasis. The once-flowing rivers combined with rich alluvial soils to produce a garden city on the edge of the desert, while backing into the Anti-Lebanon Mountains. That was a good beginning, but its precise location was always the real strength, and led to its significance and prosperity. Damascus was situated perfectly to dominate the east-west and north-south trade routes: Egypt to Arabia, Europe and Asia Minor through to Asia and principally, of course, all their spice and silk markets.[24] In the mid-nineteenth century, it was common to see camel trains of 500-600 outside Bab Sharqi, having arrived from Baghdad in forty days during fair weather, perhaps up to seventy in the winter. Once Islam arrived the city became one of the main gateways to Mecca for the devout going on the *Haj.* As late as 1906 the Hijaz Railway Station was opened principally to convey *Hajjis* to the holy cities. Out to the east lay the fertile crescent created by the Tigris and the Euphrates, another food bowl that needed its products transported and consumed via the

---

[24]A wonderfully detailed account of this may be found in C.P. Grant, *The Syrian Desert: Caravans, Travel and Exploration* (London, Black, 1937)

oasis city that distributed goods everywhere from there. That was Babylon.

Damascus effectively straddled the route from Europe to what became known as the Far East, as well as the cross-cutting routes that were as important. For that reason, Damascus grew and prospered as a trading city, and down through the ancient and medieval worlds witnessed the arrival and departure of the huge camel caravans. It became an *entrepot* city, as famous for its camel and horse bazaars as for its food and goods.

Just around from the house, in the sweet *souk*, Kamel Passage was named for the animal that in the old days helped move all those goods, and allowed all those people to work and prosper. A left turn from Kamel Passage into the *souk* leads up to the magnificent *Khan* As'ad Pasha. In the 1840s, A.A. Paton considered it the "handsomest" of all the *Khans,* the trading warehouses, the major venues for this trade and activity coming from far flung corners of the earth.[25] But they were not prosaic buildings. *Khan* As'ad Pasha is a vast space with a soaring roof rising to a series of domes, the whole thing an architectural masterpiece. Built in the mid-eighteenth century by yet another member of the Azem family, it was the number one trading spot in the city. On its upper floors it provided accommodation for travellers, who could then descend to floor level to conduct their trade.

Many of the other surviving *Khans* are easily missed, but even now still carry on the trade that gave them life. A particularly evocative one runs off the

---

[25]An Oriental Student [A.A. Paton], *The Modern Syrians* (London, Longman Green, 1844), p.13

Hamidiyeh *souk* just up from the Roman arch at the
Mosque end. Now running in an L shape, it contains a
string of shops carrying expensive up-market fabric,
especially silks, dazzling colours and beaded designs
flashing everywhere. As in centuries past, these silks
come from around the world but especially China, a
line unbroken now for over a thousand years. A
glance away from the fabrics and up towards the roof
reveals the origins: the vaulted domes and black and
white, block-checked colours of the traditional trading
centre. This is *Khan* Al Gumruk that dates from the
very early seventeenth century, starting out as the
customs centre but having traded continuously from
the beginning.

The location of these *Khans* demonstrates just how
central this activity was to Damascene life and
prosperity. They were right in the middle of the main
souk complexes, close to the opulent houses of the
beneficiary officials and the mansions of the traders
themselves. Many of these houses sit quietly awaiting
restoration   in   the   southern   Muslim   Quarter,
immediately across Straight Street from the *souks*.
These grandees could walk to work.

Many of their workers and suppliers, though, the
predecessors of today's trolley men, lived further
away, perhaps in Midan to the south or in Qanawat
across from Bab Al Jabiye, or out in *Souk* Sarouja
where the horse trade and horse supplies were located.
Like any other society before or since there was an
underclass, but they survived on the constant stream
of work available so long as the caravans kept coming
and going.

As times changed and the globe with it, so did
Damascene fortunes and practices. In earlier days, for
example, because of constant warfare and conflict,

Damascus became renowned as a centre for swords and sabres, with Damascene steel the medieval forerunner of Wilkinson. It is still just possible to buy a later-period version of these finely bladed and elegantly shaped weapons, some still in their original decorated wooden sheaths, but the antiques dealers know their value.

At more mundane level, one constant was the dried fruit and nuts that emerged from the Ghuta orchards outside the city, along with other foods. Those orchards and gardens fed their respective *souks* until relatively recently. Early visitors reported that the trees and gardens were right up to the gates of the city on that side, out from Bab Touma and Bab Sharqi. They were what set Damascus in its paradise, the river water and the soil combining to create a guaranteed food supplier for those inside and just outside the walls. Supported by that, the merchants spurred the rise of "damask" and other fabrics, particularly threaded with gold, which became prize pieces in European markets, and helped feed the craze for "Orientalism" that Edward Said would later see as so influential in forming global perceptions of the Arab world.

BUYING A SHIRT

At a roughly pre-determined point, somewhere around forty eight hours, the conviction sets in that your bags will never emerge from the airline clutches. Somehow, that is strangely liberating, an unpredictable thought because although the laptop on which your life depends is with you, nothing else is, and the entire plans for the assignment have gone out the window or, more precisely, into a black hole known otherwise as lost luggage.

The point having arrived, however, it takes over. The first venture is into the *souk* for toothbrush, toothpaste and all the rest. Mission accomplished, and positively, because the ways and layout of the *souk* are becoming clearer. The next stage is more daunting, if only because shopping for clothes is a trial at the best of times. Those lost shirts were made in Penang, Malaysia by a tailor found years earlier and whose product is guaranteed. Trousers were found by trial and mostly error. One pair of shoes will do for now. Underwear? Now that is a nightmare.

The hotel clerk was helpful. Yes, it was the main Muslim holiday today but, no, not all shops would be shut.

"Can you find your way to Bab Touma?"

Yes, I think so.

Good, because in Bab Touma the Christian-owned shops will be open. Get to Bab Touma Square then continue over the bridge. Go straight, and you will find yourself in a street with several clothes shops. They will open from about ten a.m..

Fortified with an excellent Arabic breakfast, I set off. A bright, clear morning developed into a warm, pleasant day. The local area was calm, deserted, quiet, its Muslim inhabitants enjoying their holiday. A few restaurants and coffee shops were open, the city stirring slowly. I got to Bab Touma and its square, from here on it was *terra incognita*.

A little bridge led away from the square and the traffic, while not busy yet, fed into a one-way street that spirited as many vehicles as possible away from the Old City. I would get to know this area and route well in coming weeks, but for now it was a revelation. Unlike in the Old City just a few metres back, here were what counted locally as high rise buildings, in that they reached to four or five levels. The ever-present street vendors selling jeans, socks, shirts, jumpers (because winter is coming), jackets, hats and scarves were already out. The pick of them, though, were the mother and daughter, both in *hijab,* selling their intricate brocade work while sitting and sewing on a bench overlooking a small nature strip. Their work was exquisite, one of the local hallmarks and the real thing.

On the other side of the street, a much more twenty first century version of commerce awaited. Around ten a.m. the shutters rolled up to reveal shoes and fashion shops, the window dummies decked out in fashions that would look *a la mode* anywhere in the present world. The first problem was that there were too many of these shops and they looked too, well, "hip". How could I ever buy anything there that I would wear and feel comfortable? After two or three passes along the entire three blocks, I selected a candidate shop.

There was no particular reason for the choice. Nothing in the window set that shop apart. It displayed shirts and trousers, most looked too trendy but a couple of things appeared passable. That said, it did not look much of a shop and it was impossible to see what lurked inside. This always was a doomed expedition anyway, I would just have to make do for the next few months, but the experience would be interesting. I entered trepidatiously.

"Good morning sir."

He was in his 50s probably, neatly turned out and groomed, slight, hair receding.

"May we help you?"

Had he been watching *Are You Being Served?* Surely not.

I am not sure. My luggage has gone missing, I am due

in the office the day after tomorrow and I need some clothes.

His English was excellent and he picked up the problem immediately.

"Sir, I am sure we have everything you will require."

The shop was very narrow so, from what was apparent, it was hard to see how that promise could be met. There seemed to be very little available.

"Some shirts first, sir?"

He suddenly shot round a corner to his left and disappeared. I had not seen that alcove but followed him, into a large space full of shirts in serried rows behind banks of showcases holding ties, cufflinks, even cummerbunds and pocket scarves. How had that happened?

He looked at me, measured my neck and headed over to a section of the shirts.

"This section should do sir."

We looked along the selection and it was, well, better than good, there was even a choice. Who would have thought that? Perhaps the expedition was not entirely doomed.

"If there is nothing here to your taste, sir, we do have more."

By now I was wary of making any more snap judgements, so said that it might be a good idea if we had a look at the "more."

"Of course sir."

He set off again and disappeared down a small staircase I had not noticed.

On the next floor down there was almost the Valhalla of clothes, because the entire floor mirrored upstairs, but without the interrupting showcases and all the rest. Suits, shirts, casual trousers, accessories, shoes, all burst out from cupboards and hangars and drawers.

An hour later I re-emerged on to the street, heading back to the Old City laden with four excellent shirts all made in Syria, three pairs of socks, two pairs of casual trousers, and five pairs of Turkish underpants. This level of purchase was rare for me, because I am usually hopeless in clothes shops, known to go into several in a row then go home unburdened. True, this was a desperate time but, even so….

Not that desperate, as it turned out. The next morning came a call from Royal Jordanian Airlines. My bag (complete with Penang shirts and all the rest) was at the airport, so if I would care to go out and retrieve it?

The steady project driver gave me a much calmer ride back to the airport than had the earlier cowboys involved on earlier fruitless expeditions out there in search of the bags. The man at the lost bags counter was very courteous.

"Please wait just a moment, sir, someone is coming to accompany you."

The question was where, I just needed to collect a bag.

A smartly dressed customs official burst out a door, gathered me up and took me back through whence he had come. We strode past security guards and customs agents, right back through to the immigration gates encountered upon arrival. No one looked at let alone stopped us. He took me into a busy but ordered office, and sat me down in a comfortable chair facing a row of four men at desks. One of them looked up, smiled.

"You are missing a bag?"

He stood up, beckoned me to follow him through a door behind him, and into a very large room with racks crammed with luggage. Without asking, he walked straight over grabbed my bag. He grinned:

"I was advised of your bag number while you were arriving."

That was impressive. I asked if all these bags were lost.

"Oh yes, sir, we have many bags that lose themselves."

Who could argue with that?

"Luckily, though, most of them find their way back to us."

These, then, were the most animate bags I had yet encountered.

He then took me back through the maze of corridors to the main hall.

"We apologise that your bag was delayed, sir, but hope its return helps make up for some of that inconvenience."

He might just have been the most polite lost luggage man in the world.

We said our goodbyes and I set off back into the city, now with an over-supply of clothes but some warm thoughts, which all returned in mid-2012 when came news that the airport had been shelled during the struggles. I wondered how he and his colleagues had fared.

MAN OF LA KEMBA

After a magnificent and memorable dinner provided one night by the Affable Interpreter's parents, we walked back to the Iman Mosque and its traffic circle in search of a taxi. There were few about and we looked aimless. One came along, slowed, flicked its lights, stopped, and we asked for Bab Touma. Setting off, the amiable driver asked the inevitable question of whence we came, the pickup location not belying our foreign origins. Australia, we said.

"Australia!! I love Australia. I have been to Australia. Where do you live?"

Melbourne.

"Melbourne! I love Melbourne. I went there for five days. It is a beautiful city. It is cultured, and seems English. You live in a beautiful place."

By now he was beaming as he retrieved memories of a trip obviously well treasured. He had tight, brushed back hair in the Arab style, greying a little. His face was square with a thick but beautifully manicured moustache, and eyes that sparkled as in his mind he returned to Australia.

"Why are you in Syria?"

"I am fortunate enough to be working here, and my wife is visiting. We love Damascus."

"You are welcome always in Syria. Australians are always especially welcome in Syria. Which hotel you stay in Bab Touma?"

"I have a house in the Old City."

"An Arab house?"

"Yes."

"Then you are most especially welcome in Syria."

By now, mention of the house had changed the attitudes of several inquirers in the *souks* and elsewhere from warm to radiant. In their minds, it somehow transformed me from visitor to enthusiast, and that spurred them to introduce me to others. Upon discovering the house factor, for example, my Aramaic friend in the *souk* immediately introduced me to his perfume merchant friend. I had somehow become a better person.

Our Aussiephile taxi driver was no different.

"My friend lives in Sydney now, twenty years, I went to visit him after Melbourne. Do you like Sydney?"

Not much.

"Me either, after Melbourne. Sydney is like America."

Many visitors to Australia who see only the Sydney waterfront suburbs make that observation, then reach Melbourne to find a totally different milieu, and say so. That helps fuel the Sydney-Melbourne divide, debate and rivalry. A Damascene taxi driver knew that.

"My Sydney friend lives in an area, I cannot remember. I went there and stayed with him. There are a lot of Arabs there."

Would that be Lakemba?

"Lakemba! Yes, Lakemba. Lakemba. A lot of Arabs, my friend introduced me."

In recent years Lakemba, one of Sydney's sprawling Western suburbs, has emerged as an epicentre of growing rumbles about immigration. Western Sydney is a multicultural melting pot with Cabramatta, for example, a centre for Asian communities and especially Vietnamese ones. It produced Australia's first political assassination when a Vietnamese local council member-turned state Member of Parliament was shot in his home. Lakemba quickly became the centre of the national debate about Islam and Muslims, its residents building Australia's largest mosque. Most famously, it had a radical Lebanese cleric called locally Sheikh Halili (Taj El-Din Hamid Hilaly), controversial for a series of incendiary incidents that included him describing skimpily dressed western women as "uncovered meat on a plate" on offer to local cats, and later being cleared of having links with Hezbollah. His "uncovered meat" comment came hard on the heels of an infamous and sensational series of gang rapes in the area, for which several young Lebanese Muslim men were charged and convicted. For many Australians, Lakemba was a no-go zone, a symbol of all that is wrong with immigration policy, and a means of justifying their hardening Islamophobia and racist antagonism.

"What did you think of Lakemba?" I asked.

"My friend and his friends love it there. Very good place. They work hard and do well, and they enjoy themselves. I was there for four weeks and enjoyed it, but it is not as nice as Melbourne".

"What did you do there?"

"My friend and his friends? They barbecue! They barbecue all the time. Barbecue, barbecue, barbecue. All the time barbecue. Australia has very good meat to barbecue Arab-style."

We all laughed at the incongruity of travelling almost 20 hours in a plane to spend days on end doing BBQs. In one sense it was like a bad Paul Hogan tourism ad that stereotyped Australia in the way much of the Arab world, and especially Syria has been stereotyped. At another level, though, it revealed the essentials of the human condition. Our taxi driver's friend and his friends love Lakemba because it gives them a lifestyle they enjoy and it provides their essential pleasures, maintaining food styles being a connection to home from what otherwise is an utterly different place. Sadly, their Australian critics do not understand that, seeing only strange and incomprehensible people speaking Arabic in public and attending a controversial mosque. They do not see people who share many of the same interests, like the BBQ.

We were travelling through the suburbs towards Bab Touma, the driver negotiating traffic and the one-way system while we all chatted, laughed and enjoyed shared experiences.

"Why do you not stay in a hotel? All foreigners stay in a hotel."

That is not true, of course, because Damascus had a sizeable foreign population made up of diplomats and development workers, for the most part, many of whom lived in the upper scale suburbs of Shalaan and Abou Roumaneh that lay behind us as we drove towards the Old City.

"I am working here for a while, and coming to Damascus I wanted to live in the Old City."

"You are very welcome."

We pulled into Bab Touma, reluctantly to end a marvellous conversation that was in itself a perfect conclusion to a wonderful evening. But it was not quite finished. Always carrying money in my shirt pocket, I reached to pay our new friend.

"No, no my friend", he said.

I became confused.

"This is on me. You are from Australia. I love Australia. You are welcome in Syria. This is my pleasure."

And he would take no payment.

We got out, humbled.

He grinned, waved, and drove away.

We looked at each other and grinned, too. What a great city.

AN ANTIQUE SELLER

A string of tiny antique shops line the Jabri House lane that leads to the steps up to the house. They are joined by a sandals seller, an industrial tape merchant and an outside fruit vendor selling from a cart, as well as all the restaurants. The area is cleaned meticulously by an orange boiler-suited man who starts work every morning about 5.30 am. He sweeps the alley and those nearby, retrieving the rubbish we all deposit in the lane in plastic bags, the bane of modern living—any drive out of Damascus east, west, north or south is marked by a proliferation of these bags blown hither and thither across the landscape. The few Bedouin encampments now are besieged by these things, something they did not have to cope with in earlier times.

Even in the Old City, rubbish can sometimes cause strife. One night, outside a restaurant across from Jabri, an aggrieved German dragged an employee outside, pointing to some rubbish bags lying in the alley awaiting collection. "I liff here too", he shouted at the waiter who looked incomprehensibly confused. It was not clear where the man "liffed", but he cannot have been in town long enough to catch up on local practice, because the bags were awaiting the arrival of the meticulous man in the orange boiler suit.

The laneway is normally scrupulously clean, not least because the shop owners, as elsewhere in Damascus, wash down the front of their shop areas at least twice a day. One of these owners runs a tiny shop right at the bottom of my steps, and we met very early on as I looked in to see what he had.

"Are you living here? I have seen you go up the steps."

Yes, I am in the house about half way up.

"An American man used to live there, too. Very nice, he was interested in Middle East politics."

Now, it is unclear when this might have been or whether it was even the same house. The house was empty for months beforehand and when asked later, the agent professed to be unaware of any "American". However, a neighbouring house did have an American connection.

One afternoon, a fire broke out in the *souk* and Sandi climbed up the ladder to have a look. Of course, the *souk* and the Umayyad Mosque have a long and terrible history of destruction by fire, as do various parts of the Old City and its adjoining suburbs like Sarouja and Midan, so any outbreak still produces high excitement and anxiety. An Englishman on the roof of the house at the back pointed this latest eruption out to Sandi, at which point an American woman's voice inquired as to why the man had spoken to her. The man replied to the hidden voice that he had simply responded and not initiated the conversation. This was not the normal warm Arabic inquiry or exchange, but it might just have been the source of the prior American connection.

After our initial exchange, the small antique shop became a regular stopping point for endless cups of tea (with sugar), food, and lots of discussion. My new friend's business partner was a French-speaker, and the shop was always full of foreigners of some kind, along with local friends, business associates and even family members—it turned out my new friend's father-in-law owned one of the shops further up the lane.

The antique seller defied all the stereotypes. He was certainly a practising Muslim, and the shop shutter would go down regularly at prayer times, especially in evening. And like all Muslim men, he could often be seen conducting his own prayers in the shop as the opportunity arose. In addition, he sometimes led the prayers at his local mosque.

But he was also a great fan of American movies, and American English.

"I think American English is best, don't you? The language of the movies."

Well, no, my friend, I prefer English English, but tell me more.

"American movies show a different life. People are free to do things for themselves and make a better life for their families."

But Arabs have a much better commitment to family, surely? One of the many things I admire is that family is so important. I go to restaurants and see family groups eating, playing cards, shouting, laughing, and you all look out for each other.

"Ah yes, that is true. But America gives opportunity. I would like to go to America."

Many Syrians did, and had a hard time getting there. One American consultant on the project was twice detained for twelve hours by immigration upon arrival in Damascus and that, naturally, sparked considerable discussion. One of our local colleagues remarked coolly that we would all do well to experience arriving in America as a Syrian and see just how difficult things could be. Despite such tough receptions, though, for many Syrians America remained a goal because it was thought to be a land where opportunity abounds, and that view persisted even in wake of the 2008 Wall Street crash, the housing and unemployment disasters that followed, and America's clearly waning world authority.

My antique man himself knew some of that, and thought he experienced it daily in his business. His constant comment and a recurring theme for discussion was that while more and more tourists arrived, they left less and less cash behind them. He had stories of Europeans and Americans coming in to say they had only Euros 10 or $US 20 to spend, whereas most of the stock in his shop started above that. One day, three European women walking past spied some lovely scarves he had on display as a sideline to the antiques and collectibles.

"Very nice. How much?"

"Three dollars."

There was a furious discussion among the three and it was obvious they liked the scarves. My friend was at his rock bottom price because the scarves cost him $2.50.

"How much for 3 scarves?"

"$9."

"Too expensive."

They walked off.

He constantly put that sort of response down to the "world economical crisis", and said he experienced it every day. Moreover, he said, his colleagues along the lane and further afield in the Old City reported the same patterns: business was tough even though tourism was rising. The complication was that business was also concentrating more and more in the main *souk* where property prices were escalating. He said his father-in-law had really opened the nearby small shop as a hobby, having sold his Hamidiyeh property for a fortune—it was easier to sell and take a good profit than to keep running a business that faced increasingly tough competition. That, clearly, was one of the reasons the main Hamidiyeh arcade was becoming so homogenised: the lowest common denominator was the level at which sales and income might be maintained. No one could afford to have stock sitting unsold.

America remained the goal, because the antique seller thought he might be the last of his line to maintain the shop that had been in family hands for at least four generations, and had itself shifted physically to this cheaper location only recently. In darker moments, he speculated about perhaps getting a regular job with a steady income. But those were hard to find with pay levels sufficient to maintain his family. He loved his avocation but his family more, so the decision weighed heavily.

Every day, he travelled by microbus to and from his outer suburban home, anything up to an hour each way. This was in one of the outer areas of the city that came under pressure during 2011 and 2012. He was there because, like an increasing number of younger generation Syrians, he wished to have his own family space rather than share the traditional extended family one. His family had owned an Old Damascus city property now sold, but had he moved there after marriage he would have lived in just one room and been part of a wider drama.

Times had changed, he thought. The older extended family times had been subject to fewer pressures, and relied heavily on an acceptance of the older ways. People now still maintained their traditions but also wanted newer things, like their own space.

He relayed an old Syrian saying: a mother-in-law will never fully approve of a daughter-in-law. While such a pattern might not necessarily be unique to Syria or even the Arab world, it is easy to speculate that an extended family home would help sharpen the sentiment. Hence the beginnings of change as women's education and training extended and, along with that, an increased sense of self-esteem and ambition. Add to that economic shift, changing patterns of life, and changes in aspirations and ambitions, and the social outlook began to alter substantially.

All that was faced daily by my friend in the alley trying to make a living through economically straitened times by selling "Orientals". Throughout 2011 and 2012 I would call him to see how he was—

okay, thanks, but times are hard. Those Orientals were now even harder to find. There were fabulous things to be found in many of these shops, but difficult to spot and more expensive to buy.

Like many others, my real estate agent also had such a shop for a while. His prize piece was a nineteenth century collective portrait made up of enamelled depictions of Ottoman Empire provincial governors. It was beautiful, but he refused to sell because he dreamed of doing reproductions from it—it was rare, so he might make more profit that way.

In all these shops could be found glass, old watches and cameras, old prints, some paintings, old rugs that might perhaps be the real thing from "Persia", Roman coins and artefacts, some old woodwork along with the renowned mosaic tiles that are now almost all "distressed" new ones, Ottoman ornaments, and maybe some rare silver. All that mixed with newer tourist items like boxes, scarves and jewellery. At the upper end, there might be modern versions of the swords that once made Damascus so famous, old and reproduction firearms, fine iron work in the form of birdcages and lamps, and the lovely copper work that was well worth buying. The good pieces were expensive, rightly, especially in more central locations near the Azem Palace.

Can these all survive? Well, perhaps not easily. That was why my antique seller still watched American movies and talked to people like me, to improve his English. That might just give him another avenue towards the future, in addition to the pleasure of conducting a global discussion over tea from his tiny haven on the lane along from Jabri.

ANOTHER HOME
AT BROKAR

Of all the restaurants near the house, Brokar probably announces itself the least. Its nameplate is almost missable, it has no menu in the obligatory window box outside, it has neutral colour walls framing the small and subdued doorway. Yet it became a second home, beginning on my very first morning in the house, a Friday and, so, a holiday. Jabri and the others nearby looked either closed or somehow uninviting— late mornings are not the best times at which to judge these places—and there was a guy stationed outside the Brokar, so they were at least anticipating business. "Free Internet" was also on offer, and that I was in serious need of because there was no provision in the house. By this stage, though, there was scarcely a serious restaurant in the area that did not have "free" wifi, it was now a prerequisite for business.

Brokar does not have the closed, tight alleyway entrance of most restaurants and houses. Instead, the door opens into a small landing with some perfunctory decorations, and a stand bearing mostly outdated information on Damascus. It is dark, done out at this level with deep toned wood and muted glass. That area leads to a small set of stairs that go up one level to tables and seating, as well as a small standby drinks and snacks service area. Off the entrance landing, another set of stairs heads down to another mirror image of tables and chairs. Down further, there is a small alcove done in Bedouin style. Even further down, the ground floor is partly under cover of the upper two floors, partly under the "private piece of sky" in the warm weather, or the retractable roof in the cold. It sounds large and in some respects it is, but it is not cavernous like many of the more popular restaurants. At any one time, full, it might hold perhaps one hundred people or a few more.

What it had was atmosphere. It was a welcoming place, even with little or no English spoken. It was a local community restaurant that sometimes attracted largely German-speaking tour groups, or out-of-towners in Damascus for the day and looking for a meal. Everyone was welcomed warmly and treated like a regular, though regulars got extra "treats" as I soon discovered. Constant smiles and a lot of laughter were perhaps the Broker's greatest attraction, in addition to its excellent food, and that sold the place. It was also a reminder that these people were just like anyone else anywhere else: they appreciated friendship and good food and humour. They were a

very long way from the Western media images of
Syria and Syrians.

On this first day I was shown into the upper level, the
autumn sun glinting on tables and a cloudless sky
allowing in bright sunshine. This was a day for
relaxation. A tubby young man was at another table,
puffing away at a hubble bubble and staring intently at
the screen on his laptop. That was encouraging. I
opened up mine to find I needed a password. The
waiters had no English at all so things were difficult.
The tubby young man got up, came over, smiled, and
tapped in the password. Success.

"*Sukran Jazeelan"* I said, thank you very much.

"My pleasure", he replied, "you are welcome in
Syria."

Then began the menu learning curve. It had a basic
English version that was not entirely clear, at least to
me. There was a section labelled "Continental
Breakfast", another "Arabic Breakfast". Each carried a
list of things that looked like an inclusive package, so
I opted for the local version. The waiter came up, I
indicated that section, he looked surprised—my
immediate thought was that he had predicted I would
take the Continental. He went away and soon came
back with the first edition of what would be my
Brokar staple, the Turkish coffee. It came in a
beautiful, long handled copper pouring pot, with a
small beaker and a sugar bowl. I had long since sworn
off coffee, mainly because I had become bored by it,
but also because by now it was such a complex
offering in the West it was too hard to contemplate. "I
will have an organic decaff skinny latte, and hold the
froth"—who has time for that? By now my laptop was
going and, moreover, I was on Skype back to

Australia. This was new to my password saviour so he came over to investigate, as did several of the waiters, and that led to a broken discussion about what all this meant. Within minutes we were old friends, and it might have been then when Brokar became my second home in Old Damascus.

Then the food arrived, all of it. I had made a huge mistake, of course. The "block" offering was, instead, a list of further optional selections under each category. I had form for this sort of thing. In one of my first exams at the University of Canterbury a million years earlier, I had completed all ten questions only to discover later we had to choose six. The waiters kept bringing out plates and even though I was just one person at a table that held four comfortably, it took some work to get the food on the table. There were smiles all round, and the upside was that I got to see immediately just how marvellous and varied was the Brokar offering. There were several different kinds of bread and pastries, even more varieties of cheese, especially the traditional soft white one, cold meats, *labneh* (cream cheese), *hummus* (chick pea dip), *ful* (the fava bean dip), olives, boiled eggs still in the shells, dried fruit, fresh fruit and several other things. This was an order for a large family, so some of the new friends helped introduce me to and shared all these new delights. By accident, I had the best possible introduction to both the local food range and to the Brokar's high standards. At the end of all this, during which the coffee kept coming, one of the waiters arrived bearing a plate of ice cream, the house speciality.

"For you", he said.

But I did not order this.

My tubby friend interpreted: on the house, you are very welcome in Brokar.

I staggered out two hours after having gone in, but knowing I would spend a lot more time there.

EATING OUT

In 1154 Nur Ad-Din, the uncle of Salah ah-Din and himself one of the great figures in Damascene history, established a new hospital near the Mosque, aiming to provide the very best Arab medical services. One story has it that a major attraction was the hospital's food. A citizen we would now call a "foodie" heard such good things about the menu that he admitted himself, feigning illness. A doctor soon detected him as a fake but let him stay and the man enjoyed the food. The doctor approached the "patient" after three days, suggesting that Arab protocol of providing for a guest for that period having now been honoured, it was time to leave.

Damascus has long been renowned for its food, and even now tourist guide books and articles stressed this aspect for the prospective visitor. Newer restaurants had sprung up everywhere to serve that interest,

including globalised and globalising Chinese and
Indian ones—about three minutes walk from the
house, for example, on a corner where two tiny
laneways meet, a Chinese restaurant hid behind
traditional Arabic doors and windows. Despite that
growth, however, the old food practices prevailed. In
one corner of Hariqa Square there was a tiny
takeaway food shop with room inside for three people
at best. Nevertheless, at almost any hour of the day
there would be three times that number inside with a
much longer queue outside, waiting to buy reputedly
the city's best *shawarma,* the meat shaved off a
vertical grill slab and wrapped in *pita* bread. Every
Damascene had a firm view on where to get the best
kebab or *falafel* or *ful* or *hommus* or any other
speciality. These ancient versions of fast food were
available everywhere.

Rafik Sharmi's reminiscence of the city revolves
around food, each major figure in the book
contributing a dish for which he or she was famous in
the family or its circle of friends.[26] That is a simple
indicator of just how central food has been to
Damascene life. The same may be said of other
cultures east and west: India and France spring
immediately to mind. But Damascus has developed
and maintained such a special food profile, perhaps
more than most, as a result of its history, multiple
forms of faith, geographical position and evolved
social customs.[27] That in turn heightens and is
heightened by the Arab tradition of honouring any
guest with food. Food was always at the centre of the

---

[26]Rafik Schami, Damascus: Taste of a City (London, Haus, 2005
edn)

[27]Siham Tergeman devotes several pages of her memoir to this
food aspect: Tergeman, pp. 45-53

family bonding that has been such a strong feature of Arab and Syrian life, and that still survives in Damascus, even if more shakily now than in earlier times.

On one trip back to Damascus from Lattakia, we diverted through a small town to drop a local team members at the family house for the weekend. One international colleague, perhaps not fully realising the implications, suggested we all stop into the family home for tea. That was arranged with great grace but "tea", of course, became a full meal with family members bringing out everything they could find in the house. It was excellent, and honour was served with the international guests given the proper treatment demanded by Arab etiquette. It was also humbling, a reminder of just how much of that courtesy has been lost in the West. On a later occasion that same family entertained the international team to a full dinner in their Damascus home, including alcohol so that all needs would be served. The preparation for that dinner was extensive and intensive, the result a magnificent example of Syrian cuisine and style.

While never as good as in such a family home, taking food in Damascus was always a pleasure and over time I developed a circuit of favourites.

The Al Kawahli was very near the house, unobtrusively signed and just into a little alley on the right at the end of the covered Souk Medhat Pasha at the top of Straight Street. In a huge restored Damascene house, it was worth a visit just to sit in the waiting area. About three times higher than it was long and wide, this reception space was a quintessential example of Damascene art and tiling. The large mosaic tiles on the floor were perfect, the furniture heavy but ornate in local style, the walls covered in the black and white layered paint look, and the lights soaring chandeliers. It was more like a church or a mosque than restaurant holding area and, indeed, it was common to see the faithful performing their prayers while waiting to be seated.

The place was huge and complicated. A large dining room downstairs was always busy and crowded, waiters expertly balancing laden trays while avoiding children, chairs, new arrivals, people greeting each other and other waiters either bringing or removing a bewildering array of dishes. It was noisy but welcoming, the food smells exquisite and the look even better. Just inside the tiny entrance, on the left before the main dining room and the cathedral-like reception area, a set of stairs afforded the long trek to the rooftop. On the way up, small areas with tables and chairs were tucked in behind stairs and doors and in tiny rooms once used as a conventional family home. It was a labyrinth and and the waiter serving as guide was definitely needed the first time. The stairs led all the way up to a couple of dining areas on the roof, definitely the place to be when the weather allowed. These roof terraces looked out over the domes of Khan Asad Pasha and the souk towards the hills and Mount Qassioun, a reminder of both the ancient nature of the city, and the fact that over many centuries visitors had come to both sample and contribute to the development of the cuisine. The food itself at Al Kawahli was said to be among the best in the city, in the sense that it was good quality and true to the heritage—no fusion or modernised Arabic food here, just the best traditional basics. Sitting on the roof with some of that food, looking away to the horizon and over the roofs and minarets, this was among the best places locations to remind yourself that you were, indeed, in a very special place.

Naranj was considered by some the best restaurant in all Damascus (and it was, at least in the social sense), so was always crowded, especially on weekend evenings. It was not well signed: it the modern glassed building on the corner of Straight Street near the Roman Arch with the Greek Orthodox Church nearby, given away by all the tables inside. A small upstairs terrace overlooked the Church, but was a prized space and off limits unless you were in the know. The service was good and the reputation well earned, though in all truth it was probably overpriced for what it provided. The range was excellent (the raw but spiced lamb appetiser might not be to everyone's taste) and alcohol was served, but above all it had a presence of which it was well aware.

Just a little further up the lane a nondescript building hosted many of the *Naranj* staff so that throughout the day, a stream of uniformed waiters, chefs, cleaners and others were coming and going constantly. The restaurant, then, was as much a location as a food outlet, and that added to its presence. In turn, it attracted a crowd with a presence. On one memorable weekend night, our party spent more time watching fellow diners than eating food. The game was to guess what particular characters did. The favourite subject was a man in a visiting Lebanese group, if only because he was noticeable and wanted to be noticed. In his thirties or early forties he was tallish and slim, dark with mandatory designer stubble, very well dressed and extremely self-aware. The feature was the hair. It was black and oiled and there was plenty of it, swept up in the elaborate style favoured by English "Teddy Boys" of the 1950s and 1960s, and by people like Ed "Kookie" Byrnes and Elvis Presley of the same era, only this was even more elaborate. The bets on what and/or who he was ranged from Lebanese film star or producer through to music impresario, or pimp. We never found out.

The *Al Dar* is located towards the Straight Street end of a main walk through to Bab Touma: find the Greek Orthodox Church on the first street left past Naranj on Straight Street, turn left and go around a couple of bends, and the restaurant was signed on the right hand side. It looked nothing from the outside but the interior had a clean, modern design with a very high ceiling, and a sense of space. Steps led down from the street into a well laid out and modernised dining area, looked by the kitchen behind a large window through which the neatly dressed chefs could be seen at work. Before the 2011-12 upheaval it was becoming increasingly popular with locals and tour groups alike, all attracted by the good atmosphere, reliable food and available alcohol. The food was westernised Arabic for want of a better description, but very appealing.

One favourite escape was *Al Azariyeh,* a gem in the Christian Quarter. Lazaristes Street is really more of a wide lane that runs off Bab Touma Street in the Christian Quarter and includes, among other interesting things, a marvellous little shoemaker shop in the traditional style—he was further on past the restaurant, itself perhaps fifty metres off the main street. I first ventured into the restaurant late one afternoon after a long walk around the area, and in need of a beer. Like some of these places it looked a touch forbidding. There was small door in a large lime-washed wall, a man lounging outside with a cigarette, and no real way to look inside to check out the place. The man smiled, that was a start. He was in his thirties, perhaps, casually well dressed, average build, ubiquitous brushed back and short black hair.

"Good afternoon" he said, "you need food?"

Well, a drink first, really.

"Come in, come in, you want beer?" Being a European made that question a standard one here.

He showed me into a small, L-shaped restaurant area. The first area has half a dozen tables along a wall, facing a small bar that might have been in an English village: dark wood, high stools, small bar area backed by a mirrored wall hosting the usual range of optics, including a good range of single malts. Just inside the main entrance and to the right of the bar, a set of stairs led away to the cellar and, as it turned out, the kitchen. A small television set high above the entrance doorway was showing a football match from somewhere in the Arab world. On past the bar, and the few tables in this area, stood the main dining area. All the tables had cutlery and condiments set on red and white checked cloths, the English bar now teamed with provincial Italian *trattoria*. The same football match was screening on another television set here.

He showed me to a table opposite the bar and brought the menu, along with three small plates containing peanuts, chips and popcorn, perhaps the most generous array of "free" drinks snacks to be found anywhere in the world.

"What would you like to drink?"

An Almaza, please.

By now this was the beer of choice, preferred over local brews (including the Barada whose taste matched what the water in the "river" of the same name looked like). The Almaza pilsener is a lovely beer and comes either in the bottle or as a draught.

That simple choice of a beer has some interesting global connotations, though. The Almaza company began in Lebanon in the 1930s and had a strong French brewing influence, though essentially owned by a Lebanese family. The company went through several iterations before becoming part of the giant Dutch Heineken group, then later still Lebanese political boss Walid Jumblatt bought a stake. Unsurprisingly, then, the other beers readily found in Syria are Heineken and Amstel.

The host brought me the coldest beer in Damascus. The mug had been stored in a freezer and ice still clung to the sides, so the already cold beer gained an additional chill when poured. It was spectacular and led to a second and, automatically, food.

The generosity of the snacks was matched by the quantity and quality of the food. Over several visits the *shishlick* (lamb grilled on skewers) became the favoured dish but everything was excellent, and extraordinarily cheap. A single main dish was more than enough for one sitting but, alternatively, so were two or three appetisers, including one of the many fresh salads.

Over several visits I never found the place crowded and only rarely did another foreigner turn up, even though many foreign students lived in the area. Most of them frequented a much trendier but far less value-oriented place a few streets away whose owners, cleverly, had opened up the front wall of a house so that it opened onto the street. Most un-Arab like this was, of course, very Western. In warmer weather the windowed doors were rolled back so the place became more like a European street cafe, its denizens all resolutely staring into the screens of their laptops, plugging into the world via the wifi while the Old

City went on all around them.

Back at *Al Azariyeh,* meanwhile, business remained quiet but steady, catering mainly for locals. The host said that business was good enough and kept him going but, like all the city's other entrepreneurs, he had other enterprises boosting his income. He was content, he said, to let the restaurant run its course, and was happy to see people like me as regulars because we spread the word around the locality. It was a pleasure to do that, because this was a "find".

The *Elissar* became my "treat" restaurant of choice, and where I took visitors to get them started. Just a few paces from the *Albal* hotel, in a lane off Hammam al Bakri, the restaurant had suffered lukewarm reviews in a couple of guidebooks. For some reason I ignored that: perhaps it was because the place looked so inviting from the outside, and the staff coming and going all looked so smart. It had a large neon-lit sign on a vast expanse of whitewashed wall, so was hard to miss. There was the usual small door in one corner of that expanse, and a short corridor led into the usual big space open to the sky, but with the motorised canvas retractable cover that would come over during winter or other bad weather. Immediately inside the front door, stairs led up several flights to other eating areas, including a really nice roof terrace. Downstairs the decor was traditional, and a little dark.

I met the best *maitre d'* in the city on my very first visit. He was tall, solid, big featured, sporting greased back black hair and wearing a tuxedo along with a huge smile.

"Good evening sir, welcome to *Elissar* and to Syria. You wish to eat? You have come to the best place in the city."

Well, you would say that, would you not?

"Smoking or non-smoking, sir?"

That was unusual because in many restaurants, even the better ones, smoking was assumed to be a natural habit. In here, though, non-smoking also meant that no hubble bubbles were allowed in that area, either

The place was busy even though by local time it was still quite early, mainly because at first glance there seemed to be several expats and tourists in. One of the more difficult things to adjust to for many travellers in Asia and the Middle East is the timing of meals. Breakfast is often taken late, followed by a biggish lunch, then dinner might be any time after 9 pm, and often much later—being confronted by a large dinner at 10.30 pm is a trial. The consequence, of course, is that many restaurants do not even open until after 7 pm and towards 8, so that the desperate Westerner looking for normality sometimes has a struggle. *Elissar* seemed to have worked out that it had a market.

He arrived back with a menu and several recommendations about the best dishes in the city. I settled for grilled lamb and a *fatoush,* the signal dish for me as to the real quality of a restaurant. It is a salad that features crisped-up chunks of the previous day's flat bread, along with all the fresh leaves and tomatoes and onions and olives that make Arab salads so remarkable. A great *fatoush* is one of the prime culinary experiences, so this was a little test.

"Very good choice, sir. Would you like something to drink, a beer or a glass of wine, or a bottle of each?"

I looked up to see the smile broaden even more, genuinely.

Not a bottle of wine, I think! Perhaps a glass?

"Very good, sir, very responsible!"

This guy had a sense of humour that got bigger and better the more I visited the restaurant.

We settled on a Lebanese light red that came out with the sparkling water and, soon, the lamb and *fatoush*. He might have exaggerated, but only ever so slightly because the dishes matched anything else I had encountered in the city to that point, and few if any surpassed it later.

By now we were chatting in between him attending to his other tables and instructing his waiters. Like others he was intrigued to find I had a house in the Old City, and that produced a complimentary glass of the drinkable red. Another free glass followed when he learned I was there to help improve the university system because, like most Syrians, he believed in the power of education to transform lives and help the country "re-enter" the world. Universities were very important, he thought, and "Arabia" had a long history of higher learning that was well due for restoration.

"You are most welcome in Syria. But you are alone? You have a family?"

Yes, but all over the world at present.

"Well, you have a home here at *Elissar* anytime."

I visited frequently after that.

The famous *Jabri* was literally a few steps up the lane from the house. In fact, that lane demonstrated the nature of the Old City restaurant business and, oddly, why it was so safe eating in all those restaurants. A least twice a day the narrow laneway would be jammed, two or three tiny trucks parked outside the restaurants with their drivers and assistants helped by restaurant staff to unload boxes and boxes of fresh produce: lettuce of all shapes and shades, eggplant, onions, carrots and all the rest, fruit of all descriptions along with all the meats and yoghurts and sweets. These places had so many customers that the food never had a chance to go bad, the turnover was so fast.

The house in which *Jabri* now sits has been in the lane since the late eighteenth century, according to the sign outside, and it has a commanding presence. First there is the "door within a door", like those at the main gates of many Oxbridge colleges, but on smaller scale. There is a larger door set into the building, but entrance is through a smaller one set inside that frame, causing most people to duck or go through sideways. A nondescript passageway turns sharply right into another one after a few steps, then the building opens out. The dark passageway yields to light streaming through windows and skylights to create an airy, weightless feeling accentuated by a very high roof. Around the edges, smaller dining rooms are hidden away, some up stairs and all behind doors.

The real revelation was the main dining area that was very large, yet always crowded. The noise of innumerable conversations floated up towards the ceiling and circulated, along with smoke from several hubble bubbles. The bubbling sounds from those pipes added to the ambient noise, while the sweetened tobacco gave further texture to the all-pervading food smells. In the middle was the obligatory fountain, a really beautiful one gurgling clear, cooling water into the large surrounding trough. As in all other restaurants, tables by the fountain were at a premium, because to be there was to be at the centre of attention. It was the quintessential "Arabian" scene that might have been depicted by any one of many visiting artists and travellers over the past three to five hundred years.

First time up the food was fabulous, even when sampled in a limited way—the one big drawback to being a lone traveller is that in restaurants there is no-one with whom to share a bigger number of dishes. The *falafel (*deep-fried chick pea and/or fava bean patty) was excellent. In these days of multiculturalism, places like Australia and elsewhere have come to experience the *name* of new dishes, but not always their true *nature*: think of, say, "curry" in the United Kingdom and "Chinese" in Australia. It is possible to get the real thing but, for the most part, that real thing is not on offer in Soho or any Australian country town. Among the more famous depictions of some of this is John Birmingham's book, *He Died With A Falafel In His Hand,* the title referring to a dead junkie found in a share house.[28] I have often thought that sounded more like a *shawarma* than a *falafel,* with the *shawarma* itself in some locations, like Australia, often being more technically a *kebab* (skewered meat cooked over open flames). Given all that, it is always a delight to encounter the genuine article, and the *falafel* at *Jabri* was definitely that.

Truth be known, though, *Jabri* was good for only a couple of visits, despite it being so near the house. By now, it was a tourist place both for international and domestic travellers. Large groups took it over, and the management knew it had a lot of one-off traffic. It was busy, so waiters could be brusque to the point of

---

[28]John Birmingham, *He Died With a Falafel in His Hand* (Sydney, Duffy & Snellgrove, 1994)

being rude, orders were handled carelessly, prices higher than elsewhere, and the quality could and did vary considerably. It was a wonderful experience, once, but never went on the "to be visited constantly" list because, simply, there were better options.

Haretna was definitely one of those. All the guidebooks described it as being "behind the police station in Bab Touma". Well, that was true, to a point, but it was hard to find at first. If you could locate the police station—there are usually gun-carrying policemen outside, a bit of a giveaway—then a nearby set of steps led up into then along a lane until it met a T junction. A left turn followed quickly by a right led into another lane. That then headed towards a sharp left hand turn at the *Zaetona* Hotel, marked simply by a brass plaque on the wall beside the obligatory innocuous door. A little further along, on the right a long wall funnelled down towards a crossing point for two laneways. In that wall, a tiny door gave access to *Haretna* ("our community" is one interpretation). This was different from most other restaurants in that it was low ceilinged, just two floors high, and unusually long and wide.

It was the pick of the "guide book restaurants". The food and service was excellent, prices reasonable, the atmosphere excellent and the crowd always entertaining. It had the best *fatoush* in all of Damascus, let alone the Old City. It was a "must visit" place, if only for the sheer variety of people to be seen there. A group of Orthodox priests from nearby churches and monasteries might be in to celebrate an occasion. They might be seated next to a gang of young women, scarfed but heavily made-up and all smoking the *nargileh*. Young couples would be there sharing private time, groups of men socialising or talking business or both. Family groups would be celebrating a special moment or just enjoying a family outing. People of all sorts would be playing backgammon with noticeable gusto and flair, tourists "in the know" absorbing the atmosphere and writing their logs, or Skyping home to show friends and family just how amazingly different this Syria is from the reported one. Through all this the neatly dressed, well trained and super efficient waiters scooted about carrying impossibly loaded trays bearing food and drink.

Haretna was also the natural home of The Beautiful People. One fortuitous evening, four of us arrived for dinner and were shown upstairs—definitely the place to be. We were seated next to a table full of the most stunning-looking young women and men. One of the latter, it transpired, was a rising star in the local political and governmental scene (I thought a lot about him through 2011-12—what was he up to, and how had he fared?). They were dressed impeccably, groomed immaculately, and delightfully expansive. A birthday was being celebrated, and they wanted to include us. When it transpired we were there working to improve Syrian higher education they became even more friendly, appreciative to the point of serving us birthday cake.

"Thank you for coming to help Syria. Higher education is important for our future."

Part of the reason we were upstairs was because a large tourist group had been seated below. The management had laid on a Whirling Dervish demonstration to entertain these visitors. Colin Thubron has an evocative account of seeing such a group back during his much earlier trip to Syria, at a time when the Dervishes had to be secretive because

they were outlawed.[29] Those days are gone and the
Dervishes now are more of a tourist attraction—a
poor value restaurant just around from the house
featured them nightly. This one at *Haretna,* though,
was modernised. When the music started, The
Beautiful People rushed us over to the balcony so we
could get a good view of "one of the highlights of
Syria" as they explained. The lights dimmed, a
Dervish came on stage, and in a postmodern moment
it transpired he was electrified, covered in coloured
lights blinking on and off. As his whirling routine
sped up, the stage was transformed into a series of
swooping coloured lines, the speed of his turning
blurring the lights. It was sensationally spectacular.

We retreated to the table, finished the wine, still
stunned from the performance and one of our number,
in Damascus for some time by then but about to leave,
declared it the most spectacular evening she had
experienced there.

Similar places, if less spectacular, abounded
throughout the Old City, and it became a mission to
find them. *La Guitare*, off Straight Street near the
Oriental Hotel and at the side of the Greek Catholic
Patriarchate Church, was a nice place to sit outside
with a beer and a couple of appetisers late in the
afternoon. The *Opaline* was strangely isolated in the
southern Muslim Quarter, a signpost for it high on the
wall of an inauspicious looking laneway running off
from *Souk* Medhat Pasha, just opposite the entrance
into *Souk* Al Bezuriye. The alleyway looks uninviting,
but about two hundred metres in a big square-looking,
cream-coloured building loomed up on the right.

---

[29]Colin Thubron, *A Mirror to Damascus* (London, Vintage, 1996
edn)

Inside, it was a pleasant, light and airy place in which to take some food and a beer. It was a Druze place, but the menu presented the normal range of excellent Arabic food. *Zeus,* small but beautifully done out in precise Damascene style, was on Al Quedaya in the Christian Quarter, the second main walk-through lane from Straight Street up to Bab Touma.

Leila's was renowned, near the house and overlooked the Umayyad mosque, a spectacular venue at night when weather permitted. The view from tables on the upstairs terrace was right along the southern wall of the Mosque. It was not a place to go for the food, not the best around, but one trip was mandatory for that view alone. Even so, it seemed sacrilegious now to be drinking beer and wine while taking in that view. The management decided increasing tourist numbers meant alcohol must be served. Once again, that action seemed vastly out of line with the stern, intolerant and hardline image of Syria cast so often abroad.

Aside from these and other enticing restaurants, the Old City was replete with snack and drink outlets. Just at the start of Bab Touma Street, at the police station before Hammam al-Bakri lane, there was a glass-fronted, wood fired oven place. It was dominated by the oven, attendants sweating as they worked and coped with the constant stream of patrons. Trays in the window were stacked with choices: meat-filled pastries, different breads, mini-pizzas and other local delights costing a maximum of a dollar. Point to one of those, and an assistant would scoop it up, then heat it in the oven for a minute of two before retrieving it to be placed in a paper bag. For the record, though, it was likely from there that one of my few serious stomach ailments arrived. Diagonally across the street was one of the innumerable biscuit shops to be found throughout the city, its highlight the huge bags of varied biscuits. The *Al Khair* restaurant and hotel on Straight Street near Bab Sharqi was excellent for a beer or coffee while accessing the free wifi. The *Ecological Café* beside the Citadel had a peaceful terrace looking over the gardens, and served the best minted lemon in Damascus, along with basic snacks like *haloumi* cheese in the local flat bread toasted. The café at the Roman Arch on Straight Street did good coffee and juices as well as fruit.

One consequence of this good food abundance was that the kitchen in the house remained unused. It was actually cheaper and easier to go out than buy food and prepare. The food outside was a magnet not only for its own sake but also for the enriching social experiences it offered. Why eat badly and expensively at home when all that awaited outside? The kitchen was thus consigned to providing only boring Western alternatives to breakfast, like cornflakes, housing all the olives (which I came to love in Syria after a lifetime's disdain and there is a story, allegedly, that only those who eat olives can learn Arabic—maybe there is hope yet) and other standby snacks, and on the ready to produce a version of coffee that could replicate, at least to some degree, that prepared in the restaurants and coffee shops outside.

In all those outside places, though, it was easy to see why Damascus has attracted and entranced so many people over the centuries. In almost all of them the visitor was given honoured attention, and the service was supreme. The food was invariably good, the atmosphere even better, and the friendliness of the locals noticeable. This was a place with a tradition, and wanted to share that with others.

GIVE US THIS DAY
OUR DAILY BREAD

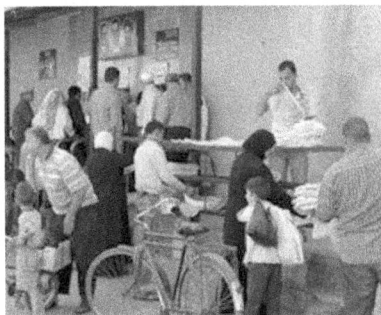

In many ways, Syria and Damascus has always run on bread, so one of the city's great emblems remains the bread shop.

There is a lovely example in an alley just off the bottom of Al Amin Street in the Old City, around from the first boutique hotel. It is stuck behind a row of shops, and at the corner of two converging and tight laneways so there is inevitably a confusion of traffic, pedestrians, hand carts, bicycles and stray animals. Add to that a lorry loaded high with sacks of flour brought in to keep up with the voracious demand for bread, and the congestion is complete. The building is squat, made out of unpainted breeze block. A few poles protrude from its front wall about two thirds the way up, so tarpaulins can be hoisted either at the height of summer or in a vain attempt to keep out the later rain. Men and boys queue at one tiny window, women and girls at another. The respective queues tail back several metres, adding chaos to confusion. Almost all that can be seen of the workers behind the windows are their hands, distributing piles of the warm sometimes hot round, flat breads straight from the oven, the staple food in this part of the world. Nearby, customers use the available metal racks to help organise their purchases, because most buy a lot. The breads are sorted into orderly piles, which the new owners walk away balancing in hands and on arms or, even now, in traditional style on the head. Throughout the less "modern" areas of the city, people might still be seen walking along with what at first glance look like a floppy hat designed to keep out the sun—it is fresh bread being carried home.

That scene was repeated all over the city and, as with anything else, citizens frequented their local and/or favourite haunt, stories abounding as to where the "best" product may be found. There was a good one just outside the Old City, over in the Qanawat market and conveniently near all the cheese, olive, and meat shops. It, too, was tiny with barely room enough inside for the man who distributed the breads, reaching back behind him to grab the next supplies delivered by the bakers toiling away in the recesses. It had to have been a million degrees in there during summer, and not much less at other times. A small crowd thronged the miniscule window, arms and hands disappearing inside in an effort to gain ascendancy over other customers. Bicycles, cars and horse-drawn carts skirted the bustling patrons. This went on for most of the morning. People arrived bearing their other food purchases, looking now to add the final piece to the jigsaw that would be lunch or dinner, or just an in-between snack. Others would buy the bread first, then head off to construct the meal around it.

There was a more peaceful outlet back in the Old City, just around from the crumbling Dadha Palace and on a main walking route that eventually led through to Bab Sharqi. Tiny lanes ran off this walkway near the shop, some short and heading for dead-ends, others winding off into a mysterious distance with old, often decrepit buildings, as always, seeming to touch each other at the top as they leaned in from each side. There were no other food shops near this baker, this was the genuine community article serving only the residents who lived nearby, and those from further afield who had learned of its reputation. Next to it, set into a wall, a beautiful drinking fountain was built in the customary soft, creamy sandstone, and was draped in vines colouring off now in the late autumn. Unlike other bakeries, the selling window here extended across the entire front of the building, so that customers could get easy access as well as chat to their neighbours, all the while looking right back into the traditional oven producing all those wonderful sights and smells. There was no hurry here, with always time for a chat either with the vendor or a fellow customer. A steady string of breads came from the baker's paddle, buyers carrying them off into all those tiny lanes and alleys.

Along the Old City's Quemariye, the main walk through from Bab Touma to the Umayyad Mosque, there was a perfect demonstration of bread's significance in this culture. Half way up a little rise in a broader part of the street there was an old, low wooden building with a step up to the selling window.

A small oven, a traditional rather than modern gas-fired one, blazed away in the darkened interior. It produced little other than the smaller seeded breads, rather than the bigger, flat *khobz*. This was because right next door stood a just as small but very well known *ful* and *hommus* outlet. A few battered round metal tables and chairs sprawled about its step landing. The hungry could sit down there and along came the dishes as well as the breads, and the snack was ready.

All over the city, newly baked breads could be seen stacked on racks, laid out on car bonnets and shop steps as well as in display cases and on empty boxes. Every food outlet had packaged breads, clearly not as good as the fresh ones but nonetheless necessary for daily survival. Snack sandwiches were available to ease people through a work day, these *sajj* options (usually cheese or salami) on offer at the coffee shops and restaurants and made possible only by the bakers. Bread runs the city.

It has been this way for a very long time, and a simple recipe has taken on cult status. The traditional bread contains only flour, dry yeast, salt, water, milk and olive oil, although some variations may see herbs added in. The human skill in making that simple combination into a product to be preferred over others underlines the importance of the bakers, and it seems their trade began perhaps as early as the eighth millenium BC up near Aleppo. Rudimentary tools evolved over time: newer and better ovens emerged from the simple, earlier use of hot stones (remarkably, the present day "inventions" of oven stones simply return to the ways of those earlier bread makers).

The rain/grain/bread/social contentment index began very early. Ibn Al-Qalanisi, for example, recorded

several examples in the early twelfth century where
shortages caused discontent through resultant high
prices.[30] As villages grew into towns and cities, the
supply chains for bread developed and grew. By the
nineteenth into the twentieth centuries, commercial
flour mills were well into production, and by the later
twentieth century government-run and controlled
bakeries were in action. The production and
distribution of bread was, in effect, a marker for social
contentment and political order.

In his marvellous book *Everyday Life & Consumer
Culture in 18th-Century Damascus,* James Grehan
devotes an entire chapter to "Bread & Survival",
reaffirming the significance of this humble product.[31]
As he points out, the city was overjoyed in June of
1749 when the wheat harvest arrived, because it
followed serious shortages and hardships. Bread was a
social litmus test for the well-being and health of the
city. Wheat was the preferred staple with even the
West's other standby, the potato (which arrived in
Syria only through the eighteenth century) struggling
to gain popularity. Wheat made bread. The fields
themselves that produced the necessary grains were
referred to simply as "bread", and Damascene bread
was renowned as the best. The major industry for the
city was, in many ways, the production of bread
because that involved growing, harvesting,
transporting, milling, production and distribution. For
the ruling classes it also represented a major form of
taxation, along with political trouble when shortages

---

[30]Ibn Al-Qalanisi, *The Damascus Chronicle of the Crusades* (New York, Dover, 2002 edn)

[31]James Grehan, *Everyday Life & Consumer Culture in 18th Century Damascus* (Seattle, University of Washington Press, 2007), ch. II

occurred. Stockpiles of wheat were already being put aside for such moments, because rulers knew that low supplies of bread meant high supplies of malcontents ready to turn out on the streets in protest. They must surely have understood the impulses of the French Revolution when it broke out in 1789. Grandees manipulated the Syria/Damascus market, and that led to suspicion and rumour of all kinds. Price controls and taxes were an attempt to regularise supply, whereas the populace in many respects still believed in a free market. Bread the staple was also bread the political barometer.

As Grehan points out, the bakers were invariably the meat in the sandwich, as it were. Governors and citizens were often united by just one thing: a high disregard for the honesty and probity of bakers who determined the state of bread consumption. In extreme cases, miscreant bakers were hanged publicly for their alleged indiscretions. Inevitably, they were caught up in the bread riots that appeared constantly throughout the mid-eighteenth century. In 1743, a severe grain shortage, exacerbated by supplier hoarding, drove bread prices high and supply was low. A hungry crowd stormed the courthouse to threaten the authorities, then raided all local bakeries in search of supplies. The intersection of supply and demand, control and discontent culminated in 1757-1758 when severe shortages produced the highest grain prices of the entire century, at the precise moment of serious political uncertainty. A governor installed by the Ottoman powers immediately encountered allegations of grain hoarding by city leaders. The general discontent led to full scale street battles. Then the *Haj* caravan was almost completely destroyed and the governor, who survived, fled rather than return to the city and chaos set in. Shops closed and bread prices soared one hundred and forty percent. A new governor set about restoring order but with a heavy hand, especially in the always-restive Midan where bakeries were deserted and bread production halted, the whole condition worsened by yet another crop failure. Again bread, its availability and price, symbolised a much deeper malaise.

There is an eerie continuity to this in Syrian and Damascene life. In 2008, for example, severe drought in the country's main wheat growing areas led to extreme shortages. By then Syria was consuming somewhere around four million tons of wheat annually, and had already gone from being self-sufficient to becoming a wheat importer. Food prices rose and inflation set in, and that was intensified by the government having to reduce subsidies on fuel and energy because of the straitened economy. Those price movements had a direct impact on bakers: petrol price rises were reflected in higher transportation costs for wheat deliveries, and rising natural gas prices added to the bakers' bills because their ovens were now all driven by gas. Bread prices went up, along with discontent, and the government had to very carefully balance the competing social pressures.

When the broader troubles broke out in 2011, it was not long before bread featured in the protests. As Homs and other centres came under siege, food price rises and bread shortages soon further stoked the discontent. In mid-2011 one demonstration in Banias, held to support those under siege in Daraa, featured the crowd lifting its bread aloft—"raise the bread to lift the siege of Daraa", they cried. By early 2012, some families in the poorer outer districts of Damascus were eating only bread (because of escalating food and vegetable prices) but needed up to four kilos of it a day, so were queuing at all local bakeries in order to fulfil their quota. The Damascus bakers reckoned they needed about three thousand tons a day to satisfy demand, but flour prices had risen by two hundred percent. The authorities, as earlier in history, saw the significance and implications here so not only attempted to guarantee supply, but also to use the opportunity to pass on their own messages. One report had bread distributed from all government-controlled bakeries carrying printed messages such as "the nation is bigger than the upheaval".

Oddly enough, then, the Ottoman rulers of the eighteenth century would have understood and may even have sympathised with the position in which Bashar al-Assad found himself.

COFFEE

At the eastern end of the Umayyad Mosque, near the end of the main walkway down from Bab Touma and just by some steps, sits Al Nofra, the most famous and most photographed of Damascene coffee shops. The Nofra has been there a long time: Karl Baedeker noted it on his 1906 map of Damascus.[32] It is always full, a crowded, bustling place that mixes ages and traditions, women included. Tourists sit writing their postcards, soaking up the ambience amidst hardened locals for whom it is still a principal social gathering point. Patrons spill out of

---

[32]Karl Baedeker, *Palestine & Syria* (Leipzig, Baedeker, 1906), p. 301.

the crowded shop and along the walls onto seats around a little well and beyond, watching anyone still walking around. There is a constant hum of conversation, and the inevitable gurgle of the *nargileh*. This is the ultimate in the modern coffee shop hangout.

Up the steps and immediately on the left through the arch, though, sits the ultimate traditional coffee shop. Its front step is really a patio, where groups of men puff and sip away. And they are only men, mostly older but with a mix of young. There is rarely a woman to be seen, because they never went to the coffee shop in the traditional settings. These guys will sit out there for hours, puffing the hubble bubble, drinking coffee, playing backgammon while watching "the life" walk by. There is another example of these traditional coffee shops off Straight Street near the Medhat Pasha end and walking through to pick up Al Amin Street—it opens in late evening and all the neighbourhood men drift in for a chat, a coffee, a smoke, and a game of cards. Outside the Old City, in the "centre", on Al Muttanabi Street that runs down from the Four Seasons to Port Said Street, there are two huge versions of these older style coffee shops. They have open windows, many tables, and perhaps hundreds of men sitting in groups.

The Azem Palace has a fixed display of a coffee shop that explains how important these institutions were and, to some extent, remain in Damascene and Arabic life. In their original form, a main attraction was the storyteller who would recount long and elaborate folk tales to help while away the hours. The storyteller may still be seen at the Nofra, but is a reminder of the past rather than a constant in contemporary life—like so many other aspects of life everywhere, the arrival of the electronic media in the form of 1920s radio was the beginning of the end for the Damascene storyteller. In the West the coffee shop has a history, too, but has become increasingly the site for a hurried stop to pick up coffee "to go" along with a muffin. That would never happen here. The Damascene shops are timeless, an escape from the outer life where, even in the Arab world, the clock has gained more of a sway. The Azem Palace interpretation depicts the coffee shop as a place for men to relax, escape the pressures of the household, get a chance to think, and socialise with people who thought like them. Modern feminists are scarcely likely to see that as an unalloyed social benefit. Nor would they appreciate the other Azem Palace display's explanation—that the coffee shop was a place for men to ease their stress while awaiting the birth of their children, because childbirth was dangerous! Well, yes, but more for the woman involved and the child, surely?

One romanticised mid-nineteenth century print depicts "coffee shops along the Barada", a time when the river ran and still retained its natural contours. The only thing that comes close now is the coffee shop in the ecological gardens, just near the Citadel along from Bab Al Faraj. It is very pleasant, but the gardens put a respectable distance between it and the summer fetid canal that is the modern replacement for the river. It runs mainly during heavy rains that are now more unpredictable in these days of climate change. What that print confirms and underlines, however, is that the coffee shop has been an institution in Damascus for a long time.

It is widely reckoned that the world's first coffee shop opened in Damascus in 1530 with the influence of the bean spreading widely and quickly throughout the region, and eventually around the globe. Some twenty five years later, a man called Shams from Damascus and a colleague from Aleppo were said to have opened the first coffee shops in Constantinople. (The term "Shami" is commonly used for "Damascene" in everyday expression, coming from "Sham" as the name of the city that dominated Greater Syria). Similarly, the roasting of coffee beans is thought to have begun in and around Damascus during this period, so in many respects "Turkish" coffee might just as easily have been "Damascene" coffee. Samer Akkach recounts how from this sixteenth century beginning, the taking of coffee entered the Ottoman and Damascene popular cultures, so that for the next two to three hundred years not only did coffee shops flourish, but coffee became a central part of leisure activities, including at picnics along the Barada river and down in the orchards of the Gouta.[33] The famous mid-nineteenth century Bartlett print captured one of these occasions, and was probably set outside the Tekkiye Suleymaniye complex and mosque that appeared in the mid-sixteenth century, and now houses the quality crafts *souk*. It stands directly across from the Four Seasons hotel, separated from it by the concrete channel that now directs what is left of the Barada.

That is not to say the tradition remains unchanged. Foreigners obsessed with the search for "good coffee", which some cynics might consider an oxymoron, are automatically shocked when asked if they want "Turkish" or "American" or even "Nescafe". For a country with such a deep coffee

---

[33]Samer Akkach, "Leisure Gardens, Secular Habits: the Culture of Recreation in Ottoman Damascus", Journal of the Faculty of Architecture, Middle East Technical University, Number 1, 2010

tradition that seems an oddity. It is, however, a simple reflection of a tradition unaffected by the arrival of ""skinny decaff latte" and "moccachino with more chocolate" via Starbucks or some other chain. There is coffee, Turkish, or the modern snap frozen varieties. But there are some concessions. One favoured coffee additive is cardamom, and the coffee shops sell prepared packs that have either a little, more, or a lot of added cardamom.

Yes, there is Arabica, but that is really the coffee bean prepared to the Arab taste, bitter (that taste for bitter is replicated in a lot of Syrian chocolate), which is why the inevitable question comes at the time of ordering: "sugar?" Even the hardened addict of "good coffee" cannot but be charmed when the coffee arrives in a long handled, beaten copper urn of varying size, and poured direct into the cup at the table. This coffee has had the sugar added to the water, if necessary, then been boiled, taken off the flame and at that time had the coffee stirred in, then brought back to the boil at least once. The more it is boiled, the stronger and thicker the brew. Then it arrives at the table by the copper express.

The ubiquitous "Turkish" tag is fascinating, a reminder of just how long the Ottoman Empire ran this part of the world, and of just how hard it is to change popular culture. Syria and other regional powers might have thrown off the Ottomans, regained independence, adopted new institutions and habits and practices, but they still drink "Turkish" coffee.

SWEETS ARE US, AND
WE ARE NUTS

Along at the corner of the lane at the bottom of the steps, behind small wired windows, a little factory space contains what look like six cement mixing machines, except that they are scrupulously shiny. Early most mornings, their whir was heard by pedestrians padding by on their ways to work, school or coffee.

This was part of the sweets-making chain integral to the Damascus scene, because these machines prepared the basis for many of the treats that later appeared in the stalls and shops just a few metres further up the lane that leads to Straight Street, and along the lane leading off it past the *madrasa* and into the bottom of the spice *souk* that by then was the sweet *souk*. Similar little factories were dotted throughout the area, outnumbering the wedding dress shop, the provisions stores and the general merchants, along with the tiny offices whose purposes remained unclear.

On my first venture into the sweets *souk,* before the advent of the house even, I was adrift in front of mesmerising choices at one stall that would become a favourite. From early in the morning the goodies were spilled out onto stands atop the cobblestones, forming an aisle into the shop where even more goods are displayed in boxes or packed in glass jars stacked almost to the roof. There were chocolates of a million varieties, jellies of all descriptions and colours, rumballs (as we might call them but probably lacking the essential ingredient here), liquorice, sherberts, gums, glaced fruits and more. You might be forgiven for thinking it was more about the packaging than the content, because these delights came exquisitely wrapped in brightly-hued wrappers, so that a box of chocolates was more a box of paper accompanied by chocolates.

As I stood confronted by this array and clueless about what I might buy, a young couple with their very young kids took pity. The mother handed her young daughter a sweet, and nudged her in my direction.

"Try that" she said, her husband smiling as the girl handed the tiny packet up to me.

Thank you, I replied, unwrapping what proved to be a stunning cherry-flavoured chocolate.

"It is that one there" said the husband, pointing to a table on the left just outside the shop, "and you will find some of those excellent as well", indicating to the other side.

The shopkeeper joined in: "You are from?"

Australia.

He smiled. "You are very welcome in my shop and you must come often. These ones are very good", and he shovelled a selection into a brown paper bag.

By now we were all good friends, and I was humbled by how easily these people had helped a stranger they would most likely never see again, although the shopkeeper probably reckoned, rightly, that he might.

That began a love/hate relationship with the sweets *souk:* love, because it embodied all the fables of the market, its long history and reputation; hate, that lay with the certain knowledge of the likely results of extensive fieldwork among all those calories. Back in my PhD student days in New Delhi, a Bengali sweetshop at the bottom of the stairs to my apartment on Connaught Circus inflicted severe damage on my cricket-playing weight in just a few short months. Now, again, and especially after I moved into the house just a few short steps away, at least twice a week a 100g or 200g bag of temptations would somehow end up at home after another visit to my friend in a vain attempt to sample all he had on offer, not to mention his colleagues' selection as well. However, with effort, I drew the line at buying sweets *en route* to the morning taxi—that would have been way too much.

Nuts are the other great casual filler in Damascus, and up on Straight Street several tiny shops overflowed with an amazing array of options: walnuts, cashews, peanuts, almonds and all the other favourites along with more exotic options. On my first foray along Via Recta I fell victim to a very clever nut salesman. I was across the road from his shop, checking out a bakery, and he sailed over bearing products.

"You must try these."

I did: almonds, not my all time favourites.

Thank you, but I do not need any.

"But you will like these." Out came some cashews which are a favourite.

They are splendid, thank you.

"Come over to my shop."

By now I was in that classic traveller position of feeling obligated having tasted the wares, so I went over. Ten minutes later I escaped but only after having bought half a kilo of several different varieties and at a price, I discovered subsequently, well above the going rate. In my subsequent walks past that shop, there were few occasions when he did not have another foreign buyer lined up. He was very good at what he did.

My favourite nut shop became the one directly across from the top of the nearest alley by which I could reach Straight Street from the house. I could be there in a couple of minutes: out the door and down the steps, left into Jabri lane, past the shops and the fruit stall, left at the sweet factory and up to Straight Street passing all the sweets shops, most of which I had visited by the time I left Damascus. Then it was across Straight Street, watching out for cars, which the legionnaires never had to do, and into the shop. I started going there because it was the closest place where I could buy drinking water, with half a dozen large bottles being my limit to carry back at once. Naturally, I began to notice more than water. It was a narrow fronted, glass windowed place stuffed full of nuts and sweets to the point where no more than about three or four customers at a time could squeeze into the narrow space in front of the counter. There was a small desk at the back where the owner did his books, and took phone calls while directing other family members to their tasks. Immediately behind that desk a set of stairs led to a mezzanine where even more goods spilled out, threatening to topple onto the floor and customers below.

Typically, people would reach their arms in and around the front door to snare their desired goods while people in front took their time in choosing. There were those who knew what they wanted, and others did not. I was mostly in the latter group, because every time in there I spied something new. After the first couple of visits the owner started giving me additional samples, and next time in there I would usually select a couple of those samples. He would then line me up with yet another new sensation, knowing he would have a firm sale next time. It got to be a game: me trying to resist (failed) and him trying to see how many new things he might sell me (succeeded).

There were other sellers, yes, but my main sweets and nuts agents, in the *souk* and up on Straight Street, were more than merchants, they became guides and I never tired of learning from them.

HUBBLE BUBBLE

On any walk along the laneway at the bottom of the steps, especially from later afternoon onwards, I frequently encountered a man walking up and down swinging a small, metal container trailing smoke vigorously in a circle from his shoulder. When the swinging stopped, it revealed a container of glowing hot coals that were then fanned to keep their intensity and heat while being taken inside one of the restaurants or a shop.

This was one of the *nargileh* men who provide Damascenes with one of their most distinct pleasures, the water pipe or hubble bubble.

Throughout the city, but especially in the *souks*, a profusion of shops sold nothing but *nargileh* and all the necessary *accoutrements*, including the coals scuttle. Rows and rows of the metal pipes were lined up in all shapes, sizes and colours. Then there were the smoking attachments themselves, and the mouthpiece reeds that go in the end of the flexible hoses. And, of course, there was the tobacco.

The principle is simple enough. The tobacco is placed in a small concave container at the top of the pipe. That tobacco is mostly fruit flavoured, so gives off a distinctive smell wherever it is used. The *nargileh* man then places a piece of foil over the top of the tobacco, pierces that foil then tops it with some of the prepared coals. That creates heat inside the concavity and smoke comes off the tobacco. Meanwhile, a mouthpiece has been attached to the smoking tube attached to the bottom of the pipe, near the base on which it sits upright. The smoker draws a breath through the tube, the smoke travels down through the pipe and through water, creating the sound that gives the pipe its popular name, the hubble bubble.

These modern pipes are all brass and other metals with flexible pipes. In 1822, Robert Richardson reported on the earlier Damascene models. At that point, according to him, there were no long pipes, so he thought the shape unwieldy to the point of being "hideous". It had a head like a *hookah,* but there was a long cane stuck in the side of the body whose stalk was so short it could not be placed on the ground. He was not attracted to it or its product, the smell of tobacco drawn through "dirty water" being "terrible", in his view. It was taken only because of fashion, he opined, "poison and stupefaction" coming from "the end of a stick" hardly being a useful social habit.[34] Well over a century later Bob Newhart, the American comic, created a sketch (available on YouTube) in which a functionary at the court of Queen Elizabeth I takes a phone call from Sir Walter Raleigh, promoting new products from America. Raleigh is unheard, but is clearly explaining the attraction of this new substance he had discovered, tobacco. The courtier says, "so you take these leaves, stick them in your mouth, and set fire to them? It will never catch on, Walt."

It had taken in the Levant because the pipe was a social glue, as it remains. Couples might share one. Groups of people will have one each. Young women are now particularly prominent smokers, and may be found practising in all the smart café/restaurants late in the afternoon. The traditional, men-only coffee houses produce a cloud of smoke whenever they are open. Pipes are on hand in the *hammam* for a post-bath smoke to go with the tea or coffee. Shopkeepers will be outside in their chairs, paper and or coffee in hand, and the hubble bubble alight. It is common to see people walking through the souk, new *nargileh* or replacement part in hand. Hubble bubbles are always on the move, the *nargileh* men taking a fix to a customer somewhere.

All over Damascus the sight, sound and smell of the *nargileh* was ever present. A few lanes away from the house, one small juice shop had an independent contractor in attendance. Every day, his small van would draw up to the shop, and the back door opened to reveal racks of pipes and all the rest. Outside the door, even in winter, he would fan and protect the

---

[34]Robert Richardson, *Travels Along the Mediterranean,* pp. 475-6

coals for his customers inside. Every so often he
would check on his customers, replacing those coals
burned to ash. A good *nargileh* man will keep a pipe
going for an hour or so.

Smoking is ever present in Syria, as throughout the
Arab and Asian worlds, a constant shock to
Westerners now reconciled to smoke free
environments, and to social outcast status for any
wretch who continues to smoke. Even though
government buildings are allegedly smoke-free
throughout Syria, some senior official or other will
always light up a cigarette. The Vice-President at one
of the universities always lit a cigarette when we
arrived, an impish grin daring us to say anything. He
was in Homs, so would have had little to grin about
not that much later. Young people of both sexes
smoked freely and furiously, their elders, too, if they
could still breathe. Smoking in restaurants was
permitted, but non-smoking sections were available,
especially in the places used to greeting Westerners.
In smaller and less compromising places, the non-
smoker is at the mercy of the horde.

While most cigarette smokers took the hubble bubble
almost automatically, non-cigarette smokers would
also frequently take it, too, not so much because of the
smoke but of the ritual. The time it takes to smoke a
pipe suggests it was almost made as a form of ritual
interaction. Once the pipe starts, people stay until it
finishes, and that provides a lot of talking and
friendship time. It is common to see different
individuals within a group take the pipe at different
times so that the total time involved goes well beyond
an hour, ensuring that everyone joins the
conversation.

Watching the veterans confirms this view of it being a

ritual. There is a studied steadiness and rhythm to their smoking. The coffee, sometimes a pastry is at hand. Talk, smoke and listen. Talk, smoke and listen. It creates a conversation pattern, perhaps a more elaborate version of the "peace pipe" smoking always observed in the old cowboy movies.

But it is clearly a health risk, some critics reckoning that one pipe produces the same amount of tar as a packet of cigarettes. The choice of tobacco was always an important matter, though. Karl Baedeker reported that the Lebanese variety was prized around the turn of the twentieth century, but because of the Ottoman rule it was banned in favour of the Persian strain which was excellent for the *nargileh.* Even so, he added, smuggled-in Lebanese was readily available.[35] Tobacco was an important commodity then as now, not just for the smoking but also for the occasion. It was for that reason a 2008-9 proposed "smoking in restaurants" ban in neighbouring Jordan raised such a controversy—it was not about the tobacco, but about the *nargileh.*

---

[35]Baedeker, *Palestine and Syria,* p. xxix

BACKGAMMON AND CARDS

On any given evening, a quick walk into the Old City confirms the continued existence of another great social ritual. It is most noticeable in Straight Street. Shopkeepers along there, even those fully reliant on the tourist trade, very rarely press their goods. They prefer to let the potential client look around, and will turn the lights on and off to enable a better view, but there is no hard sell. It is tempting to think they have a more urgent mission, and in many ways they do. On those evenings the shopkeepers, their neighbours, colleagues, friends and even passersby will be engrossed in what is theoretically leisure, but in reality is almost their main preoccupation.

For some this will be playing cards. All along the street, small tables are set up. Grander affairs will have folding or even the highly ornate and stylish Damascene chairs brought out from the sale stock, but others get by with upturned milk crates or fruit boxes. The tables all have coffee or tea cups strewn about, often a little gas burner nearby keeping up the supply of caffeine. Ashtrays abound and cigarette smoke is palpable, and many players bring out their *nargileh.* This is games season on the high street, and it is serious business even though the banter is incessant. The play is intense, along with the concentration. Hovering experts pass knowing looks and even comment on the play. Winning players flourish their cards, perhaps slamming them to the table to emphasise victory. Comments and counter-comments fly. Scores are kept or argued. Having started early in the evening, the games stretch into the night with either shop lights or oil lamps allowing continuance. Depending on the state of the game, any customer may or may not get served.

Card playing has a long history around the world and the Levant, Syria in particular, is no exception. Almost all visitors throughout the ages commented on the presence of cards in the coffee houses and restaurants, along with the accompanying tobacco. As with so many other aspects of life, though, the long Ottoman reign produced change. Many of the older forms of card games became more codified, and different forms of games appeared. By the early nineteenth century, for example, *tarneeb,* a form of bridge, had appeared, remaining popular but not exclusive in Syria and in the Old City. The commercial opportunities in all this were soon realised and, even now, the Khabbaz Industrial Company in Aleppo describes itself as the Middle

East's leading supplier of playing cards, with several different varieties on offer. Another trader carries a pack bearing the ubiquitous "I [heart] Syria" message, yet a further reminder that for a country allegedly isolated from the world, Syria carries a lot of outside trappings. Interestingly, Khabbaz stresses that one of its strong points is its attention to European detail in the cards, an indication of just how long, how pervasive and how continually surprising the forms of that cultural interchange have been and remain.

Over in *Souk* Sarouja, there was a small alleyway between the main arms of the Saturday flea market. It hosted, among other things, an exotic junk/antiques shop that features old oil lamps from the 30s, battered *ouds* (the Arabian guitar-like instrument), branded ashtrays, Russian books from the 60s, some interesting pictures and old bicycles. Elsewhere, the lane contained audio cassette and DVD shops, some clothes shops, and several coffee shops where those not interested in the market could while away a couple of hours. Outside one of these, in the middle of the lane, the same four old men seemed to sit everyday with their coffee or tea, cigarettes or *nargileh,* and their cards. They were certainly there every Saturday, each of the four with his own playing style: one sat back relaxed and open; another closed up and literally with his cards to his chest; the third cautiously laying his cards flat on the table, then raising a corner to check if he really had the cards he thought he had; the fourth a variation on all the others depending on how his game progressed. They sat literally in the middle of the alleyway, pedestrians laden with goods and bags streaming around them while they obliviously got on with their game.

Cards continue to be significant, not only as a playing

form but also as a representational one. During 2011, Paris became a centre for the myriad forms of oppositional alternatives that sprang up in the latest version of the "Syrian Spring". There were the usual reports of meetings, coffee and tea. One intriguing story, though, announced the arrival of Syrian "revolution" playing cards. The Kings and Queens had their heads removed and blood trickled down their necks. The only form still with a head was the Joker. In true Syrian style, the meaning was open to interpretation, but there was no coincidence about the use of the cards as a vehicle for the message. There was military intent in Iraq when the Americans issued their troops with playing cards bearing the pictured faces of those most wanted within Saddam Hussein's entourage. Here, the Syrian version was about passing a coded message, and using one of the oldest forms of Syrian pastime.

The greatest Syrian participant sport, however, has to be backgammon. There were versions of the game found in the Levant, where it emerged, as early as pre-Christian times. In one of those curious paradoxes it then found its way to Europe, by way of the Arab arrival in Spain, where it took on more developed forms and became known as *tabula* (meaning, literally, "board"). Ironically, the Crusaders took that form back with them to the Levant, so the circle had closed. This was rather like the British discovering a horseback game with stick and ball (a skull in the purest form) in the Himalayas, taking it back to England, renaming it polo, then returning it to India for the princes to adopt as an elite sport. Over time, the Levantines again modified the European rules of backgammon, partly as a form of rejecting the Frankish overlord, but retained the Arabic form of the name, *taawli,* which it still largely remains today.

Backgammon has a deeper, even superstitious aspect embedded in the representation of the board. In total it has twenty four points, taken to represent the number of hours in the day. Each side of the board has twelve points: the months in the Zodiac. The thirty counters match the days in the month, the two dice represent day and night. The number seven is the most frequent score set up by the dice: the days in the week. Given this direct connection to daily life, it is scarcely surprising that backgammon is found everywhere: homes, offices, cafes, shops, restaurants. Every night at Brokar, clients would arrive either clutching their own boards or asking for a house set. One gang had a regular meeting three times a week and sat at a particular table, their noise and merriment filling the place for hours, the sounds of the counters indicating precisely why the French called the game *tric-trac.*

The Ottomans were again instrumental in the growth of the game, and its commercialisation—well, to be precise, in the commercialisation of its equipment. In the Khalili Islamic collection based in England there is a beautiful board dating from the turn of the nineteenth century, painted on wood then varnished over, the artist thought to be the court painter, Muhammad Hasan. It has three interconnecting boards that, when unhooked, create a box in which the counters and dice were kept. It is beautifully coloured and designed, the Ottoman influence evident in the presence of two apparently European couples and a Persian couple. This was part of a new artistic expression of the backgammon board, and Damascus was to the fore in that production. Over time, the design thinking was reversed: instead of the board being transformed into a box, an opening-out box was created to contain the board inside and be able to carry counters and dice. This box became a renowned

Damascene product, and especially in marquetry form.

My favourite Damascene marquetry shop remained the very first one I went into, a tiny place in Lazaristes Street (alley, really, if a wide one) in the Christian Quarter, where much of the amazing wood ware comes from. On that first visit I met the brothers who now run the place, having taken over from their fathers and grandfathers. The really chatty brother habitually wore a singlet rather than shirt, had a pot belly, a balding head, Marty Feldman-like eyes and the loveliest smile and sense of humour, neither of which ever left him. The Damascene box boys showed me not only the showroom but also the workshop where the dust of ages lay amidst the huge range of works in progress. Unlike some of the more traditionalist makers, they had a bandsaw and other modern equipment to speed things up.

Their work was stunning. At the top of the range were the marvellously intricate games tables that disassembled down to a small flat pack ("Excellent for travel, sir!"), but when assembled had tables for cards, chess, checkers, and backgammon. That design was startling enough, but was outdone by the craft work in the pieces. Damascus has long been known for the beauty and brilliance of its wooden furniture and right down to smaller items like boxes, coasters, pen boxes and, of course, backgammon boards. All of these items piled up in the shop, the few visitors who could cram in to the showroom at once being surrounded by a dazzling array of options. The quality and variation of colour in the woods glued together then shaped to make these items was impressive, but what makes the work really distinctive is the mother-of-pearl inlay. That practice began in the early Ottoman period. By the nineteenth century, Damascus was the acknowledged centre of excellence for the work, though the mother-of-pearl itself is these days more likely to come from Taiwan rather than Deir ez- Zor as it did back then.

One afternoon we sneaked into the tiny showroom on yet another visit, skirting the massive German horde crammed into what was the not-much-larger factory area. We selected a box for a gift and Marty Feldman began to wrap it up, just as tour group members drifted in to check what was available of the things they had just seen being made.

"How much?" I asked.

He looked up, this short, ageing and balding man with the mirth-lined face, and whispered,

"For you, 600."

He looked meaningfully towards the tour group and grinned—that was a very, very fair price, one he anticipated more than making up for in the succeeding minutes. He even added in a gift of a small box that sits now on my desk. We grinned back, paid, and fled before the fleecing frenzy began.

This family business has endured at least three generations, probably more, and will survive longer because our conspirator's son is now involved, a serious salesman who loves a beer. On another occasion, this younger entrepreneur showed us some exquisite examples of the larger games tables they were making and exporting to the USA, the latest variation in a trade his family had been running for well over a century. It was he who sold my two project colleagues an elegant backgammon board each. These were medium-sized, and in the now-customary form. Each of the points was marked out in alternating coloured wood pieces, all invisibly fitted together, and interspersed with the mother-of-pearl, inside and out. These stunning pieces now sit in England and Oregon.

These boards and their variations are not just showpieces, because they are also the ones that appear all over the city, surrounded by shouting players who smash dice and counters at each other in an almost physical confrontation. The game has a long history and still serves a social purpose—throughout the events of 2011 and 2012, media reports routinely referred to Damascene shopkeepers sitting around drinking tea, playing cards—and backgammon.

THE ANIMAL KINGDOM

A remarkable sight appeared one Friday night on the main thoroughfare between Bab Touma and Straight Street in the Christian Quarter. In amongst the normal bustling weekend crowd looking for supplies, a restaurant, or just a promenade this pair stood out. They were young, late twenties or early thirties, extremely attractive, well groomed, impeccably dressed. He wore a sharp suit, neat silk tie and clearly expensive shoes. She was perched on high heels, wearing a white shirt with the collar turned up, black jacket and grey skirt to just below the knee. They were riveting enough, but that alone did not attract the attention—"beautiful people" were plentiful in the Quarter and in the city. Between them, though, they led a pair of fabulous Siberian Husky dogs, those normally seen on film pulling sleds in the Antarctic or Arctic. These are the dogs that power the legendary Iditarod Race over a thousand miles between Nome and Anchorage, Alaska. Yet here were two out for a stroll in the Old City of Damascus that was again living up to its reputation as a place of surprise. This was a statement of some kind.

It was not unusual to see dogs in the Christian Quarter. Back in the mid-nineteenth century, one report had dozens of them prowling the area.[36] A walk around on any evening now might produce a sighting of a Pekingese, a King Charles spaniel or a Shitzu, lapdogs all. Some of them might be carried rather than be walking themselves, they were house pets. At one point, a young man began parading a silver and grey German Shepherd through the main thoroughfares. These Siberians, though, were something else, these were serious dogs.

The underlying wonder, of course, was this scene's absolute contrast with the well-known Muslim aversion to dogs, few of which are to be seen in Damascus other than in the Christian Quarter. This aspect of Muslim life provides an interesting perspective on change and tradition. Tradition has it that dogs are impure so Muslims should not keep them, though dispensation is given where dogs are needed for herding animals or guarding crops. For that reason, dogs are more commonly seen in rural areas, but outside rather than in the house. Some argue, technically, that the dog's saliva is taboo rather than the dog itself, for obvious health reasons. The anti-dog tradition became powerful, early, although Mrs Mackintosh suggested that at the time of her living in

---

[36].*A Handbook for Travellers in Syria and Palestine*, p. 481

Damascus in the mid-nineteenth century, some Muslims fed the street dogs.[37] Any man before whom a dog passes preceding prayer, for example, immediately has his purity compromised and his prayer nullified. Black dogs were thought to not just symbolise but to *be* evil. They, in particular, were to be killed. Selling dogs to make a profit is forbidden. In fact, keeping a dog was said to lead to a daily loss of "credit" towards the afterlife.

Most of this is said to be written in the *hadith,* the rulings of the Prophet and later interpretations, rather than laid down in the Quran. Inevitably this has become the subject of debate. One Islamic scholar in the United States took to keeping dogs as a symbol of the struggle between rules and customs, because he believed the *hadith* made no such restrictions. Indeed, he even pointed to one Quranic source that had the Prophet himself praying in the presence of his own dogs. Islamic veterinary surgeons also stress that animals are all part of Allah's will, so need to be treated well. As in the West, these vets lament that people tend to abandon pets at times of holiday or other inconvenience, and may even have them destroyed. Those Siberian Huskies were certainly well looked after, but clearly belonged to Christian owners, a further reflection on diversity in the city.

Cats are another story. On my second or third morning in the house, the weather still warm and clear, the sun cast a shadow over the top floor parapet that was projected onto the wall against which the stairs stood. Because of that, I could see the shadow of what became the house cat walking along the parapet, tail high and agile. Then came a thud as it

---

landed on the roof above me, on its way to what was a daily routine of visiting the local area. Every day after that, its distinctive cry heralded its arrival, usually accompanied by a clatter as it leaped onto a loose tin awning over an upstairs bedroom. A splendid ginger and white that was well nourished, it spent its days foraging and hanging out with colleagues of whom there were several. Imperious, like all cats, it looked me over from afar but never stooped to visit—perhaps it knew what was (or, more specifically, was not) in the kitchen. In every laneway and cul-de-sac in the Old City, cats and kittens are legion, and they are all very healthy. People put out food to feed the animals whether or not they own them.

The "Damascus cat" is a known phenomenon and often the subject of conversation. There is evidence that the cat was revered in the Arab world before the arrival of Islam, perhaps even to the point of worshipping a Golden Cat. Certainly, the cat is widely believed to have been particularly approved of by the Prophet, and there is an often-told story about his own cat, Muezza. One day, at the call for prayer, Muezza was asleep on the Prophet's sleeve. Rather than disturb the cat, he cut off his sleeve, then stroked the cat three times which is said to have endowed the famed seven lives, and the ability to land on its feet at all times. During the nineteenth century, one old mosque in the city was said to have been given over to housing cats. Under Islam now, to mistreat a cat is a severe sin because they are meant to be looked after extremely well. They may not be sold for money or exchanged for goods and, unless the cat has obvious problems, its saliva is considered harmless to humans.

As a child, Siham Tergeman adored the "fat pampered cats" that jumped on to her *Souk* Sarouja house roof from neighbouring properties. She also remembered her own cat, Shama, and its kittens, one of whom was killed by Harun from the "fat pampered" and allegedly father to the victim. Her grandmother explained this tragedy away: Harun did not want to " bring up his children to eat at the banquet of others".[38] The child seemed unconvinced by this explanation.

Marius Kociejowski extends this issue of animals in his confusing and frustrating but always stimulating book, *The Pigeon Wars of Damascus.*[39] The "at large" pigeons live abundantly in the city, notably around the Umayyad Mosque and especially so on Saturday mornings when visitors feed them generously. They wheel about in great flocks, constantly on search for food. The pigeons to which Kociejowski refers, however, are the "kept" or homing type and, again, in Islam there is a view on these. They were thought to disturb neighbours and, in particular, create in the owner's mind, via the pigeon, a glimpse into a neighbour's courtyard privacy from on high. That is, the pigeons were regarded as emissaries from and even an "eye in the sky" for the owner, and that was seen as an affront to the principles of Islam. For that reason, latter day pigeon fanciers are what Victor Turner and others would have labelled as "liminal" members of society, tolerated but suspected.[40] From there, Kociesjowski uses them as an allegory for the evolution of modern Syrian and Damascene life, with all its complexities and consequences.

---

[38]Siham Tergeman, *Daughter of Damascus,* p.17

[39]Marius Kociejowski, *The Pigeon Wars of Damascus* (Emeryville Ontario, Biblioasis, 2011)

[40]Victor Turner, *The Forest of Symbols* (Ithaca, Cornell University Press, 1970)

Many of these birds fly over a building across from the entrance to *Souk* Sarouja. It stands out on its own now, cut off from everything else by the freeway on one side and a shabby park on the other. It is, however, always busy, on its ground floor, at least. There are three or four pet shops there and, as usual, the cages and other goods for sale spill out into the covered walkways. Inside, there are birds of all descriptions—one shop once had a pair of Macaws for sale. The birds were joined by rabbits, guinea pigs, tropical fish and a range of other animals. Parents brought in their kids to choose a family pet from among the host of bright, healthy animals that were all kept in clean conditions and extremely well fed. Just like anywhere else in the world, it was always touching to see a beaming kid carefully carrying away a kitten destined to be well loved.

The Siberian Huskies, the house cat and all the others, then, were not just curious facts in Damascus, they were another set of social and cultural markers indicating issues in Islam, as well as changes in the modern city being undergone by its inhabitants. On the other hand, the owners of the Huskies may have just been *flaneurs*.

A FIGHTER PILOT
AT THE BAKERY

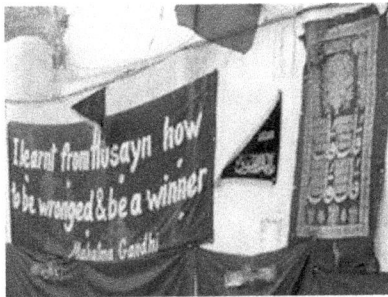

Up past Jabri, just around the corner towards Straight Street and before Maktab Anbar, stands one of the busiest Old City bakeries. It is open almost continuously. People stop their cars in the alley and lean out the window to make a purchase, often upsetting those drivers behind whose horns rapidly move from "Hello" to "shove off." There are always people at the windows, half windows really at the bottom with transactions conducted over over the top of them. This is a separate display and sales room, the baking done off in another space seen from a door alongside. The goods are frequently outside on trays, though, ready to be shipped off somewhere else as part of this highly successful operation.

The owner invariably sits on a chair under a small tree opposite the shop, discussing daily events with a couple of pals while watching proceedings. The bakery's location is perfect, dominating four major ways in and out of the Old City that carry considerable vehicle and foot traffic. As they say in real estate, he has "location, location, location". The bakery's decision-making process about precisely what will be on sale remained a mystery throughout. True, the chocolate-filled *croissants* were always present, the stock in trade for all bakers because Damascenes revert to them automatically. They are extremely rich to some tastes. Sometimes the round, chocolate-topped and *sauce Anglais*-filled donuts and/or the *éclair* version appeared. The plain biscuits were excellent and always there, along with the even better and addictive coconut drops. There was also a coconut cake cut in small squares, moist, delicious, very filling, and undoubtedly "bad" in the modern sense. Then, suddenly and unheralded, sensationally good jam tarts emerged—maybe that was a winter thing.

The word "bakery" needs a little explanation. There were two types, really, the bread shops, and ones like this that baked no bread and would be more likely known in the West as "cake shops." Bread in Arabic is *khobz,* but perhaps predictably, *ka'ak* (baked goods) can also be used to refer to those seeded bread rings made by the small shop in Quemariye and taken with the *ful* from the tiny snack place next door. That said, these two types of outlets were to be found all over the city, and all doing an excellent trade. Another favourite *ka'ak* outlet, for example, was strategically located along the walk towards the taxis. It was one of the establishments more or less embedded in a section of the old Roman wall on the way to the ATM in

Hariqa, and its window was well above ground level. Customers looked down into the small shop area and its gas-fired oven that was always well alight by the time I walked past in the mornings. Its range was relatively limited, but high quality. The main man there looked like he had sampled a lot of the product to ensure quality control, and always had a big smile on the afternoons I stopped to buy something. After the first couple of times, there was always an additional sample to carry away as well from what became known as the Other Bakery.

It was no wonder the place near Maktab Anbar was so popular, though. Buying was a great experience because the Arab queue was always in operation, meaning no queue. Someone else might be mid-purchase, but a coin or a note would appear over the shoulder along with a request and an instruction, and then another might well appear. The server would choose whether or not to take any notice of these anarchic practices, but would always continue conversation with the initial buyer. People on bikes stopped in front of the window, kids were sent with money, the odd foreigner strayed in bewildered, the process continued day and night.

A curious paradox pervades Arab culture. There is a heavy emphasis on hospitality and care of the visitor when immediately-met, but that is as far as it goes. No one takes any notice of whether or not another person was "there first", because this is a fight for survival. While waiting for taxis, for example, someone else would frequently and languidly drift past to be a little further up the road in the hope of snagging the next available cab. Similarly, anyone walking towards you in a lane or alleyway would rarely deviate from their line, even if it was directly at you. It was a little like playing "chicken" on foot, scarcely life threatening but occasionally aggravating. In crowds, people would frequently cross immediately in front, to the point of tripping anyone daring to come the other way.

None of this is done with malice, it is just a way of life for people intent on being somewhere to do something. Much the same principle applies on the roads, so that someone wanting to go left off a traffic circle will think nothing of going all the way around on the right then cutting across five lanes of traffic. It is just being expedient.

This rule applied at the bakery, then, and the person usually dispensing service, balance, wisdom, commentary and consideration on the evening shift was the personable fighter pilot, met very early on. He was tall if now a little stooped, slightly balding, heavy set, strong Arab nose and distinctive cheekbones, no moustache, dark and deep-set eyes with a calm exterior that coped with everything coming along. His house was a little further away in the Old City, the standard extended family abode where his kids grew up surrounded by relatives.

He had served in the air force and recalled flying jets at fifty feet in contour navigation through mountains and deserts. That excitement took him overseas and gave him an interest in the world but did not, it seems, turn him into the full warrior. When he left the military he had ambitions of becoming a commercial pilot, but the money was not there to get him started so, now, he was philosopher in residence at the bakery rather than global aviator.

His view on that was striking. He considered himself lucky to have a family and an avocation, a regular life that caused him no stress. He wished nothing but the same for others. Conversations were invariably about family, especially after he met Sandi because that helped him place things more. His other great source for thanks was health and happiness, *Alhamdulillah* ("Praise To God"), and the wish that every day be peaceful.

That led to politics and, again, his view was universal rather than nationalistic. He had no love for Israel, but believed everyone in the world wanted nothing but peace in which to conduct their affairs and bring up their kids. He was kind to the Americans in this respect, as a lot of ordinary Syrians were—no one in their right mind wanted conflict, thought the Fighter Pilot and many others like him. There was no future in that. That was why people like George Bush were anathema, because from this standpoint he seemed to represent nothing but a thoughtless commitment to violence with no idea of consequence. And the concern was as much for the American as for Arab victims. There was a hinted desire for more "democracy" in Syria, but also a strong sense that Syria was a very young country in terms of dealing with independence, despite its ancient history. Greeks, Romans, Mamluks, Crusaders, Mongols, Ottomans, French and all the rest had taken their turn, and the country had been run by Syrians only for a short period during which further considerable change had occurred.

This was a constant theme in debate at that time, immediately before the 2011-12 uprisings. One of the translators at the office, for example, pondered whether it would simply take time for more democracy to arrive, or whether it would have to be forced perhaps by revolution. After all, he observed, the French required a revolution to bring about dramatic change. This turned out to be a highly prescient comment with a future much closer than it appeared at the time.

The Fighter Pilot might have been no revolutionary, but he was also a peacenik with a wicked sense of humour.

One night, while I was buying coconut drops, three Scandinavian women stopped to ask directions for Straight Street, presumably because I looked a bit like them.

"Straight up there, to Straight Street".

Off they went.

He looked at me.

"How come all these women ask you?"

No idea.

"You must have something."

A sense of direction.

"They seemed to like you."

They needed help.

"Do you get lonely?"

No, the Old City is too interesting and, besides, I have friends like you to talk to.

"You are too clean. I think a lot, but do nothing, unlike my father."

Too much information.

The coconut drops changed hands and we bade our goodbyes, subject to be resumed at later stages.

Sometime later a new, more groomed version of the Fighter Pilot appeared. The hair was slick, the face newly clean shaven.

"I thought I needed to smarten up", he said.

I complimented him on looking younger.

That was a good thing, he thought, for old men like us!

FATHER, SON AND
HOLY GHOST

One early foggy morning in January 1994, Basel al-Assad relegated his chauffeur to the back seat of the Mercedes, and drove himself to Damascus airport. At high speed in poor conditions he careered through a traffic circle and flipped the car several times. He died, the chauffeur and another passenger survived, and life changed dramatically for his brother Bashar, then a young doctor specialising in ophthalmology.

Something that struck all visitors to Syria immediately before the troubles was the ever-present symbolism of leadership, principally in the persons of President Bashar, his late father Hafez, and late brother Basel.

Hafez shaped the new Syrian Arab Republic following the coup that brought him to power in 1970, Basel was his heir apparent, Bashar became the unexpected successor.

Bashar appeared in picture or profile on the windows of probably three in every five cars in Syria, if not more. This was certainly so in Alawite-predominant areas like Lattakia whence came the Assad family, but the images were also strongly visible elsewhere, and in Damascus. There was the military leader version, all combat fatigues and aviator shades with the general's determined look. The international statesman in Savile Row suit look had the engaging smile. Then there was the guide, the man looking forward confidently to the future. Sometimes Bashar was paired with Hafez, a reminder of the leadership continuity. Sometimes the two of them appeared with Hassan Nasrallah of Hezbollah, a pointer to the complex regional role Syria had assumed in its ever present desire to see Lebanon disappear and the "true" boundaries of earlier times be restored. Hafez himself appeared in military image frequently, and sometimes the "lost" son and heir apparent appeared as well. These photographs, outlines, prints and other images adorned every prominent building and even apartment blocks. Photographs of Bashar appeared in every room of every official building and in the corridors. A favourite trick for every new consultant come to the office was to have a photograph taken sitting at work under the gaze of the President. There was a continuity, too—the "Bashar waving" photograph was identical to that of his father, even if the "wave" now had unfortunate reflections of the Saddam Hussein imagery that emerged from the Iraq war.

Some commentators had compared this phenomenon

to that of the North Korean leadership cult, suggesting even that Hafez might have modelled the practice from there. Likenesses certainly flourished throughout Syria, and must have kept many artisans employed: statues huge and small dominated traffic circles and elsewhere, busts appeared outside buildings. On the way to Homs, two huge statues of present leader and father occupied prominent sites, and there was an even larger edifice between Homs and Tartous on the way to Lattakia. The "wave" was a favourite pose for these. It was suggested, however, that even then Bashar had already begun quietly discouraging the indiscriminate proliferation of statues, and that said something interesting about his perception of a necessarily changing role and associated "image".

When Bashar al-Assad came to power in 2000 at his father's death, then, it was an accident caused by an accident. Following his brother's death, Bashar the aspirant ophthalmologist returned from London for military training to gain not only the skills but also the network of military influence he needed as leader and politician. In particular, Bashar had to cement his social networks inside the minority Alawite community of which he was part, and which his father had delivered into power by co-opting other minorities like the Christians and the Druze, along with the urban Sunni Muslim merchants. This coalition ran Syria, with social and intermarriage networks further cementing the bonds. Bashar had little time to learn all this and to make the career switch, just six years before his father succumbed to cancer.

Many thought Bashar would not last when he assumed control, suggesting he lacked the "killer streak" and some early commentators, especially

Israeli ones, depicted him as weak, impulsive, and dangerous.[41] His father had become President in 1971 as leader of a more moderate wing following the Baath party split in 1966, the more radically conservative elements ending up in Iraq under Saddam's version of the ideology. For the first couple of years under Bashar, observers discerned him leading a liberating "Damascus Spring" in such things as open political dialogues, but those disappeared quickly. The suggestion was that the older generation, his father's contemporaries and colleagues, reined in the younger man whom many considered merely a transitional arrangement. Bashar then began carefully opening the country to development by encouraging wider use of technology, and moving towards a market economy.

There has to be some sympathy for the position in which he found himself. Here was an educated and intelligent man, with a background in the West and a naturally liberal outlook, thrust into leadership. Despite that profile, however, even before 2011 he endured such lurid headlines as being named one of the world's four most dangerous leaders by *Reader's Digest*, of all things, in 2008—because he allegedly aided *jihadists*, supported Iran because of the Shia dominance there, was close to Hassan Nasrallah, and was reckoned to be developing nerve gas and biological weapons.[42] That latter issue recurred in commentary throughout his tenure, and as his regime seemed poised to fall in mid-2012, the Western powers raised the fear he would use such weapons.

---

[41].See, for example, Eyal Zisser, "Does Bashar al-Assad Rule Syria?", Middle East Quarterly, X, 1 (Winter 2003)

[42]Dale van Atta, "World's Most Dangerous Leaders", Readers Digest (July 2007)

Yet, despite the provocative Axis of Evil provisions, he reframed relations with important powers like France, and won the tentative appointment of a US Ambassador to Syria after a long absence. By 2010 as a result, a BBC report suggested that despite the odds, he had survived and would most likely last, having by now placed many of his own people into influential positions.[43] There was still, however, the murk surrounding the 2008 car bomb death of Rafik Hariri, the former Prime Minister of and revered figure in Lebanon. From the outset, the Americans led suggestions that this was down to Syria as part of its design on Lebanon. The Syrians denied it vigorously but it was a blight, the slowly emerging United Nations investigations and mainstream media reports pulling back from full accusations of guilt, but leaving heavy implications. Alongside that, Bashar and Syria had to balance a position with Iran, little admired but unquestionably influential in the region, even more so under the post-Bush rise of the Shia in Iraq that changed much of the entire regional balance. Given all that, on balance, Bashar might have been reckoned to have done "alright".

When it comes to assessing all this, the mythical "average person" is at a complete disadvantage because, in our daily lives, we readily ascribe easy labels to actions taken in, say, "Canberra" or "Whitehall" or "Washington" or, of course, "Damascus". From there it is an easy transference to "Australians" (are all sports mad, for example), the "English" (all anti-Europe), "Americans" (all evangelical right wingers) and "Syrians" (all terrorists). Looked at like that, we as individuals

---

[43].Jim Muir, "Bashar al-Assad's Tightening Grip on Syria Ten Years On", BBC News, 17 July 2010

immediately recognise the absurdity of such ascriptions, yet they have an abiding power, especially when repeated daily through modern communication means. Following 9/11 the word "terrorist" became the short hand marker between "them" and "us": "we" are fighting to spread freedom, "they" are terrorists who oppose us. In all this fog, the dilemmas facing someone like Bashar—a young, inexperienced but willing reformer—were subordinated to a need to demonise him as the worst person on earth bar just a few. The obvious question is, then, how does someone like Bashar deal with that as a person? Might things have been different had the White House and State Department zealots adopted an alternative discourse? Could the man who was already discouraging statues in his honour perhaps have constructed a different dialogue with the West, given more encouragement? Things might well have been very different.

Bashar's wife played a large part here, too. He, an Alawite, had married the similarly reformist-minded Asma, born in London to distinguished Sunni parents from Homs, and gone on to a career in merchant banking. Asma al-Assad became one of the "smart glamour" wives of the world, joining her southern neighbour Queen Rania of Jordan. She supported the development of many NGOs, and was said to have toured the country *incognito* to get a real sense of living conditions. When their children arrived, Bashar and Asma were known to turn up unannounced, with the kids, at city restaurants where they played at being just ordinary citizens. There is always an act in some of this, of course, but Bashar was thought to be working hard at cultivating an approachable "man of the people" persona.

This all petered out, and especially so once the 2011

disturbances began, when his image transmogrified from well-intentioned leader to cynical butcher. That switch was swift and substantial, as demonstrated by what happened to Asma. As the Kofi Annan/United nations peace plan to settle Syria petered out and the shelling of places like Hama and Homs resumed in early 2012, the international focus on Syria focused momentarily on a sideshow, the mysterious disappearance from the *Vogue* website of a flattering March 2011 profile on Asma al-Assad, along with a similarly flattering view of her husband and the future of Syria.

The piece appeared in *Vogue* as the Syrian troubles started assuming ominous lines.[44] Asma al-Assad was portrayed as a glamorous, smart woman intent on doing good things for her country. The later criticism, leading to the article's disappearance, focused on the paradox between this "illusion" and the "fact" of her husband's apparent crack down on the citizenry in ways reminiscent of his father, Hafez al-Assad. The article was predominantly about Asma's clothes, and spectacular items like the Christian Louboutin shoes she was wearing at the time of the interview. That latter item is a wonderful weapon in attack journalism—in the uptown stores in New York a cheap pair will go for around $US600, while most are over $1,000 heading towards $2,000. By definition, any stylish wife of an identified dictator must be wearing these off the back of an oppressed people. Never mind the fact that Asma al-Assad herself made a lot of money as an investment banker before her marriage, and had independent means. She was guilty

---

[44]Joan Juliet Buck, "Asma al-Assad: a Rose in the Desert", *Vogue* (March 2011)—the piece may be seen at www.seraphicpress.com

by association, in other words.

Critics, in hindsight, considered the piece ill-conceived, so *Vogue* management was considered sensible when the article suddenly disappeared from public gaze. Opprobrium was distributed all around, consciences salved, mainstream political views satisfied.

This little *frisson* highlighted one of the enduring problems in dealing with the Syrian condition, and in getting a balanced and sensible view about Bashar and Asma. When media attention turned more fully upon Syria as the strife escalated so, too, did the superficiality of coverage and analysis. In part that was due to the difficulties of getting into Syria (which later cost the wonderful Anthony Shadid of the *New York Times* his life), and partly because, frankly, many of those providing coverage had clearly read little. From the outset, a highly complex and specific social structure and political condition were regarded as simply the latest domino in the "Arab Spring" set to fall, and for a long time it was reported that way. At the same time, Bashar was cast as the evil monster, and Asma the fatuous consort.

Never mind that the article was developed then appeared during a period when the United States had reinstated its Embassy in Damascus on the grounds that Syria, under Bashar al-Assad, was showing clear signs of wanting to return to the global mainstream by way of a more market-oriented economy and more political interaction. French President Sarkozy and other Western leaders were taking the same view. The disturbances in Syria were in their infancy, and few if any noted international analysts of Syria and the region really thought that the situation there would develop to what it had become a year later.

When the controversy arose the author of the *Vogue* article, Joan Juliet Block, was quick to say she now thought she should not have "gone near the Assads," and that it was "horrifying to have been near people like that".[45] In a derogatory rather than complimentary way, she described Asma al-Assad as speaking "like a banker with a degree in computer science", and implied that Asma had no real interest in the Syrian people. That was very different from the tone of the original piece, and close to the strident views of Andrew Tabler who, once having worked closely with Asma on some of her NGOs, was by now in the Washington hawk camp on Syria.[46]

Asma al-Assad conveniently became "the Marie Antoinette of the Arab Spring", her husband the "Demon of Damascus". That became accentuated when a cache of their e-mails became public, apparently showing them carefree while Syria raged, him downloading music from iTunes and her ordering thousands of dollars worth of jewellery online. There was further accentuation when Wikileaks released another set of e-mails, with Bashar pilloried as "sexist" and a "misogynist" for having passed on jokes of the kind traded daily by millions of people in offices all over the world.

This is important, because the later media descriptions of the pair, that have a big influence on public

---

[45]Transcript of interview with Joan Juliet Buck by Melissa Block: "A Look Into the World of Syria's First Lady", www.npr.org/2012/4/20/151058724/a-look-into-the-world-of-syria's-first-lady

[46]Andrew Tabler, *In The Lion's Den: an Eyewitness Account of Washington's Battle With Syria* (New York, Lawrence Hill, 2011). His website would carry some of the most strident calls to action for the West on intervention in Syria: www.andrewtabler.com

perception, were so far from removed from earlier ones that they must be assessed carefully. In all the recent portrayals of Bashar the cynical, almost megalomaniacal despot, for example, few if any journalists paused to wonder about that gulf between now and before. The man remains an enigma, and it is clear that what has happened on his watch, especially of late, has been terrible. A mystery remains, though, about who he is and what he was thinking. Was he, perhaps, really just a puppet with the show run by ruthless brother Maher at the head of the feared Republican Guards? Patrick Seale, long-time observer of both father and son, thought that Bashar gained a taste for control that clouded his understanding of the growing desire for freedom arising within the country. Seale also suggested that Perhaps Bashar was not strong enough to rise above the myriad of self-interests and fears and create a new way.[47] Perhaps we will never know the real state of affairs, but the chasm between the ophthalmologist and proto-reformer of 2000, and the "fight to the end, hardline Alawite" of 2011-12 is unbridgeable.

The man in the images on the back of those car windows ended up a very long way from the one in the international newspapers, and from the loved figure depicted in the thousands of Bashar souvenirs displayed in the specialist shop near the Roman Arch on Straight Street. Perhaps it was symbolic that, shortly after I bought it, my "map of Syria" key ring broke into several small pieces.

---

[47]Patrick Seale, "Is This the End of the Assad Dynasty?, *Viewpoint,* 13 July 2012, Online Issue 109, www.viewpointonline.net/is-this-the-end-of-the-assad-dynasty-patrick-seale-html

AL MIDAN

Because the house lay in the heart of the oldest inhabited capital in the world, it was sometimes easy to forget about other areas outside the walls that are as ancient and have their own histories, charm and attraction.

One walk was through to the Gate Al Jabiye, dodging the traffic across Al Beit Street then disappearing down what looked like a narrow lane left, marked by some *nargileh* shops, then reaching the top of Al-Midan street that winds down through Yarmouk Square and under the Hafez al-Assad Street motorway to eventually peter out near Al Kawakbi Street. The most important stretch was from Yarmouk Square, dominated by the huge and modern Abdulla Ibn Rawaha Mosque, down to just past the motorway, because this was the core of the Midan. Centuries ago, this had begun as a racecourse for the early Muslim rulers, then later developed as an identifiable quarter.

In earlier days the area got a mixed press from visitors, at best. By the mid-nineteenth century it was the largest Damascus suburb according to the John Murray guide. Around the same period, Mrs Mackintosh reported that it was badly paved or not even paved at all, so that it practically impassable in winter—and was full of corn dealers. She clearly believed them an evil to be tolerated. A decade earlier, the Thomas Cook guide suggested that the people in the Midan were more interesting than their surrounds. Baedeker was more generous: it was newer [relatively, of course] and poorer than the Old City proper, and while it was full of corn dealers and blacksmiths, it had the very great attraction of the massive camel caravans that carried goods and pilgrims all over the region.

For many of those travellers, the only reason to go to the Midan was to watch the Haj departure. For the month prior, the area was crowded and a bustling centre of commerce as pilgrims prepared for the arduous journey. When the time came, there could be as many as four thousand horses and eight thousand camels setting out for Mecca, carrying many thousands of the devoted. It was still one of the great migrations to be seen anywhere in the world, and it was one of the most arduous.[48]

The eminent scholar of Syria, Philip Khoury, provides a deeper analysis of the Midan's profile.[49] He argues

---

[48]Paton, The Modern Syrians, ch. XIV

[49].Philip S. Khoury, "Syrian Urban Politics in Transition: the Quarters of Damascus During the French Mandate," *International Journal of Middle East Studies,* 16, 4 (November, 1984)

that throughout the nineteenth and into the twentieth centuries the Midan was one of the least coherent quarters in the city. Because it was on the edge of the Hawran grain growing plains, it hosted a mixture of very wealthy Muslim grain dealers who doubled up as moneylenders, Druze highlanders, peasants from the Hawran, a small Christian community of merchants and moneylenders, and desert tribes who came in for the winter. Its main trade was certainly based around the Haj, but by the turn of the twentieth century it was largely poor, itinerant and with a low rate of property owning. It also had a higher crime rate than other quarters. In short, this was a largely dispossessed and rather misunderstood section of Damascus. Those patterns would have an impact in the 1920s, and recur well into the twenty first century.

The Midan nowadays seems to have been described by the same person in almost all contemporary Damascene guidebooks and travel stories: the Midan is very conservative. That may be so, but it is also extremely friendly. Asking to take a photograph would almost always elicit a "yes" with a smile, and frequently an invitation to tea. Despite its reputation, the Midan has always been at the centre of change. On the one occasion when it seemed the Crusaders might breach the defences in 1126, Ibn Al Qalinisi reported that men and youths from the area, and from the neighbouring Shaghour, banded together to see off the Franks.

In late October 1925, the Great Syrian revolt reached Damascus via the Midan and the area now divided from it by Al Beit Street, the Shaghour, which spills over from its heartland inside the walls. Generally speaking, these two southern quarters immediately outside the walls of the Old City were at the heart of the resistance to French rule.[50] Two rebel raiding parties came in through these areas, gathered supporters and headed towards the Azem Palace, just around from the house and then the home of the French Governor. Merchants and others, led by the quarter bosses who really had quite organised networks, supported the rebels who reached and entered the Palace where a fire broke out. The Governor escaped and the French sent troops into the Old City, separating it from the rest of Damascus. The French troops then entered the Hamidiyeh where fierce fighting broke out involving local leaders and gangs loyal to the revolt.

Late that afternoon the French troops suddenly left, and two days of fierce shelling and air raids began. The areas in and around Al Jabiyeh, the Shaghour and all the way down to the Midan were particularly targeted, and to this day the Hamidiyeh retains the bullet-riddled roof created at that time. Hundreds of houses and shops were destroyed, and the Hariqa of today was constructed in the aftermath—it was once like the rest of the *souk*, but is now a series of block and concrete office and commercial outlets perched between the Hamidiyeh and remnants of the old *souks* that survived the onslaught. The official number of dead was put at 1,500 but that was widely believed to be a serious and deliberate under-estimate, perhaps by both sides for their respective reasons. That was bad enough, but the destruction was followed by public hangings, more fighting and a complete shutdown of social services. The French set about destroying the Midan, because they considered it to be at the heart of the revolt.

---

[50]12 See Sami M. Moubayed, The Politics of Damascus, 1920-1946 (Damascus, Tlass, 1999), ch. II.

In May 1926, just a few short years after King Feisal and T.E. Lawrence thought they had entered Damascus to establish Arab independence, the French further surrounded the Midan and began looting homes before launching more air bombings. Fire broke out, but the French had cut off water supplies and the conflagration spread for two days. A further 600 people died in the raids, and perhaps 1,000 homes were destroyed before international pressure helped force the French to halt the assault. The revolt was over, but memories were strong and would endure.

That experience remains just a couple of generations or so back in the Midan mind, and some of the urban scars remain as the area rebuilds around what was one of the oldest sections of Damascus outside the walls. There is now a profusion of concrete and block tenement buildings, but among them are much older buildings, like commercial grain centres and other retail shops. They look young compared to some other survivors. Tucked almost under the motorway is Al-Tinbekeya Mosque that also has a *madrasa*. It was built in 1417, taking in the tomb of the Damascus Governor Tinbek Al-Hassani. Its distinctive facings and gracious lines show what much of the area must have been like before 1926, and before the subsequent urban regeneration. Further down the street stands another mosque built in the thirteenth century, a fourteenth century *madrasa,* and a sixteenth century Ottoman mosque.

A couple of kilometres further down the road, the Qadam mosque provides one of the best stories from Islam. That story has the Prophet himself reaching the point on which the mosque now stands, on his way to Damascus. Seeing the city from afar, however, he decided to stop, then turned back. He declared that because a man could only enter Paradise once, he would eschew divine Damascus and await his heavenly reward. Legend has it that his footprint is preserved in the Al Qadam mosque. It should be said that there are a few versions of this story, with each quarter seemingly taking ownership. Whatever the true location, it is still a great story.

The Midan, then, has a history, and retains a character. These days it is famous among Damascenes for its sweet shops, restaurants, *shawarma* and *falafel* stalls. Early on a weekend morning the shutters come up, the coffee is brewed, and the day begins. A coffee supplier extends an invitation to tea, a nice paradox. Butchers invite inspection of their wares. Old men sit outside a humble mosque, taking coffee in the weak sunshine. In a myriad of shops the sweets are piled high, as staff in famous outlets like Daoud Brothers ("a taste of heaven on earth") ready themselves for hectic weekend trade. The piles spill out of the shops and onto the pavements, where packages and mountains of sweets glisten in all directions. Counters are polished, shop fronts washed down, tables and chairs appear on both sides of narrow Al-Midan Street.

Sometimes, the traffic is halted by horse-drawn fruit and vegetable drays still common in the Midan. The quiet horse is draped in the colourful traditional rugs and ropes of red and white. Customers surround the cart which is covered in everything from onions to pineapples, and the *keffiyeh*-clad owner/driver doles out supplies, haggles over prices, and sends customers on their way, all while the banked-up motorists behind wait, for the most part patiently.

In some ways, this is a readier and more connected version of what the Old City was once like in its entirety. There are no boutique hotels down here, scarcely any hotels at all. This is a district, a community with a heritage and a shared outlook. Stop to peer inside some of the ruined facades behind which elegant grave markers stand, and a local will attempt to explain the story. Greetings are warmly welcomed and easily given. People go about their business, but take quiet pride that an odd foreigner is interested enough to come and have a look, even if attracted by the sweets. Despite the post-French buildings, this place has a living past that stretches back a very long way.

That attitude of resistance abides, too. As the 2011-12 unrest filtered in to Damascus from the provinces, the Midan was soon in the news for hosting demonstrations in support of change and, later, witnessing struggles and physical conflict. The reports about the Midan being a centre of support for the conservative Sunni cause could have been written at any point in the past few hundred years. All that had changed was the technology—rocket propelled grenades, mortars and modern rifles were deployed throughout the area as Syrian Free Army fighters met troops loyal to the regime. Some of the FSA bodies were described as bearded and dressed in black, clear reference to the Sunni orthodox strain thought to be coming to the fore as words like "sectarian" and "civil war" began to enter the discourse, supplementing the earlier "freedom fighter" descriptions.

It was hard to imagine all that occurring in a street and an area that, despite its reputation down through the ages, had been so welcoming and warm, and where a quiet horse had helped carry on trading in a location where the practice spread back over several centuries.

QANAWAT
AND OTHER HERITAGE

It is sobering to think that over forty years ago, Colin Thubron already considered the "real" Damascus to be dying.[51] That, it must be said, is the lot of writers lucky enough to encounter places early enough to recall something of what they call authenticity. Of course, neither Damascus nor anywhere else was "authentic" at any given point. Rather, they were just places encountered that told stories different from those of other more accustomed locations, and before the latest changes were experienced. Penang, formerly "the Pearl of the Orient" in Malaya now Malaysia, has transformed into an international free industrial zone

---

[51].Colin Thubron, *Face to Damascus* (London, Vintage, 1996 edn)

in the interests of attracting foreign capital. Batu Ferringhi turned from a one-hotel beach with pristine water into a high rise haven with dishwater in front. Yet, if you look hard enough, something of Penang's essential character still remains. Damascus, too, has always had those willing to declare it "gone". And in some ways they are right. It will never again be the pleasure garden from which the Prophet retreated, in the belief he could never attain Paradise twice. Freeways and suburbs arise, the modern global world intrudes, cosmopolitan lifestyles spring up, traffic clogs the arteries, and people flock to the burgeoning metropolis.

Our project's wonderful and ever-smiling driver took us safely on all the long journeys out to Lattakia, Homs, Aleppo and, occasionally, all the way out to Deir Ez- Zor. He was a Damascus boy, having grown up in that part of Sarouja now separated from its main section by the busy highway that fronts the Citadel and the Hamidiyeh *souk*. Whenever we drove by that part of Sarouja he would recall the large family home of his youth, wistful to the point of sad as he considered his present home, a much smaller affair on the outskirts of the now-sprawling Syrian capital. Like many families unable to sustain the rising costs of inner-city living, his had cashed up and moved out, but with considerable regrets. Some of these outer areas became the Damascene version of the modern Parisian *banlieues,* or at least the more disenfranchised ones and, like their French counterparts, these ones blew up in 2011-12 for similar reasons: unemployment, lack of services, rising costs, miserable conditions.

This is a common story, a local variation on transformatory global patterns that see customary inner city residents displaced by gentrification and social change. Many Damascenes with whom I spoke had grown up in Old City homes, but their families had realised the assets either because they now wanted a different lifestyle, or the offered price was simply too good to resist, or both. That was exacerbated in the aftermath of the Gulf wars, oddly enough. Many incoming Iraqi refugees were well cashed up, considered Damascus prices as very cheap compared to those of Baghdad, so bought up property wholesale, including in the Old City. The Bashar al-Assad regime soon clamped down and legislated to prevent the sale of property to foreigners, though it was still possible to take over a 99 year lease. Regeneration of properties began all over the Old City and, wandering about, it was frustrating not being able to see inside a few of the more famous ones.

There was one such place down a *cul-de-sac* on the other side of Straight Street from the house. It was large but no longer in full local style. Windows had been inserted in the normally blank exterior wall, higher up rather than in full Western style. The door, though, was genuinely European in appearance. Reworked walls incorporated local stone and retrieved artefacts, including a piece of Roman stone with an inscription. Tucked with flair and style onto a corner of two intersecting narrow alleys, it was a stunning discovery in amongst a flotilla of drab blank walls with small doors. This was not a new act, by any means. Foreigners have long been among those renovating: the Burtons retained a notable house up on the hill during the mid-nineteenth century, and a century later at least two Europeans had refurbished Old City houses, well before the current fashion began. Those houses were on the walking trail from the Mosque to Bab Touma, wall plaques hinting at the changes made inside. Another was the wonderful renovation done on an old house by a Danish research centre just in behind the Medhat Pasha *souk*. Some of this movement was reflected in the rush to boutique hotels that preceded the troubles. Down in the Jewish quarter, for example, the bland walls of the Talisman Hotel hid an opulent and luxurious interior.

Much of this points to how somewhere like the Old City retains its authenticity and charm, while dealing simultaneously with pressure for change. One early twenty first century example of this involved a traffic issue, namely the rising pressure of vehicle flow about the walls of the Old City. One solution involved taking a swathe of houses from just outside the wall on the eastern side. That raised a storm of protest ranging from the owners involved all the way through to international conservationists. Yes, the city has a special quality; no, it cannot resist change totally.

Across the busy road from the start of Medhat Pasha, and in behind a small mosque, the beginning of one of the most delightful lanes in Damascus outside the Old City was just ten minutes walk from the house. This was Qanawat Lane that gives its name to the area in which it is found, immediately up from the Midan. Somewhere back around the seventh century, under the Umayyads, a sheep market in the area began developing a commercial and residential centre to take the overflow from within the Old City walls, and Qanawat was the result. It boomed under the Ottomans, and by the eighteenth century featured several fine homes for senior administrators, prosperous merchants and others who did well out of the Turkish overlordship. It was close to the *souks* and the major political buildings, and created its own social networks for people "in the loop".

It is frequently the lot of these once-prime inner city locations to fall on harder times and Qanawat was among them, but it is still part of a "genuine" Damascus. Qanawat Lane is narrow, a reminder of its origins and its location. There is a lot of greenery, shrubs and bushes and trees surviving in the modern, harsh, degenerated inner city, a further reminder that it was once a far grander place. Crumbling houses, some four stories high, threaten to subside into the street and many remain standing only at crazy angles. Small shops and traders lurk in the bottom of these places, serving people who live in nearby houses and apartments. These people are relaxed and clearly "local", politely and without overt curiosity welcoming strange wanders to their locale.

The lane backs into a significant market whose main entrance runs off at an angle from the start of the lane itself, so that the whole area creates something of a triangle. This is a genuine market. A hole in the wall serves out steaming bread. Butchers carve meat from carcases suspended from hooks outside their shops, cats awaiting the cast-offs. Sweet shops have pristine windows behind which are piled more kilos of processed sugar than might be seen in a Barbados sugar factory. Mops and brooms stick out of another stall, next to a kids' clothes outlet that is next to a mobile phone shop. Shopkeepers sit outside with coffee, catching the watery sun and watching for potential customers who are welcomed, not hassled.

At the base of the triangle, there is a large fruit and vegetable market through which drivers propel small trucks drive while people walk or wheel bicycles. The produce is fresh, unloaded from the trucks that come in loaded so heavily they dip at the back and strain thin tyres. These vehicles are often seen out on the highways loaded with everything from lettuce to aubergine, via carrots, onions, oranges and bananas. In the tiny cabs may be crammed up to four men, along to load and unload.

This is Qanawat, and having survived a thousand years of change it is likely to change again, because it is the pilot district for a significant restoration project. Over the course of the twentieth century the area changed significantly, influenced by developments like the 1930 establishment of the first Damascus cement factory that helped transform building design and practice. Urban usage changed along with those new designs and practices. By the later twentieth and early twenty first centuries, even though Qanawat was provisionally under heritage protection, the quarter had declined. While around twenty five percent of the inhabitants were in upper income brackets and still retained the old, and mostly crumbling houses, there was now a predominance of low income families. Traffic and noise had risen, and courtyard houses were deteriorating. One significant change from the 1930s was that the private gardens in all these houses had largely disappeared, also contributing to environmental change. International agencies and heritage groups combined with local bodies, and the slow start was made to regenerating Qanawat.[52]

Further away, down on one of the main thoroughfares in the Jewish Quarter, just along from the magnificent

---

[52]Aisha Darwish, "Qanawat Quarter: a Strategy and Instruments for Sustainable Rehabilitation", SB10mad Conference Proceedings, www.sb10mad.com/ponencias/archivos/b/B005.pdf; and Kotsuko Matsubara, "Urban Conservation Based on the International Cooperation—a Case Study of the Qanawat South Area, Damascus, 2011 International Symposium on City Planning, http://infoshako.sk.tsukuba.ac.jp/~matsub/2-11.pdf

bread shop next to the elegant drinking fountain, a faded and insignificant notice announces the location of the Dahdah Palace, another reminder of just how much has to be considered by the conservation movement. Press the bell pointed to by a hand-drawn arrow, and the door opens on to a remarkable sight. As usual, the first glimpse is from the gate down the narrow and covered passageway into what is a courtyard. It is only at the end of the passageway that the true scale of the courtyard and the house built around it becomes apparent. It is huge, hidden behind unpretentious walls and, unlike most other major houses now, it is still privately owned. There is no entrance fee, but there are quality craft goods available to buy in part of the house, so visitors contribute to further upkeep through their purchases.

The courtyard has the obligatory open reception areas and wonderful gardens, and is dominated by a big reception area. The house is somewhere around three hundred years old and provides a direct link with the grandeur of the early Ottoman period. The opinionated Mrs Mackintosh visited the Palace during the later nineteenth century, applauding its grandeur, and complimenting the wisdom of the rich banker owners who maintained it in what she considered the dirtiest part of the city. Off on one side there is a large and lofty public reception room with raised areas on either side of the entrance. It is here that the true nature of the house can be appreciated, and the reflections of wealth, power and prestige that it generated. The roof is highly embellished with wood mosaics, the walls are hallmarked with exquisitely carved stone decorations, the whole effect mirrored in the elaborate tiles and mosaics that make up the rest of the décor. It clearly took time and money to achieve this remarkable statement and now, of course, the need for the sale of goods shows just how much is required to maintain such a place in the modern age.

As another example of this change and compromise, Bab Touma is now a traffic site rather than the great gate it was once. However, just along the wall nearby there is an interesting regeneration. A small park is being created at the foot of the wall, and a whole series of houses being refurbished with spectacular effect. The differences in style create an immediate focal point, and the idea of the wall now reaching out to rather than repelling the world is thrilling. As a result, windows have appeared in what were once blank spaces, courtyards adorn the top of the wall, and there are even French windows looking outwards. This is a living wall in effect, the latest version of how this city has adapted to change, pressure and time.

During a walk along from this modernisation towards Bab Sharqi, the originally monolithic nature of the wall reappears, broken here and there by a new house built into the surroundings, including one notably modern version of a Damascene style, with elegance and power enmeshed in its projection. Bab Sharqi manages to retain its ancient role at the end of Straight Street, all the while pouring traffic out into the circuit road that now swings past. The Orthodox Church dome peeks over the top of the wall. The past is never far off. Along an underpass to this circuit road there is a fenced- off section of the original Roman wall, a few metres below the modern road level. Motorists pass over it every day, pedestrians scarcely give it a glance.

From there around to Bab Kissan, where Paul allegedly jumped over, there is a long run of successive era wall building stages, piled one on another to create what once was a seriously good defence of the city. At one point there are Roman blocks scattered carelessly about, at the base of a wall that reflects all those who have been and gone from Damascus. Even here, though, there was a touch of adaptability. Just before Bab Kissan, a small area at the base of the wall had been fenced off, and a garden created. Away up at the top of the wall was a small dwelling with an outside landing. From that descended a rope ladder, obviously to aid in the tending of the garden. Paul was not the only one who jumped the wall.

From the oddly out of character Bab Kissan, the view over the road is further reminder of what Damascus has been and how it has evolved. There is a church within the same camera viewer frame as a mosque, and around the church there is a cemetery.

The wall then immediately changes, a remnant rather than a presence. It encloses what is oddly open space in a city where that commodity is at a premium. For a few hundred metres there is an amalgam of styles and periods, but some excavation shows much of the original wall now lying some way below the present levels. Base and superstructure: Damascus invented that before it was discovered by the cultural Marxists.

The line peters out on the way through to the bottom of Al Amin Street and its residential area. In fact, the wall cuts in through residential areas so that tantalising glimpses appear through fences, over other walls, through open gates and even incorporated into buildings. Bab Saghir is almost hidden amidst this, off to the right of the road that feeds through the bottom of the *souk* from the main road. It is a fabulous gate, still used every day by people who pass beneath the beautiful ancient Arabic calligraphy and never give it a thought. This gate is especially important in the history of Damascus, because it is the main portal to the Saghir cemetery where lie some of the most significant people in Syrian history and, indeed, in the history of Islam. They include the husband of Halimah, the Prophet's wet nurse.

From there the wall winds through and around to Bab Jabiye that is now so incorporated in the souk that it is almost impossible to find. It is low, squat and impressive, even if festooned by clothes from the nearby traders who have adapted it into their lives. The massive iron doors are still there, as they are at Saghir, but they have not been shut for a very long time and probably never will be—the succeeding levels of asphalt layers are now well above the base of the doors.

Bab Al Jabiye really turned up of its own accord in that, such is Damascus, I had walked within a few metres of it almost every time I returned through *Souk* Medhat Pasha. All I had to do, by accident one day, was go just one more alley coming from Hamidiyeh, turn left, quickly right then further still left, and there it was. It is the classic gate, solid but low in height with a squared-off arch, thickly-stoned and graced by fantastically heavy iron, decorated gates that have now not closed for many years. The trading stalls are now built all around those gates, that lead to yet another maze of commercial activity behind Medhat Pasha.

Every day, then, produced yet more heritage treasures, often in the most unexpected ways and places, a central part of the allure and mystery of Damascus.

SALAH AH-DIN'S SHADOW

An impressive statue sits in front of the Citadel, just along from the entrance to the *souk* Hamidiyeh. A distinguished-looking, bearded and helmeted soldier is seated on a horse, guarded by two watchful soldiers. Huddled immediately under the horse's backside, literally ready to be shat upon, cower two vanquished foes. The rider is Salah ah-Din (known more straightforwardly in the West as Saladin), the great scourge of the Crusaders and whose memory is still revered, demonstrated daily by the stream of visitors paying homage at his nearby tomb beside the Umayyad Mosque. The two vanquished Crusaders are Guy de Lusignan, who was the King of Jerusalem, and the unlovable Renault de Chatillon who commanded the mighty Karak Castle, further south of what is now Amman in Jordan. Renault de Chatillon is said to be the only Crusader prince killed by the otherwise saintly Salah ah-Din: the Frenchman had hassled Salah ah-Din's sister, and was also said to have tried to steal the Prophet's remains from Medina.

A couple of years earlier, during a break while on assignment in Jordan, I spent an afternoon wandering the impressive Karak remains, probably now the second-best Crusader castle to visit. It is south of Amman on the King's Highway, a switchback ribbon that threads through the towering hills and swooping valleys of the chain that falls precipitately to the Dead Sea and so, by definition, gives a clear line of site over the West Bank and into Israel. This is the fulcrum of world history both ancient and modern. The first approach to Karak is through the town itself, and the stroll into the castle from that side is anti-climactic to say the least. A little wooden footbridge leads over a modest moat to a ticket box, tucked under an equally modest wall and in an undistinguished staging area.

It is only when you start wandering through the levels and along the walls that the true power of the place emerges. Karak sits right on the edge of a sheer drop of perhaps two thousand metres but looks a lot more. The castle was first built atop this, then over the years its inhabitants created a catacomb of levels, rooms and hidden spaces underneath at the same time as they started building up. Originally, of course, the castle was out on its own,, but over the ages the town built towards the giant, so now it is actually in an urban setting that helps underplay its initial impressiveness. One guide book hinted that for a fee an attendant might just show off the magnificent hall that lies underneath the main courtyard. Sure enough, for a small fee, he showed me to some stairs that led to wooden doors opening into a cavernous but impressive space once used for major occasions. Along its outside walls, a series of windows both let in light and gave a breathtaking sense of the drop into the valley. This was why Karak was so important, and so substantial.

While exploring the chains of rooms that were once Crusader residences, the grander halls assigned to the greater nobles, the kitchens where lesser folk toiled, and the servants' quarters that made up the bulk of the castle, I thought not once about Renault de Chatillon, but frequently of Salah ah-Din. Exploring the site and standing on the ramparts looking miles off into the distance, it was almost as if his spirit was there on my shoulder.

There was an historiographical journey at play here. G.M. Trevelyan,the pioneering English social historian, once said that his craft required its practitioners to own a stout pair of boots (these days the reference would be to sturdy Keens or Eccos, no doubt). My addiction to social history was fired by reading Sir Steven Runciman's three volume *History of the Crusades* while an undergraduate student at the University of Canterbury in far-off New Zealand.[53] While no apologist for the Western invaders, Runciman did not necessarily provide the story of the "Other", as we would now term it—many years later, Amin Maalouf's *The Crusades Through Arab Eyes* provided that insight magnificently.[54] Rather,

---

[53]Steven Runciman, *A History of the Crusades* (Cambridge, Cambridge University Press, 1987 edn)

[54]Amin Maalouf, *The Crusades Through Arab Eyes* (New York, Schocken, 1989)

Runciman provided a clear sense of what it had been like and, by definition, raised questions concerning how it all worked and how people ran their lives. The iconic T.E. Lawrence's work on the Crusader castles did something similar, but the combined effect was more of an idealised view about those days.[55] That was especially so for a young, country town New Zealander for whom the seventy five kilometre shift to Christchurch was in itself an adventure. My subsequent intellectual journey has been about trying to locate the "historical view" from the other side: India, sport, Asia generally, the Caribbean and, now, the Levant.

At the outset I had one great advantage, the extraordinary J.J. Saunders of Canterbury's History Department and who, although I did not then realise it, began developing that view of the "Other" both in his writing and through his teaching. John Joseph Saunders (identified behind his back as "JJ" but addressed always as "Mr. Saunders") came to New Zealand from England after World War II.[56] He had begun his academic career in what was then the lowly centre of Exeter between the wars, and developed a sense of the grand sweep overview of history, especially of the medieval period in what is now known as Central Asia. He spent some of World War II in military intelligence in India but, soon after that

---

[55]T.E. Lawrence, *Crusader Castles* (New York, Oxford University Press, 1989 edn)

[56]Geoffrey Rice, a classmate of mine at Canterbury, student and later colleague of "JJ", kindly gave me a copy of a memorial volume he edited in memory of the great man - G.W. Rice (ed.), *Muslims & Mongols: Essays on Medieval Asia by J.J. Saunders* (Christchurch, University of Canterbury, 1977). It contains an excellent account of the Saunders career.

conflict concluded, decided a better future lay in New Zealand at the Canterbury University College of the University of New Zealand, which would become the University of Canterbury in its own right before I arrived there.

In truth, JJ was a daunting figure, intellectually rather than physically. He was short, broad and a little portly when I first encountered him but he carried himself well, his eyes through thick glasses pitched at a level well above his nose as he rolled into lectures, the aura strengthened by the strong, well-articulated and distinctive Devonian voice. The first lectures I took from him were in the big first year introductory course, where he discussed medieval Europe and included a taste of the Crusader story. He made an impression, no mean feat because those lectures were on Monday evenings through winter in the old university site in Christchurch. It was cold and miserable, both getting to and even inside the hall, but he had something, the ability to spark an interest in events a long way off in time and space. Up close, as in the Tudor-Stuart course he ran by tutorial only in second year, he was demanding, especially if you had not done the reading. However, his specialist courses at senior levels on the Crusades and, wildly different, the intellectual origins of the Russian Revolution, were eye-poppingly wonderful, enriching demonstrations of why history was interesting and important. JJ was a gifted teacher. He had eschewed the PhD which is now *de rigueur* for any historian envisaging an academic career but his knowledge, insight and analysis was formidable. That allowed him to produce some outstanding works from far off New Zealand, including a history of the Mongols that must be reckoned as one of the original insights into the "Other".

At Karak, then, I remembered JJ and his role in getting me there—and I was not the only one. Geoffrey Rice was in my year and eventually served the history department at Canterbury long and honourably. Under JJ's tutelage he wrote an honours thesis on the role of the Assassins during the Crusader period, before going on to British and then New Zealand history. While doing that work he, too, visited the Levant and some of the Crusader sites. At the same time now, though, I thought about Salah ah-Din and those medieval conflicts that still resonate.

Arriving in Damascus later, I recalled those thoughts at Karak further to the south. Being so firmly located near the Umayyad Mosque, the house site never saw a Crusader because none ever got inside the city walls. That was not for the want of trying. In 1113 a force led by Baldwin I was so confident of victory that, in advance, it allocated who would get which of the city's houses and contents as booty. The city held out. That provoked a sequence of attacks, the last major one being in 1148 when Louis VII of France and Conrad of Hohenstaufen led the whole of the Crusader army against just this single city. They suffered terrible losses, marauding forces from inside the city picking them off at will. Damascus was never threatened again.

However, the city did figure in later Crusader manoeuvres, in curious fashion. Later that century, Salah ah-Din faced his equally idealised counterpart, Richard I "The Lionheart" of England, in what was long regarded as a "civilised" struggle for Arabia. El Adil, both Salah ah-Din's brother and one of his generals, happened to befriend The Lionheart who lit upon an ingenious plan. He would marry his own sister off to Al Adil, give the couple Jerusalem and

Acre as a separate kingdom, and so end the Holy War. It did not work because, after Salah ah-Din's death, Al Adil turned on the Crusaders and drove them out. It is interesting to imagine what his wife might have thought. El Adil is entombed in the Madrasa El A Deliya, a few hundred metres from the house, a memorial to the man who, besides marrying Richard I's sister, also built the nearby Citadel and strengthened the walls of the old Roman city of Bosra (near the Jordanian border) to protect them against attack.

That curious marital alliance is a reminder of just how important this period was in determining the shape of the world as we know it now. Right across Europe large armies, along with their baggage trains and retinues, were encouraged to give up several years and quite possibly all of their lives to ride towards the Holy Land, part of a "liberation" movement against the Muslims who allegedly threatened civilised religious and social life. This was fewer than five hundred years after the Prophet established what now ranks as one of the world's three great belief systems. In just five hundred years, then, the great clash of ideas and ideals created what would be another three hundred years of intermittent bloodshed, bigotry, hatred and misunderstanding whose ideological reverberations, in turn, still influence our present lives.

There is a further turn to this history and the study of the "Other" in my own life. As a New Zealander I am an avid rugby union fan, and as a Canterbury man I support the Christchurch-based franchise in the Super 15 competition. That causes me discomfort. The team is phenomenally successful but, for me, its name is abrasive—the Crusaders. Before each of its games a group of horses and riders parade the ground, decked out in *faux* Crusader uniforms with the riders brandishing swords. Attending fans wear replica Crusader helmets and also wave the souvenir swords. At a time of so much conflict in the Middle East, and given the history of the Crusades, it might be time for a re-think.

My Karak experience of Salah ah-Din was repeated in Syria. It was simple to achieve in Damascus, simply by standing in front of the statue and remembering that the great man was entombed nearby. A two and a half hour drive to Homs produced something very different. Like Damascus, Homs never fell to the Crusaders. Instead, it was the centrepiece for a three-way struggle through that entire period involving the Crusaders, the Turks, and JJ's Mongols. The city was younger than Damascus, dating from about the 1st century BC, and serving a dual purpose as regional centre for a rich farming area, and strategic site on the trade routes that criss-crossed the region. From its earliest days, Homs (or Hims) has been a centre of resistance, including throughout the Crusader period. Over nine hundred years later, as the French were on their way out of Syria, Homs became a major support base for the rising Baath Party that would twenty years later produce the Assad dynasty. Not too long after that Homs and nearby Hama became Baath opponents, and then in 2011 re-emerged as major centres of resistance against the Bashar al-Assad regime.

Project work took us to Al Baath University in Homs, on the southern edges of the city and very close to the area known as Bab Amr that would flash to global attention in late 2011. Regime forces shelled the area, and foreign correspondent Marie Colvin lost her life.

All that had been unimaginable not too long before. As I sat in a restaurant one evening on my first visit to the city, the streets were suddenly devoid of traffic as huge crowds of young men took to the streets. They were celebrating an important victory by one of the local professional football teams at a nearby stadium. The flag and scarf waving, chants and songs, and sharing of joy with anyone who showed an interest were the displays of victory common around the world. They were no different from anyone else.

The University's warm-spirited Vice-President, who also pointedly flouted the University's "no smoking on the premises" rule, saw an opportunistic gap in our program, and laid on transport for us to visit the old city. There were all the usual reminders of Syria's complex past and present. The main mosque was a splendid example of an earlier style, clean lines and a lovely interior. Not far away, though, stands the Um al-Zennar Church, a Syriac Orthodox centre going back hundreds of years, and famed because it holds what is said to be the belt worn by Mary, the Mother of Jesus. Homs, like elsewhere in Syria, has a heterodox population that, for the most part, has been harmonious.

It is also highly hospitable, despite forever having been the butt of the sort of jokes the Irish tell about the Kerryman:

Homsi: "Do you sell colour TVs?"

Salesman: "Yes."

Homsi: "Great. I want a green one."

These Homsi jokes are legion, but the Homsis themselves are warm and friendly. While there on one occasion my local mobile phone managed to switch it off and, of course, I did not have the access code. We drove to a phone centre and the next thing I knew, four assistants were dealing with the phone that was taken away while I and my colleagues were plied with tea and sweets. In a few minutes the phone arrived back, in full working order. I went to pay but that was refused, politely but definitively:

"Thank you for coming to Homs and we hope you have a nice stay."

Who knows now what has happened to those marvellous people?

About three hours away, out on the coast, Lattakia presented a different but as instructive story. Almost closer to Cyprus than Damascus, the city has been a port from somewhere around the fourth century BC, and in 333 BC was taken by Alexander the Great to later became an important Roman centre. When Islam arrived, one especially important development for Syria was that Lattakia and its region became the main centre for the Alawite community, an offshoot of the Shia but largely disowned by most of the major Islamic groups. The Assad family came from the Alawite, and Lattakia was the major centre.

Lattakia did fall to the Crusaders, in 1097 at the start of the long period of conflict, and for almost a century was traded as part of alliance-building among the major crusading partners. In 1188, however, that man Salah ah-Din retook the city for Islam. As at Karak, his presence is evident in Lattakia, and even more so a little further down the road where the huge Crusader castle known as Marqab still towers over passersby. Lattakia, though, now has a different feel, particularly in its conflicting roles as a military centre and a tourist one. While I had heard whispered expressions of support for more "democracy" in Damascus, sitting one night at dinner in the naval officers club in Lattakia overlooking the western end of the Mediterranean, the talk was of the need for more "control" to better manage the rising youth movements and lifestyles considered a challenge to the normal order. People needed to be given direction and certainty.

There was a radically different picture at the beachside hotel nearby. One afternoon, we decamped across the road to a bakery where tasty mini-pizzas and meat-filled pastries streamed out of a traditional oven, all to be washed down with good local coffee. We had come from a session where policy issues became tinged by political correctness, so the conversation now was about the political condition and its likely scenario, all against the growing actions in places like Tunisia and, especially, Libya. The consensus was that Syria would not take the same path, because although the regime had tight control it was also interested in returning Syria to the global political mainstream, freeing up the economy and loosening control. Those last two words were key, because they appeared often: there was a widespread view Syria should not speed towards full democracy because it had done well under Bashar, steady development would be much better than chaos. A few months later, that discussion would be recalled, especially because of what happened immediately after.

On re-entering the hotel we were treated to an extraordinary sight. Across the lobby sashayed two tall, beautiful women wearing high heels—and bikinis! It stopped the hotel that afternoon , even in this beach environment. This was in Syria. It would not have occurred in, say, a Jordanian hotel on the

Dead Sea or most anywhere else in the Arab world, but it was happening in Lattakia. It was clearly unusual, perhaps even unique, but the point was that it happened in Bashar al-Assad's Syria before the rise of all the bloodshed and mayhem. (There is an interesting point here—some of an earlier generation suggest that the more conservative dress styles came with the rise of the Assad regime, and that life was simpler and less rigid before that rise). It would be a stretch way too far to interpret this beach incident as a sign fundamental change was already occurring in Bashar al-Assad's Syria but, still, it indicated some of the options and choices some Syrians were making already. However, can only imagine what Salah ah-Din might have thought.

Imagining his thoughts was far simpler back along and off the main road between Lattakia and Homs. About sixty kilometres from Homs towards the other port city of Tartous and its Russian naval presence, a notable shape appears on the top of a hillside. As you leave the main road and drive closer in towards it, the shape sharpens into a castle that becomes ever more massive the closer it looms. The road follows a valley and its slopes, along which the now standard modern apartment blocks, shops and houses appear. One of these profusions is the whacky Al Wadi hotel, built progressively in what is vaguely described as "Crusader style". Balconies on its western side rooms provide an uninterrupted view up the hill to what by now is a hulking presence that belittles everything else—Krak Des Chevaliers or, locally, *Qalaat el Hosn* (stronghold castle).

Krak Des Chevaliers is the best example of a Crusader castle, and has survived for over a thousand years. It began life as a Kurdish castle commanding the important valley trade route from the interior to the Mediterranean coast, and it still overlooks vast plains away towards the coast, now covered in buildings but back then a significant and fertile food bowl. The Crusaders recognised its strategic significance as they moved slowly south towards Jerusalem, their ultimate goal. Over many years Krak was added to, strengthened, fortified, made more sophisticated, and in all the Crusading years it was never taken by force, such was its impregnability. The castle finally fell to the Mamluk Sultan Baybars in 1271, when he fabricated a letter from the Crusader commander in Tripoli, advising defenders to surrender because no more European reinforcements were available.

At its high point, Krak Des Chevaliers hosted a population of over two thousand inside its walls, and perhaps only two hundred of those were knights—this potent attacking force was highly expensive to run, so commanders controlled the numbers. This defensive stronghold was turned over to the Knights Hospitaller in 1144, the body that began supporting Christian pilgrims to the Holy Land, then eventually emerged as a military body aiding the Crusader cause.

The castle symbolises the seriousness and complexity of this cultural and religious clash of wills that haunts us still. Even now it is a very steep climb by car up the hill to the entrance, and the sheer size of the place is best judged by how puny the huge tour buses parked at its base appear. The convoy of camper vans driven by a party of Europeans looked even smaller. The main entrance thoroughfare was built to accommodate two fully equipped knights mounted on warhorses, riding side by side up the winding incline to the interior. The architecture, design and engineering are still breathtaking. Massive, soaring walls up to fifty metres high enclose a labyrinth of accommodation and service areas, complete with well-thought out sanitation. Given that it developed over a long period, several architectural and cultural styles are now evident, notably the elegant Norman-style hall in the main courtyard at the top of the entrance way. Elsewhere there are enormous bathing and baking complexes, and the layout shows what a bustling place it was.

It remained that way for a very long time, too. When that intrepid traveller Gertrude Bell visited Krak in the very early twentieth century she, too, rode up the long keep to the courtyard. The horses in her party "stumbled and clanked" their way over the cobblestones, as a thin light filtered in through the "few loopholes" in the walls. The villagers were then still living in the castle—they would be shifted out very much later—and a butcher was still plying his trade at the gate.[57]

The ideological heartbeat for all this development and campaigning now looks paradoxically puny. The chapel is away in the northeast corner of the complex, a narrow but high-vaulted space which would barely have held all the knights at their most numerous. When Baybars took the castle, he had a *mihrab* added to the space to make it a prayer hall, as it is still now labelled.

It is hard here to avoid the thought that, as symbolised by the relative sizes of fort and chapel, this huge undertaking was based flimsily on a small amount of understanding and appreciation. From that time onwards, relations between the Christian and Muslim

[57]Gertrude Bell, *The Desert and the Sown* (London, Virago, 1985 edn)

worlds have never really recovered, those initial frosty relations reinforced by crass, early twentieth century political stupidities that saw outside forces carve up Arabia and the Holy Land with no input from the inhabitants. More latterly, the same strain of misunderstanding and self-interest has ensured that division, decay and destruction continue.

Being at Krak, though, helps convey the complexity of all this. It could not have been built and defended without substantial interaction between invader and resident. Local populations supplied it with food and services. Local industry provided the huge stone masonry, and local labour fashioned that into the fort. Local skills and knowledge informed the design and construction engineering. There were, then, long periods where invader and resident came to know each other well, to understand the other perspective, and to gain more detailed knowledge. There was rapprochement, and throughout the Crusades there were times when a Christian outpost at Krak was surrounded and ignored by the forces of Islam.

The relationship between Salah ah-Din and the Lionheart might well have been idealised but, within it, there were moments of peace and understanding that showed how things might be in a better world led by people committed to understanding and negotiation.

CAR CULTURES

There were no cars in the immediate neighbourhood of the house because the lanes were too narrow, permitting only the small rubbish truck whose driver amazingly navigated the maze a couple of times a day, and the similarly small delivery vehicles that pitched up to the restaurants throughout the day. Qasr Ath-Thaqafeh, however, streamed traffic in from Straight Street then directed it back out again via the street along from the bakery, where yet another stream entered having wended its way down from Bab Touma Street or up from Quemariye. This was a bottleneck created by history, and social practice.

Imperial regimes might leave, but the cultures attached to them take longer to do so. For a place that loathed French rule, the loathing doubled by the knowledge that French sovereignty stemmed from a doublecross schemed up with the English, the persistence of things French is fascinating. To see the "Musee National", for example, seems odd and so, too, do many of the signs in French on houses and monuments, on *madrasa,* public buildings and streets. Strangely, that persistence came in handy, however, because the French—perhaps trying to recapture earlier glory days amidst these now economically depressing ones—provided a good proportion of the tourists who were appearing immediately before the upheaval.

Among the things that the French left were Peugeot, Renault and Citroen, new models now mixing along a surprising number of old ones. Over in a Christian Quarter back alley, a perfectly maintained example of the old frog-eyed, long and slung-back Citroen from the 40s and 50s with the distinctively box-shaped boot sat proudly, tight into the wall on the alley. Modern Peugeot 206s squeezed past it, in a stream of the latest models from several *marques.*

The most spectacular vehicles were the old tanks and spaceships made by the Americans in the fifties and sixties, the Dodge, Studebaker and Chevrolet behemoths that look huge on any roads let alone those in the Old City. Under the Hafez al-Assad motorway, just off Al Midan Street and parked near a cleared lot, there was a magnificent Cadillac—how did it get there? Or what about the marvellous, faded Studebaker parked up a laneway near all the sweetshops nearby? It takes a good many three point turns to navigate the Old City narrows in these beasts, as well as the affectionate sympathy and support of fellow road users and pedestrians. It is almost as if the old cars have somehow become the modern symbols of the city's history, because in some quarters these cars are revered.

One day, a new face appeared in the antique shop for tea. His occupation was arranging car rallies, and he reported a big and enthusiastic following. He had just returned from a rally in Turkey where there were also active discussions to create a Turkey-Lebanon-Syria-Jordan run, a parallel to all attempts at gaining strategic unity in the Arab world. Every year now, he said, there was a "Welcome to Syria" car rally run for charity, and it included celebrities from the worlds of Arab public life, films, music and popular culture. It arose, he reckoned, from a combined love for culture and cars.

On Thursday through to Saturday nights, areas like Straight Street and the stretch through the Old City emerging out along Hammam Al Bakri Street onto Bab Touma Street, became an open air car display room. On one memorable night, the Jesuit Church in Hammam Bakri was the scene of a wedding that required a fleet of eight white Audi A6s to come the wrong way up the street. Traffic was backed up in all directions, there were elaborate parking and exit manoeuvres, and considerable organisational intervention from both guests and passing observers. Most people simply admired the cars, as they do when there are other weddings throughout the Quarter where vehicles turn up festooned in flowers, the brides decked out in fashionable dresses made in small shops like the one around from the house in the lane up to the sweet *souk*.

On weekend nights, particularly, the boy racers were everywhere. Windows down, both in summer and winter, stereos at full throttle with the latest Arab techno or rap damaging their own eardrums and those of all within a few hundred meters, the racers sat, usually at a standstill. One authority reckons this to be part of "feeling" the music, and part of the evolutionary clash between old and new.[58] Like counterparts around the world their mufflers were modified, if not always the engines, attracting the same disapproving looks dispensed by elders everywhere. Their cars were festooned with the local variations on cultural icons that appear around the world: crosses, crescents, scimitars, medallions, prayer beads, and an explosion of soft toys.

Like their global counterparts, too, these guys chatted to all the young ladies who sometimes responded, but mostly looked baffled at encountering a carload of young guys seemingly able to tolerate huge amounts of noise. On the open road, these same *poseurs* sometimes attempted to recreate every car chase ever set in film on the hilly streets of San Francisco, but settled mostly for weaving in and out of traffic on the semi-freeways, or for the occasional speed limit violation out on the highways.

Kia, Hyundai, GM, Chevrolet and Mazda dominated the market with Mitsubishi, Ford and a gaggle of others making up the numbers. Around the city and out in the country, along the main roads, long stretches of car sales yards full of vehicles awaited the-then ever increasing numbers of buyers. Some of those buyers had exotic tastes. Seeing a Hummer in Straight Street was a challenge to the senses, especially given its military connection that had been so prominent in the desert conflicts. The same

---

[58]Jonathan Holt Shannon, *Among the Jasmine Trees: Music and Modernity in Contemporary Syria* (Middletown, Wesleyan University Press, 2006), , pp. 2. 24

applied, in lesser degree, to the Land Rover Defenders that appeared all over the city, many used by military personnel but others by people obviously from rural areas. The "4WD/SUV in the city" syndrome was as apparent here as anywhere in the west, with desert-capable vehicles patrolling Old City streets but clearly never having been off the tarseal.

This provided unique visual opportunities. One was the modern black VW Beetle parked at the top of Al Amin street in front of the poster suggesting Mahatma Gandhi "Learned From Husayn." That was on the occasion of the Shia Martyr's anniversary at nearby mosques, which produced a host of such inventive placards, and somehow the incongruity seemed to work.

The ultimate incongruity, of course, is that the streets and alleyways of the Old City were designed for pedestrian traffic but were now dominated by these modern vehicles. Over in the Midan, those streets developed to service the camel caravans that headed in and out on trade missions or on the Haj. The city has adapted as it has done to all else, but these cars still seemed alien. No doubt, the in-flow would have ceased once sanctions imposed in wake of the 2011 disturbances set in, so perhaps all the new models will become the surviving Cadillacs and Studebakers of the future.

THE MOVING IMAGE

There was something surreal about watching *Jarhead* in a house in Damascus.

That film, of course, has Jake Gyllenhaal in a brilliant portrayal of Anthony Swofford who wrote the book of the same name, and this is a rare occasion when the film might just be better than the book. The story has Swofford joining the US Marine Corps prior to Desert Shield and Desert Storm, withstanding the bastardisation to become a sniper. His outfit is shipped to Kuwait, its days filled with mindless trivia before entering Iraq. He fires not a shot in anger, the war ends, but by then he has seen the carnage inflicted on Iraqis, and the irrational behaviour of a military intent on killing. The film evokes sympathy for the innocent victims of war but little for the alleged Arab perpetrators, with one maddened American grunt ranting gleefully about dozens of dead "ragheads", one of the many contemporary variations on the epithet: towelheads, mad mullahs, camel jockeys, sand niggers, hajis and all the rest of the demeaning and derogatory terms.

It seemed ideologically odd to be able to buy the DVD for the equivalent of one dollar, along with just about every other Iraqi war movie made by the Americans, most of which depict an American honour or righteousness even when evoking sympathy for victims and what happens to individual American soldiers. Series like *The Unit* and *Over There* that play up the same values were not readily available, but almost all the films were. Similarly available was Spielberg's deeply flawed *Munich,* with Eric Bana as the Israeli avenging angel against the Munich Olympics massacre masterminds in Black September and the PLO. In that film, the Arabs appear singularly one dimensional, unreasonable and inflexible as well as vengeful. Again, the only sympathy is for a potential Arab child victim, and for the Bana figure who goes through post-traumatic stress, brought on by non-support from his own side as much as by his experience of killing Arabs.

The odd presence of these films in the cheap DVD shops along Quemariye and throughout the city was offset occasionally by the appearance of one from "this" side of the fence, like *Paradise Now*. Here, two lifelong but young Nablus friends commit to a suicide bombing raid in Israel. One finally goes off, having managed to get his friend returned home, and the film ends with the volunteer sitting in a bus full of Israeli soldiers and civilians. Allegedly the best insight into what drives this behaviour the film, successful at the Oscars, looked an amateurish, almost shallow attempt at understanding the driving forces, despite its setting in the ravaged West bank where people eke out a miserable living in bleak conditions.

The central question was this—if Syria was as closed a society as generally described, how come these films were available for viewing in the old Arabic house? That house was not far from the spot in the main thoroughfare where a metal Israeli flag was fastened to the ground, so that thousands of people could trample on it daily. This was also a reminder of how closely the Americans had aligned with Israel and so complicated regional politics for generations. The Americans and the Israelis were the popular villains, yet their fictionalised versions and interpretations of events were freely available for viewing.

This seemed remarkably tolerant, especially when the general depiction of Syria was so negative in all these films and series. In the 2011-12 American TV series hit, *Homeland,* the main character returns to the United States eight years after having been captured in Iraq, but with most of his terrible incarceration spent in Syria. In both *The Unit* and *Over There,* Syria is the *motif* for all that is the worst in terrorism and "fundamentalism". In *Body of Lies,* the CIA operative played by Leonardo de Caprio is taken out of Jordan and into Syria, so he can be "processed" properly by Jordanian intelligence agents released from their own rules. That is, Syria is portrayed generally as a lawless, "anything goes" zone. In the earlier *The Sum Of All Fears,* the action proceeds from a missile-carrying plane being shot down while flying over Syria. This bleak, narrow and stylised American view of Syria, then, was freely and surprisingly available inside Syria.

A superficial reading might put that down to the enterprise of local small business people who see a chance to sell American movies, with no consideration of ideology. After all, President Bashar himself was a leader in the rise of IT and the internet in Syria, considering it an essential piece of modernisation. Some things were suspiciously unavailable on the web locally, like Amazon—but there was inconsistency, because ABE books could be accessed. Then, the availability of those films might have arisen from the difficulty of policing the internet and its attendant DVD proliferation. However, it might also have been perceptible recognition that the spread of information was inevitable.

The rising number of Damascene cafes and restaurants with "free wireless" was an excellent demonstration of this process. On any day in these modern (or modem) times a young, scarfed Damascene woman might sit in a café drinking Turkish coffee, smoking the *nargileh,* and surfing the net. At the Brokar, one striking young couple could be seen almost every night, passing two or three hours in this fashion.

In part, too, the appearance of these films reflected the views displayed by people like the antique seller down the steps, a sort of irrational admiration for America, its films and its culture. Of course, toleration for the films could also have been a deeply cunning way of showing how much disdain there is in America for the Arab and Islamic world, thereby reifying resistance. That was possible, yes, but seemed far too intricate a reading.

Running through all this, and through all the broader issues was the theme of perception and depiction. In *Jarhead,* the only time "Swoff" gets close to a kill is looking at a control tower through his telescopic sight, lining up two Iraqi officers arguing with and gesticulating at each other. Now, viewed in a cultural context where that sight is viewed every day, as in discussions with the landlord, for example, then it seems natural enough. But viewed in the context of a Western cinema, this depicts "Arabs": all wild drama, hotheadedness and a lack of discipline. We know it is only the movies, but these images have resonance. Think back to all the British war movies in which determined officers were neatly turned out, calm, reserved, confident and instilling confidence, heroic, great leaders in the face of overwhelming odds. This was the making of popular belief, and it is a rare film that goes beneath this to see the complexities and the inanities either from both sides or neutrally.

Even the mavericks have heroic and leadership qualities in the English movies, like Lawrence of Arabia. That film portrayal takes on even greater symbolic moment when watched in the house in Damascus. David Lean's interpretation shows Lawrence so clearly having all those qualities and great insights that even sceptical fellow officers came to appreciate him. In that film, essentially, Lawrence sets out to save Arabs from themselves, but fails. Near the beginning, Alec Guiness' marvellous Prince Feisal is seen magnificently dressed and mounted on an equally magnificent Arabian horse, riding up and down in a pre-modern, futile attempt to see off Turkish aircraft. Lawrence has to lead Feisal and the Arabs into the new world. He does all that, only to be betrayed by two things. The first was the secret 1916 Sykes-Picot Agreement that effectively carved up the

Arabian components of the Ottoman Empire between France and Great Britain. The Arabs would never get their united nation and, worse, under the associated Balfour Agreement ,they would endure the establishment of the Jewish state.

But the second betrayal in the Lean representation is even more interesting: Lawrence is let down by the Arabs themselves. After their entrance to Damascus in 1918, just ahead of the British and Allied forces, they establish the Arab league "parliament". It is depicted in the Lean film as a total free-for-all in which clan antagonises clan, personalities bicker petulantly, order and procedure is completely absent, strategy and vision non-existent, and purpose on permanent leave. That inability to impose order and process is symbolised in Lawrence's shocked discovery that his colleagues have made no attempt to run the hospitals, where prisoner of war patients suffer dreadfully as a consequence. In short, the Arabs cannot rule themselves and even Lawrence, the revered "Al Awrens" realises that, so leaves Arabia physically as well as symbolically. This is a central part of Said's *Orientalism,* of course, the way in which an entire culture is characterised by another, and it has had a powerfully enduring effect.

The description of the "Arab" by modern media is, in many respects, a necessary shorthand in an age when subtlety, nuance and detail are expendable, but at least in part it can be arguably rooted in this Orientalist tradition. Despite all the variations depicted by the truly knowledgeable, like Freya Stark, Gertrude Bell, Richard Burton, Lawrence himself, Wilfred Thesiger and, more recently, Timothy Mackinolty-Smith, a blurred and generalised image of "Arabs" remains to stalk the popular world. It might be argued that does not matter, because policy-makers are informed, know the nuance, and can be relied upon to make the right moves. Unfortunately, Desert Shield, Desert Storm and Operation Iraqi Freedom—remember "Mission Accomplished"?—suggest otherwise. Two remarkable books underscore this sense of doubt.

David Finkel's *The Good Soldiers* follows an army unit through its terrible trials on the outskirts of Baghdad, clinically recording their tragic losses and accompanying trauma. The overwhelming image that emerges is of a mission out of control, not because of the soldiers but because of the "thinkers" in Washington and up the chain of command supposedly directing them.[59] It is a sobering readjustment of any view about just where knowledge and authority might lie.

Vijay Chandrasekeran' s book on the shambles that was Baghdad in the immediate aftermath of American "victory", and under the control of Paul Kramer in what can only be described as a post-imperial "Viceroy" regime, confirms those doubts about the existence of a clear-minded, informed and sophisticated post-conflict view on how to reframe Iraq and, with it, Arab-West relations.[60] That would swing back into view when the Americans announced in mid-2012 they were taking the lead in planning for a post-Assad transition of power in Syria. Their track record in Iraq and Afghanistan did not stimulate optimism. Worse, in some ways, was the image of the "insurgent" that emerged from all this: the

---

[59]David Finkel, The Good Soldiers (New York, Farrer Strauss Giroux, 2009)

[60]Vijay Chandrasekaran, Imperial Life in the Emerald City: Inside Iraq's Green Zone (New York, Knopf, 2006). The book formed the basis for the film, *Green Zone,* starring Matt Damon

unpredictable, unfathomable and almost if not totally maniacal "Arab" who passed up an opportunity for change and opted for a return to the past, urged on by the twenty first century versions of those nineteenth century villains, "mad *mullahs*" like Moqtadr Al Sadah and Hassan Nasrallah. Interestingly, even in a film like *Paradise Now*, there is an unnerving sense in which the martyrs are led on by calculating leaders with no sense of humanity or decency, so driven are they by the pressures of politics and deprivation.

Yet it all seemed so different and so much more complex on the ground. Even in Syria people talked in subdued ways about the need for change, and there was strong debate about the regime under which they existed. They loved Syria and would defend her. Some Westerners in Syria under-estimated this powerful pull of the nation, arguing that a Syrian was loyal to country only after family and clan and town, and even then would support Syria in a perfunctory way. That view was remarkably close to the one conveyed by British intelligence around the time of World War I:

Syria is a land geographically distinct which has never achieved national or political unity.[61]

The spies put that under-achievement down to the pull of tribes and cities overwhelmed by self-interest.

But that denied the fervour with which even casual and new acquaintances would ask how you liked "Suria", or promoted their country with obvious pride. It denied the devotion accorded the leadership in the form of the al-Assad family, even if some of that was

[61]*A Handbook of Syria (Including Palestine)* (London, Naval Intelligence Department, 1919), p. 109

manufactured. It denied the very real pride in Damascus, or in Homs or in Aleppo or in Lattakia that was then eventually subdued in the interests of "Suria" which had a prominent regional leadership role.

And there were very real differences in local perception about the rest of the Arab world, denying the "Arab" stereotyping that flows through the popular films and media. Many Syrians, we know, consider that Lebanon should be part of Syria. Relationships with Saudi Arabia are perennially fraught. Relationships with Iran and Turkey have long been complex. Syria has a sense of itself being far more important in the Arab world than it is sometimes reckoned by its neighbours, let alone the rest of the world. Syrians wanted to be recognised, and to be accepted.

From early 2011, all those questions about identity and ascription came under further scrutiny and pressure, as an atomising media divided the country essentially into two camps: those zealots for Bashar, and those freedom fighters with "the revolution". As in ages past, those typologies were and remain inadequate, and bedevil helpful popular analysis of what is really happening in Syria.

BOOKS AND MUSIC

Down Port Said Street from Hijaz Station, that splendid reminder of times past even if the trains no longer leave from there, sit several bookshops on the street itself and up side alleys, spreading through the Shukri Al Qwatli underpass on the way towards Shalaan. They are a reminder of the learning culture that Damascus has always been, their shelves piled high with great bindings and wonderful calligraphy, a throng of people constantly looking for this or that book. Right next to the project office, there was another well stocked shop, but mainly with university texts, especially in "professional" areas like medicine, dentistry and law.

To begin with, the presence of these shops is an

excellent reminder of the Arab world's long standing commitment to learning and culture, and that starts with the part played by education and the *madrasa.* The term *madrasa* in the West now, unfortunately, is taken automatically to mean "school for terrorists". Report after report depicts such places in Pakistan, Afghanistan, Indonesia and elsewhere as centres for the blandly labelled "fundamentalism" held to be at the centre of global instability. This powerful shift in the symbolism of meaning blurs the distinguished history that the *madrasa* has had and continues to have in Islamic life, especially in Damascus.

Within a one kilometre radius of the house there were at least a dozen former or current *madrasa,* testament to the central role they have long played in Islamic life. Just around in Kamel Passage, a walk to the taxi on a week morning usually saw me accompanied by a stream of kids heading for school as anywhere else in the world: sneakers, schoolbags, expressions ranging from bored to expectant. A young girl might stand at the door, all smiles, farewelling the mother who had accompanied her on the short walk through the nearby lanes and alleys. Another would look far less amused. Taxis would arrive in the sweet *souk* to *debouche* more students, while a microbus unloaded what looked like a regiment of them. This school has been running since the mid- eighteenth century. Nearby was the now-abandoned Azem school, given over to an art gallery stocking paintings for tourists—it dates from the eighteenth century. Salah ah-Din's tomb lies in a former *madrasa* to the side of the Umayyad Mosque. His brother lies nearby in the Al Edilye *madrasa* that dates from the 13th century. The list goes on.

Learning and culture lie at the heart of the Muslim

experience, and the reverence for learning has driven growth of the rich Arabic literature conveyed in prose, poetry and song. The cross-generational reverence for the singer Fairuz, for example, is one simple reflection of this deep-seated love of learning and the power of expression.

From the beginning, the *madrasa* were simply places where learning was promoted within the context of Islam. In Damascus, this became particularly important under the long stay of the Ottomans who made little if no concession to the need for education, at least until very near the end of their rule. Into the breach stepped great families like the Azem, philanthropists who founded or maintained schools so that the power of learning might continue. This was important work, and allowed for the spread of literacy and knowledge where it might not have occurred otherwise.

This lies demonstrated in areas like medicine. The current Medical Museum, located just beside the Hamidiyeh *souk*, dates from 1154 when it was founded as a hospital by Nur Ad Din. It remained a hospital for over 700 years, and was always regarded as one of the great centres of medical science. Its work challenged much of the conventional wisdom then in vogue in the West and controlled by the clergy medicos.[62]

In all these present bookshops, however, there were few works in English, German or French or anything other than Arabic. Up in the Abu Roumaneh

---

[62]There are interesting references to this clash of knowledges, for example, in Ken Follett's literary work set in the 14th century, *World Without End* (London, Pan, 2007)—Newman Burdett put me onto this.

diplomatic enclave one shop sold more European materials, mostly novels. Just near the Cham Palace Hotel in Shalaan another carried works in European languages, but with an odd range: great books on cake design and shop fittings, for example, or how to craft a patio, or the history of automobile design. One shop had the great find, though: *The Secret Meaning of Pink Floyd Lyrics.*

There was no reason why there should be any works there in languages other than Arabic. But it was paradoxical to then encounter on the project such marvellous English language translators like the Affable and other colleagues. The universities did a wonderful job turning out all these people, yet there was very little available for them to read in English, it seemed. The further paradox was that in order to learn more about Syria, the search had to be outside the country, and Amazon.com was not available via the web.

Therein lay part of the answer, of course. Syria was in transition and had taken enthusiastically to the web, modernisation and the market economy, but with limitations. That stemmed largely from transitional politics, too. It was fascinating to read on the web all the references to excellent works on Syria and Damascus, but then not automatically be able to find them in-country, unless they were of the coffee table variety about the "Big Three As": art, archaeology and architecture. There had yet to develop a culture of critical tolerance that allowed free flow to works that questioned and critically analysed. One guide book, for example, carried a nice story about a book on Hafez al-Assad written by a foreigner.[63] That book

---

[63]The book in question was Patrick Seale, Asad: Struggle for the Middle East (Los Angeles, University of California Press, 1990)

appeared in the UK, but because there were concerns over alleged inaccuracies by the author "on some points not connected to his subject", it never appeared in Syria.

That experience has not been unique to Syria, of course, over the past fifty years. Singapore during the Lee Kuan Yew years, for example, saw critical analysis controlled strictly, and people not "conforming" asked to modify their behaviour or even leave the country. Syria was by now past that stage, but still evolving, with the options still for either greater or lesser openness. The current conditions of control had, however, had created the circumstance where Rafik Schami wrote *A Taste of Damascus* from Germany via telephone conversations with his sister in Damascus, where he himself had not been able to live for many years.[64] His memories of Damascus are powerful, though, as his great detective novel based in the city illustrates.[65]

As with many things Syrian or Damascene, however, the situation was not straightforward. In mid-2010, foreign news outlets began reporting the raging success of a new play then appearing in Damascus. It was said to lampoon the overtly corrupt aspects of public life and the manipulations of bureaucrats, even taking a swing at President Bashar al-Assad. The play survived, a clear indication that blanket assumptions about Syria being unrelievedly oppressive could be misleading. That is not to say it was as fully open as might be found in London, Paris or elsewhere, but neither was it as closed as, say, Beijing.

The literary culture of any society or polity is a

---

[64]Rafik Schami, *Taste of a City* (Berlin, Haus, 2006)

[65]Rafik Schami, *The Dark Side of Love* (New York, Interlink, 2009)

marker of its intellectual and social climate and Syria, as part of the Arab world, has a very long history in this. The storyteller, who now survives more as tourist attraction than social necessity, was the earliest example, replaced in time by the poets. The subtleties and nuances of Arabic mean that the skilled use of words by poets became one of the main vehicles for social and political expression, as would again be discovered in 2011-12. Nizzar Qabbani, the Damascene poet whose 1998 death was lamented throughout the Arab world, was then just the latest to have had a profound effect on thinking and outlooks in Syria and elsewhere.

It is to be anticipated, then, that the poets and writers of the next generation will be just as influential as those of the past, and the same goes for music.

Fairuz, the Lebanese diva who is the icon of the Arab world and who can sing anything, returned to Syria in 2008 for the first time in many, many years, and in 2010 released another album of jazz standards that pitched her at world level, again. One of the best places to buy her music, and much more besides, was a tiny music shop next to another music shop about half way along Quemariye. It was easily found—its small window was full of CDs featuring jazz greats like Ella Fitzgerald and Nina Simone along with contemporary Arab-inspired jazz musos, like the Azerbaijani-born pianist, Aziza Mustafa Zadeh, who has recorded with international stars like guitarist Al Di Meola. For the *cognoscenti* , however, the real giveaway was the presence in that little window of a Stephane Grappelli album, he of the legendary Hot Club of Paris and magical association with the stupendous gypsy jazz (*manouche)* guitarist, Django Reinhardt. The French presence in Syria, as elsewhere, is bitter/sweet, with cultural benefits ranged against still-strong memories of the violent end to colonial rule.

The young man in charge of this shop was magnificently informed about all this music, saying he had learned from his father who was a jazz *aficionado.* Stephane and Django were great musicians before they were French, that is, so the music was universal in the father's mind, and the son concurred. Our discussions about gypsy jazz, from that era and the present, were intense and enjoyable. In turn, he introduced me to the skills of a truly talented Syrian musician, the classical pianist and composer, Malek Jandali. The opening bars of Jandali's 2008 album "Echoes of Ugarit" are breathtaking, as is the 2011 "Watani Ana (I am My Homeland)" that he performed in America as his stand against the Assad regime. Having Homs connections, in 2012 he released "Emessa (Homs)" in solidarity with those who suffered there, as did his parents who were beaten up by the regime. All that was still a long way off as I stood, mesmerised by the sound, in the jazz seller's shop.

On that visit, the first of many, the jazz man was chatting with a friend carrying an *oud* case. In a crass sense, the *oud* is the distinctive Arab version of the guitar. Baedeker remarked that it was a "kind of guitar", used mainly to accompany the "shrill falsetto" Arabic singing he thought "very unpleasing" to European ears.[66] He was echoing Eli Smith from half a century earlier, who had said that "we find the singing of the Arabs no music to us."[67] Neither

[66]Baedeker, p. 312

[67]Eli Smith and Mikhail Meshakah, "A Treatise on Arab Music,

description really did the music or the *oud* great justice because it has a long history and wonderful music. Smith, however, did go on to produce a detailed account of what made Arab music sound so different, and to provide a better explanation of the *oud.* It was suggested to have five strings at that stage, an advance of the four in earlier periods, but it was not clear whether or not they were double strings. While there is a fair degree of variation, most Syrian *ouds* would now have five pairs of strings along with a single string, making a total of eleven. Another major difference from the guitar is that the *oud* has never really had frets.

The *oud* has some stupendous players, like Marcel Khalife to whose music I was introduced by my new friends. That became another new album purchased, and now travels on my Ipod. Outlets for the *oud* were to be found all over the city, including a Hamidiyeh specialist music shop which had a thoroughly modern one, done in black and sporting an internal pickup to plug into an amplifier. A couple of these were in evidence a few weeks later, at a Saturday night gig in a park along Straight Street. A more traditional style was on show in a tiny little shop close to the Umayyad Mosque, near one of the best sweet shops in the Old City. On most days, the owner would test out his new instruments, creating a calm atmosphere so close to such a busy place, and welcoming curious strangers who wanted to listen for a while.

Not long before I left, some friends bundled me into a taxi and we set off for—somewhere. It was away from Bab Touma and across from Sarouja. That was about as close as I could pinpoint where we went, eventually pulling up in a busy street across from a row of extremely narrow shop fronts. In one I spied some *ouds*. We had come to an instrument maker. The door opened into a tiny reception area with room for about three people, who all had to duck to avoid hitting *ouds* suspended from racks by their headstocks. They were craft works. Elsewhere in the shop were the shells of instruments under construction and, even deeper into the back, a bandsaw was surrounded by dust from woods being shaped to make even more instruments.

While *ouds* are relatively simple to make, they require the maker's magic to induce tone and timbre. A seriously good gypsy jazz guitar, or any other variation on the instrument, will these days cost thousands of dollars. A top shelf *oud* might cost just a few hundred. In local terms that is a lot of money, but even the professional players suggest that their instruments are relatively inexpensive. Mind you, souvenir sellers along the main arteries will suggest that the instruments they have are priceless. So will the Orientals sellers along Straight Street. One had an especially garish one, covered in green stones, and that he reckoned dated from the fifties. He required a small fortune for that, which he did not get.

He most certainly would not get that asking price from anyone else who had seen the *ouds* at which I was now looking. They were magnificent. Despite their lightness, they were strong—the first step was to bond the desired woods together with epoxy and shape the gourd-like body. The fret board was then added in, along with the sound board facing. This last was highly decorated, and these days made mainly from templates although the really serious artists still work freehand. There was another maker in the

Tekkiye Sulemaniyye crafts complex near the museum. There, up close, you could watch him make and finish the instrument, etching patterns and colours into the lemon wood, then drawing that distinctive Arabic sound out of what was essentially some wood and nylon strings.

Like the poetry and writing, the music has a long history, strolling players being mentioned down through the ages. These makers were simply the latest in a long line of distinguished contributors to the musical life of the Old City, and to its impact on the movements of social change.

WATER

The house "bathroom" was both rather more and rather less than that, in the Western sense. It sat on its own, up the stairs in one corner of the top landing. Its rooftop provided an excellent view of the Umayyad Mosque, if through a forest of antennae, tanks, pipes and wires and, occasionally, junk dumped on the top of other roofs.

Physically it was a large, tiled space measuring five metres by three. The floor tiles were a dull orange, those on the wall off-white with the odd flower pattern. In the corner furthest from the battered door, three strips of masking tape were stuck across a small window, creating privacy against possible interest through the latticed block fence separating the house from the neighbouring upstairs patio. Even further protection was provided by the rag stuffed into the hole in the window's bottom right hand corner.

Immediately in front of that window was the water heater, straight out of Heath Robinson. It was once a coke/coal or even wood burner, the old door still there under the cylindrical water tank, the whole thing standing on the tiles thanks to four squat metal legs. An electrical switch had been grafted onto the wall in the corner, from where wires disappeared off in mysterious directions. The switch was counter-intuitive with up meaning "on", down meaning "off". It was connected to the tank by a dodgy-looking set of wires running into a connector that obviously fed electricity straight into the tank. Any occupational health and safety provisions applying elsewhere had no jurisdiction here.

The tank fed water to a shower that looked like a refugee from a military barracks, an Australian outback facility, or a building site temporary fixture. Pressure was related directly to the water temperature. In the warmer weather, just half an hour of switch "up" created hot water service at good pressure, but by late November and early December, wintery conditions made that more like two hours. By then, the one advantage of being awoken by early prayers call at 4.45 a.m. was the chance to brave the cool air to "up" the switch before disappearing back to the warmth.

The floor sloped down and away from the top corner containing the heater and the shower, and in the bottom corner a wash basin had no drainage pipe. Water just poured straight onto the tiled floor and into the hole that gathered all water from shower and basin, channelling it downstairs into the waste system. A hazy mirror over the basin, a few hooks on the wall, and some plastic tubs strewn around the walls completed the arrangements. Based on the idea of a *hammam,* the bath houses whose huge heyday was when very few private homes had their own bathing facilities, this bathroom was a reminder also of detached facilities on relatives' farms back in New Zealand which, admittedly, lacked this run-down exotic appeal.

The *hammam* remains a fixture in modern life. Around the middle of the eighteenth century, Andrew Archibald Paton gave his English readers a vivid account of a visit to one of these bath houses that have long been so important in Damascene life. He described it as an ordeal, a theme repeated by visiting travellers and writers before and since.[68]

It was, Paton argued, an experience to be had no more than once a week because the nervous system could not tolerate more than that. He visited the *hammam* Nur Ad Din in the sweet *souk,* which still plies its trade to this day. Paton described the entrance and the waiting room where the manager (to whom monies must be paid) awaited, then recounted the sequence of events. The victim, (as Paton described himself) was laid on the marble floor clad only in a brief towel, then soaped and lathered all over. The soaping down and rinsing off was repeated in rooms of different temperature, in some cases with a difference of thirty to forty degrees Fahrenheit. The victim, he said simply, was "parboiled and flayed alive". In some cases ropes were used to massage the customers, but at the very least they were subjected to vigorous arm

---

[68]*The Modern Syrians,* pp. 151-4

and leg stretching accompanied by a severe beating of the back. At the end, a sherbert and a *nargileh* were supplied as the victims recovered from their ordeal. Paton considered the bath house a "levelling republic".

There are Roman baths in the ruins at Bosra down near the border with Jordan, and Roman remains elsewhere in Syria also contain many large bath facilities that show just how important the practice was. In 1175 Ibn Asaker recorded fifty seven baths in the Old city, with another seventeen already outside the walls. By 1217 Ibn Jubayar reckoned the total had climbed to one hundred. In 1285 Ibn Shaddad counted at least eighty five inside the walls alone, and by 1503 Ibn Abdul Hadi counted one hundred and ninety seven in total. Baths were a way of life in Damascus. Richard Boggs has written an extraordinary book on this, *Hammaming In The Sham: a Journey Through the Turkish Baths of Damascus, Aleppo and Beyond.* As he writes, the *hammam* "survives as the greatest monument of town life; bathing was civilization".[69]

In her memoir of growing up in *Souk* Sarouja, Siham Tergeman likened her family's weekly *hammam* visit to going on a picnic.[70] Every Thursday afternoon she, her mother and sisters would head to a ladies session at their favourite Qaramani area bath house, anticipating sliding across a soap-sudded floor, luxuriating in water and experiencing the familiar ritual. They had all the famous ingredients: soap and a bath mitt from Aleppo, a *loofah* sponge, pumice stone,

---

[69]Richard Boggs, *Hammaming in the Sham: a Journey Through the Turkish Baths of Damascus, Aleppo and Beyond* (London, Garnet, 2011)

[70]*Daughter of Damascus,* pp. 11-16

powders and combs—and fresh clothes. They also took food, hence the picnic. She recounts territorial disputes, rows over young boys being brought in, different bathing approaches for women about to be married, and for those having given birth. For her, this was a joyous centre of life. Some modern travellers do not see it that way, nodding more toward the Paton view of a bath being an assault on all the senses. That said, European Union heritage agencies, prior to the troubles, were funding a project to resurrect the *hammam* as an essential institution in re-building Damascene community life.

The bathroom in the house was not as grand as some of those old *hammam,* but it came in the context of a long history of Damascene bathing. Its only real problem was that it had too much appeal. The space was luxurious, if cool in winter, the Aleppo soap lathered up magnificently, the Heath Robinson affair actually worked, the hot water provided as much therapy as in the *hammam,* there were clean clothes awaiting, as well as olives and flat bread. The natural result was that I frequently spent too much time luxuriating under the shower, and worrying about how much water I was wasting.

Water is a global issue now, but obviously far more so in a country like Syria and a city like Damascus. In 1901, when the city's water supply was normally said to be "lavish", at least compared to somewhere like Jerusalem, a very dry summer caused all water to dry up in the Barada a few miles out from the city. Some of the traditional pools were so low that "huge quantities" of fish were collected from them and sold at very low prices in the markets.[71] Early in 2010, international news

---

[71]E.W.G. Masterman, "The Water Supply of Damascus," *The Biblical World"*, 21, 2 (February, 1903)

agencies reported that as many as eight hundred thousand people had been displaced in Syria's northeast because of water failures. This was in the Tigris-Euphrates basin that flows down into Iraq, historically one of the most productive food growing regions in the world. During 2008 and 2009, rainfall was as much as sixty five percent lower than normal. That caused additional drawing on river waters to supply the flood irrigation needed for crops. In turn, that drained the rivers, while wells drew heavily on underground aquifers. Unfortunately, all that water raiding did not solve the problems and Syria, normally a wheat exporter, was now an importer.

There was a knock-on effect for Damascus primarily, although Aleppo and other cities also incurred problems. Perhaps three hundred thousand of those eight hundred thousand drought refugees relocated to the cities, living in temporary accommodation on the outskirts with little humanitarian assistance available. On the road to Homs, not that far out of Damascus, a large tented village off in the distance housed some of these people cut adrift by water failure. In the meantime, Damascus developed its own specific problems that an even bigger population increase would only aggravate.

Some reports from as early as 2004 suggested that if Damascus then needed two hundred and seventy four million cubic metres of water a year, it was getting only one hundred and sixteen million, about forty two percent of requirements. The daily shortfall in the summer of 2004 was four hundred and thirty three thousand cubic metres. The city's main water source, the Al Fijeh Spring, like its source the legendary Barada River, was drying up. Whereas in 1985 groundwater was being tapped at just fifteen metres below ground level, ten years later the depth was down at almost two hundred metres metres. And in the Gouta, the orchard area that has forever marked Damascus out as special, there was now a limited lifespan for the water supplies that gave it life.

Climate change, population growth, unreformed irrigation practice and policy complications have combined to give Damascus and Syria a problem. As always, too, there is a political dimension. Among the many reasons Syria desires to reclaim the Golan Heights are the water sources that area provides. Israel is just as concerned, because those sources feed the Sea of Galilee, its main water supply. Up in the now-beleaguered northeast, the rivers are shared with Turkey and Iraq, raising further complexity.

Nowhere is this better seen than in the present state of the Barada River that allegedly "flows" through Damascus. The grumpy Mark Twain, visiting in the 1860s, remarked that water was now the key if Damascus was to survive as a paradise because, in his opinion, the city was already the "very sink of pollution."[72]

In October 1918 an Australian soldier, among advance forces moving on Turkish lines as part of the push that put T.E. Lawrence and his Arab army into the city, reported his first glimpse of Damascus:

The Barada river wound like a silver thread through the town and the surrounding country, with numerous small water channels passing through the beautiful orchards and vineyards which enclosed the city on all

---

[72]Mark Twain, *The Innocents Abroad* (New York, Library of America, 1984 edn)

sides.[73]

That a soldier in the thick of battle could see this simply underlines how impressive the Barada was less than a century ago, and just how much change has now occurred with serious impact upon the city and its surroundings. It also suggests that Twin might have been exaggerating, underscoring his dislike for Damascus.

Given the scale of the problem, its direct impact now is surprisingly light, at least on the one person who was living in the house. The city system supplied water until midday so people made sure their tanks were filled. From then until midnight or so, the water tank provided for all needs until the town supply returned. The tanks depend on rain water in the "off" period and if that rain does not appear, as is now the Damascene norm, then surviving until the town supply reappears will become more of a challenge for large families, and for businesses or others for whom water is a priority.

For that reason, the luxurious pleasure of the shower, and the Aleppo soap, was marred by the knowledge that this water could well be used for more productive purposes, and that knowledge usually meant taking a quicker shower than desired.

We need another tank!

---

[73]Tom Darley, With The Ninth Light Horse in the Great War, (Adelaide, 1926), pp 156-8

A PROBLEM OF PERCEPTION

At some point of an extended stay in the Islamic and/or Arabic world, even the most sympathetic observer will be challenged, perhaps even affronted by something that, well into a post-Germaine Greer and Gloria Steinem world, seems anathematic to all but the most convinced misogynists.

It is possible to meet a man who has an open approach to strangers and displays, if anything, more than the normal Arabic warmth in hosting those strangers. In his daily life he displays strong interest in the goings-on of the world, keeps up to date with international affairs, has a not-too-intransigent view of the world from a regional and national perspective, makes no great secret but no great moment either out of being a practising if not zealous Muslim, and shows compassion for those people who come to his world bereft of insight. He might be bothered by the monolithic view of "Islam" and "Arabs" such people bring with them, but be no "fundamentalist" as the more ignorant of those strangers might leap to conclude. He will be warm, concerned and anxious to help, generous, and open.

Then he invites you to his house for a meal. The food is excellent and plentiful. The home is made yours as a "member of the family". The conversation is rich and long, there are agreements and points of difference. It is relaxed. Coffee and sweets follow the fruit that was preceded by a delicious selection of starter dishes. You finally say your goodbyes, and this excellent host accompanies you to find a bus or a taxi. Then you travel back to the house, walking the final stages through the Old City where some lanes are quiet, but others bustling with the young of both sexes mixing readily in the thoroughfares.

You reflect that throughout this pleasant evening, you had not seen let alone met your friend's wife. You sensed her, heard her, appreciated and admired her efforts, but had no opportunity to thank her for them directly. Your friend had proudly announced his wife was renowned as an excellent cook, which she was, clearly, but there was no opportunity to praise her for that. She and you had been in distinctly different places.

And you might even have seen some of the socialising origins of this. Say the man has a son and a daughter. It is entirely possible that the daughter, no matter how charming and accomplished, will be clearly in second place behind the son. It is entirely possible that your friend might even look sad for you when you tell him you have no son, but are blessed with marvellous daughters.

In all the debates on the "Other" of the Islamic and the Arabic worlds it is, arguably, the role of women that generates most heat in the West. Early in 2010, a BBC report from Damascus suggested that although the city was "relaxing" its social boundaries, most women in Syria and even in Damascus were restricted by religion, tradition and family. The report concerned a young woman school teacher whose marriage was arranged by her family, so that the wedding day would be the first time she saw her husband-to-be. The reporter professed shock at discovering that what she had thought to be relaxed unveiled dancing in the hall before the groom arrived was, in fact, really just a "meat market" at which prospective mothers-in-law might survey the field. The further suggestion was that most women in Damascus were harassed almost every day by men, especially the "frustrated teenagers" among them. To put it plainly, the reporter was dismayed by what appeared to be a social system within which women were suppressed, controlled, and intimidated.

Many privileged female nineteenth century travellers (and their male counterparts, it should be said) took a dim view of Damascene women. Catherin Tobin thought all the women of the "better class" she met were "splendidly attired" and naturally pretty. However, they pulled out all their eyebrows, replacing them with a dark line of makeup. That, she considered, "would spoil the handsomest face in the world." Worse, though, was their indolence: they were given over to clothes, gossip, smoking, drinking and eating, had no education and, as a result, went about with a "silly expression of countenance." They were, she continued, too lazy to take off their clothes before retiring at night, or to bathe more than once a month![74] That last point was a telling one, because her report was of a visit to a rich Jewish family that, perhaps, was not in the habit of visiting the local *hammam.* Or, perhaps, Catherine Tobin just got it all wrong.

This idea of the subjugation of women has been a common Western analysis of the Arab world generally and of Syria particularly, but belies that change is occurring and that it has a long heritage. In 1892, the Damascene woman writer, Hind Nawfal, began editing in Alexandria, Egypt, a journal called *Young Girl.*[75] By World War I there were twenty five such women's journals throughout the Arab world, all seeking to place women more centrally in modern Islamic life, and raising doubts about whether the Quran really did sanction the veil and polygamy, among other things. These journals kindled women's networks throughout the region, including in Damascus, and that in turn led directly to the 1928 formation of the Arab Women's Union. The main drive was to assert the rights of women within the context of what was positive for women within Islam and Arab culture, although lessons were also to be drawn from the rising women's movement in other cultures. This attempt at balance has made promoting the cause of women a difficult task within the context of a changing Islamic and Arab world but in Syria, at

[74]Catherine Tobin, *Shadows of the East* (London, Longman, 1855)

[75]Bouthaina Shaaban, "The Hidden History of Arab Feminism", MS Magazine, May-June 1993. Ironically, in 2012 Bouthaiana Shaaban, the feminist, was placed on the UN's list of individuals to be subject to sanctions because of her work as the Assad regime's international spokesperson.

least, has led to the formalisation of equality for women under the law. Critics, however, say that such laws are honoured more in the breach than in the observance.

As a result, it is still possible to see stories emerging in the early twenty first century about the need to establish in Damascus a women-only taxi service. The organiser of the service explained that she was driven to it by daily harassment from male drivers as she took her children to school, and as she herself proceeded to work.

There is no doubt that, in a Western sense, women are not considered to be as "free" in Syria as outside reporters might wish them to be, and that Islam's long practice of conservatism in gender relations, to put it mildly, is a major stumbling block to better international understanding. As always, things are sometimes not what they appear to be or are, at least, a little more complex than that. The West's view on this has a long history and much of the "Orientalist" literature, for example, proceeded from speculation and even prurience about the *zenana* and the *harem.* When Robert Richardson went to the Levant in the early nineteenth century, he was a member of the touring party got up by the second Lord Belmore, who used the affair as a means of escaping pressing financial problems back in Ireland. Belmore later became a controversial Governor in Jamaica, and his grandson a Governor of Victoria in Australia. On this trip, Belmore was accompanied by his wife, the former lady Juliana Butler. She was a character— Richardson describes her as dressing like a Mamluk and walking freely about the *souks,* drinking coffee in the riverside coffee houses, and smoking the *nargileh.*[76] She was in the long line of such Western women that would later include Freya Stark and Gertrude Bell, but it was not an approach that local women could adopt.

In one respect, that is a clue to the essential difference between the Arab world and the West—the women's movement in the West has been much about emphasising the need for gender relations to be normalised in the publicly visual sense, things not only have to change but have to be seen to be changed. That is a vast generalisation, obviously, but if it has any standing, it helps explain some of the frustration encountered in dealing with Islam in this area—change might well be happening, but it cannot be seen to be happening. There has always been commentary about the real power of Muslim women behind the veils, where the veils exist, but for the West that is unconvincing.

The related point arises when the *hijab* and the veil begin to appear in places where they have not been seen before and, for the West, that is automatically assumed to be an imposition by males. As usual, it might not be that straightforward. In Jordan, a young woman anthropologist suggested to me that the increasing appearance of the *hijab* among young university women there could be traced, at least partly, to a conscious decision by those women to do so as a statement about their commitment to Islam in response to American actions in Iraq. A similar story came transpired in Syria, and there was much spirited discussion about who had taken the *hijab* and why, and occasionally who had forsaken it and why.

The *hijab* and the veil were evidently not widespread

---

[76]Richardson, pp.472-3

in Damascus at this time, except in the Shia section, yet another gap between the broader reporting and the ground conditions which were, as always, more complex. Some local observers suggested that the *hijab*, at least in its milder form, was quite common a generation or so ago, and in Sunni as well as Shia quarters. Sunni-dominant cities like Hama have always had women wearing the *hijab* commonly. Again, the al-Assad regime has had a shaping influence on practice, as in Rifat al-Assad (Hafez's brother) leading his troops into Damascus during the 1980s and ordering women to remove their veils. Even against that background, however, now Jordan had the reputation for being more liberal yet was not, at least in this respect, while Syria was cast as the oppressive state, yet many of its women had more freedom than anywhere else in the Arab world.

Whatever the truth in any of this, there is no question that the role of women in Islam, and in Syria, will continue to be a major blockage to mutual understanding.

TRYSTING

Over in the Christian Quarter, one little restaurant offered a welcome escape from the streets with the pleasant proprietors offering excellent food and very cold beer at very reasonable prices. Just off Bab Touma Street and on the edge of the tourist sections, it was well situated.

Its ambience had also attracted young couples wanting to get away from it all. That was partly because the back section of the restaurant had several tables tucked around a corner and out of sight. It was discreet. Consequently, late in the afternoon and especially at weekends, it was common to see couples sitting back there spending time together with coffee and food, sometimes the Lebanese wine. The restaurant, like many others in the area, carried Ksara wines from the Beqaa Valley, that area known also for hosting military bases.

On one occasion in the restaurant the proprietors and waiters were intrigued, interested and amused because the couple of the day became very, well, close, with a considerable amount of mutual body searching conducted. The male headed for the gents toilet at one point particularly flushed in the face, surreptitiously rearranging his clothing as he went. After he returned, a little while later the lady in question retired to rearrange what was clearly a serious state of *dishabille.* Having thus rearranged themselves, they then proceeded to undo the good work, necessitating further expeditions later before they could brave the outside world. This was not a unique occurrence, either. A few weeks later another couple became similarly involved, the woman with a head scarf that was subject to considerable rearrangement.

The café provided a service as such places do all over the world, but its importance here was accentuated by the relative absence of private space in traditional settings, especially joint family homes, the still somewhat personal restrictions on the freedom of women, and rapidly changing modern attitudes towards relationships. In 1906 the Karl Baedeker guidebook to Palestine and Syria was forthright on this general matter in relation to Damascus:

In this jealous and fanatical city it is impolite and even dangerous to be too observant of the fair sex.[77]

At the same time, however, the guide book also referred to white-garbed women in the drapery *souk* "coquetishly" raising their veils to emphasise haggling

---

[77]Baedeker, p. 306

positions on purchases. Once again, these were not straightforward matters.

Well over a century later, that complexity found its way into the *Damascus For You* guide which carried a curious reference to this general area:

Sexual relations between young men and woman [sic] are correct and socially acceptable, only if they occur within the social habits regarding engagement and marriage.[78]

If that was so, then naturally the café couples were at least engaged, if not married and simply escaping the strictures of home in order to display their affections in public!

One local male made an interesting comment. In discussion, he suggested that the young American in the discussion group stood a better chance of getting a "date" (clearly code for something more) with/from a local girl, because any Syrian male given the same opportunity would shortly thereafter be served with a notice for marriage.

Casual observers are frequently struck by an odd phenomenon in Syria that is relevant to all of this. Throughout the *souks*, windows frequently display the most risqué women's underwear, bordering on or right in the territory occupied in the West by straight-out sex and porn shops.[79] There it is, all bright colours, loudly displayed and given regular and prolonged inspection by men and women alike. It is sold only by men, as are all goods in all shops, including the more

---

[78]Ayman Debes, Damascus For You (Damascus, Trans-Orient, 2009)

[79]Malu Halasa and Rana Salan, *The Secret Life of Syrian Lingerie* (San Francisco, Chronicle, 2008)

regular women's clothing and underwear outlets—women rarely run shops in the Old City. Heart-shaped pieces of fluff on impossible strings and all the usual variations of the genre are to be seen everywhere.

By definition, that means there is something very interesting going on in the field of social relations here, because it is otherwise hard to match the black veils with the black G-strings.

TONY BLAIR SHOULD LIVE
IN THE HOUSE

This fantasy arose during a conversation sparked by a BBC World News report about the latest collapse in "Middle East Peace Talks", as they are now honoured and which have now been going on for a very long time. The "Middle East" has been the subject of some intermediary action or other, perhaps, from the moment of its emergence as a labelled entity. In its more modern sense, the process dates from the collapse of the Ottoman Empire during World War I, and the subsequent carve-up initiated by the 1916 Sykes-Picot Agreement that saw Anglo-French interests best served, and from which Israel eventually emerged as a separate Jewish state at the expense of Palestine. The world has not been the same since.

The "Middle East" as a term is really the starting point for the problem. Because it was "east" of the major metropolitan powers, and because it was between the Turks and the "Asians" (another ascriptive term), it was just easier to describe the entire area as the "Middle East." That was defendable, except that, the term became a readily monolithic means by which to describe a whole set of peoples, no matter how significant their internal divisions.

At the popular media level now, there is still a conveyed sense in which Israel is surrounded by a unified team of Arab/Islamic opponents. Some media commentators work hard to nuance that view, and academic specialists know only too well the complex contours, along with the dangers of trying to flatten them out in search of a "story". Persistently, however, those nuances escape the general viewer and reader, so that the "Middle East" becomes a game of goodies and baddies.

Take, for example, the issue of Syria, Iran and Lebanon. These three are superficially reckoned the leading hawks against Israel, and at some levels that is a fair enough analysis. But the deeper search opened real fissures in that bloc view on the eve of the 2011-12 struggles. First, Syria scarcely recognised Lebanon as a separate state, because what is now Lebanon was once all Syrian (at least, in the Syrian view), and the country still believes it should be that way. Second, while Iran is predominantly Shia, Syria is not. In fact, while Sunni constitute about seventy percent of the population, the government remains controlled by the Alawites, a disputed offshoot of Shia. The Assad government ruled by drawing strongly on other minorities such as the Christians so the balancing act, a delicate one, was threatened by the rise of the "Syrian spring". Third, the tussle over Lebanon was intense, hence the anxiety over the inquiry report concerning the assassination of Rafiq Hariri that was anticipated to cite direct Syrian involvement—prior to publication of that report, complex diplomatic negotiations sought to prevent the emergence of undue chaos.

In amongst that manoeuvring lay what was probably the best example of nuance going unnoticed in the outside world—Hezbollah. Along with Hamas, this is the group most vilified in the West, and that applies also to its leader, Hassan Nasrallah. Yet behind the scenes, Syria and Iran and others like Saudi Arabia have a constant struggle to control the group's evolution and position. Nasrallah is effectively a Hezbollah moderate, and Iran would have preferred him to be replaced by a hawk. Syria did not, wishing to avoid being caught between the two. Nasrallah was a constant and obvious presence in Syria, his photograph appearing everywhere, and alongside that of President Bashar al-Assad. It was also common to be in a restaurant, eating along to the latest live televised Nasrallah oratory that, significantly, few people appeared to watch seriously.

So, all this was obviously far more layered in reality than portrayed by the mainline media. Yet, major world leaders and their representatives (increasingly ex-politicians themselves) seemed to spend inordinately short periods on the ground in any attempt to gain understanding. On one of his first "peace" missions to Syria, Kofi Annan spent something like eight hours in Damascus. Yes, they

have professional diplomats to do background
analysis. Yes, there are discussions preliminary to the
pre-meetings that negotiate the agenda, structure the
actual meeting, and pre-plan the communiqués. Yes,
these are intelligent people with good goals at heart.
Somehow, though, it all goes badly. People like Tony
Blair fly in and out, diplomats shuttle back and forth,
Secretaries of State come and go, but the conditions
endure.

So, having reached that point in the analysis one
night, up popped this idea: what about if Tony Blair
were to spend a month in the house? Why him? Well,
because in amongst all the interfaith foundation work
and speaking engagements he takes on in amassing
what is an extraordinary income for someone now
being revealed as shallow and disingenuous, he is the
Middle East envoy for the Quartet: USA, the
European Union, the United Nations and Russia,
where they meet as a consortium on the Middle East.
Since his 2008 appointment, his work has been
sporadic and largely futile. He has been reduced to
making largely meaningless pronouncements, flying
in for very brief visits, visiting the odd school, and
generally playing about on the fringes. By mid-2012
the Palestinians, at least, thought his efforts "useless",
and that he was actually more an apologist for Israel
than genuine arbiter for all parties.

This fantasy became even more pertinent as the
Syrian crisis worsened because, again, Blair seemed
to deal in slogans and assertions rather than substance.
In one mid-2011 interview, for example, he opined
that the Arab Spring gave new opportunities to re-start
the Middle East peace process—just how would that
be possible, and who would be involved? On Syria, he
suggested that Bashar al-Assad would find it difficult

to retain any legitimacy without a "truly credible reform process". That was just playing with words and bore no relationship to reality, because what a "truly credible reform process" might be, or need to be, was nowhere to be seen. It looked suspiciously like the envoy had no clue as to what was happening in Syria.

Quite apart from any qualifications he may or may not have had for the envoy role, a good part of Blair's problem, then, rested with the fact that he saw little or nothing of any of these affairs "up close and personal". By spending some time in the house, he might get a more interesting view on things. He might not be able to travel to and from meetings by taxi, perhaps, because of the inevitable security issues. But if he did get to stay in the house near Brokar, what might change?

He would meet people who would surprise him with their love of American movies and American English. And he would encounter people who want peace more than anyone, so long as it involves justice for Palestine. Tony Blair would see surprisingly few people corresponding with the stereotyped image of a fundamentalist: full beard, local garb, and *haj* hat. He would, however, see a lot of people with considerable knowledge of the outside world, and a genuine desire to see Syria more involved with and connected to that world. He would see a commitment to education as a generator of future prosperity and peace. He would meet people who welcomed him, even if they disagreed with his views. He would encounter people wary of Iraq and sceptical of Iran. He would meet people with very different views about the best ways to develop the Arab world, from Pan-Arabists to hardline nationalists.

Would he find sympathy and understanding for Israel? That is unlikely, given that metal Israeli flag fastened to the cobblestones in the Old City and trampled upon by thousands every day. The continuing Israeli hold on the Golan Heights is an on-going embarrassment and irritation for Syria, as is the Israeli grip on the West Bank for Jordan. Quneitra, up in the Golan Heights, is preserved as a ruined Syrian town, following its destruction by the Israelis during the 1974 war. Given the history before and after 1948, there is much ground to be given up before any sort of rapprochement might be possible.

Yet, by not being in the house, Blair has achieved little or nothing. So the question inevitably arises, would it do any harm to try? Maybe they could even move in President Bashar as well. That way, he and Blair would at least get to know each other. They would get wonderful service and food at the restaurants nearby, especially Brokar. They would have plenty of people ready to give them a street view, including my friends at the bakery and in the antique shop.

It was a fanciful idea, borne out of frustration between what seems an increasing gap between decision-makers and those who live the life, but if it happened, living in the house would educate even more people, important ones this time.

AN ARABIAN HORSE JOURNEY

Wilfred Scawen Blunt was one of those odd Englishmen who came to Arabia to become obsessed. In his case it was the later nineteenth century and mainly in Egypt, but his obsession was distinctive in one sense that had a huge influence around the world. Most visitors then got hooked on the desert, but Blunt did not. He returned to England with several of the horses known as Arabians. In their original form they were wiry, compact, long distance and endurance specialists, although over time they sometimes had more height bred into them. Arabians are super-smart and beautiful, the distinctive dish-nose on the pure-breds immediately identifying them to horse people everywhere. They also have a history.

For the Bedouin of pre-Crusader times, these horses

were a gift from Allah in the service of war. A particularly high tail came to represent pride, the greater the arch of the neck the greater the courage, and the greater the bulge in the forehead the more blessings from Allah. As a result, the breeding genealogies of horse lines became as important as those of the people who owned them. When Gertrude Bell visited a Damascene nobleman's house early in the twentieth century, she paid an early visit to the stables. There she found two magnificent Arab mares, from the great bloodlines developed by the Rualla, among the most famous of the desert tribes and who made up most of T.E. Lawrence's army.[80]

Mainly a poet and polemicist, Blunt established what became the world-famous and still extant Crabbett Stud back in England, in addition to one in Egypt, and run in partnership with his wife, Lady Ann Noel, granddaughter of the poet and tragic traveller, Lord Byron. When they divorced following one mistress too many (he attempted to shift this one into the family home while Lady Ann was still in residence), the stud became the centrepiece of a messy battle between him, his wife and their daughter that lasted until his death in 1922 at the age of 82. Blunt's part-solution to his consequential financial woes was to asset-strip as many horses as possible, and several were sold to Australia. Being isolated, the Australian Colonial Arabs, as they became known (from an imperially-minded English perspective, of course, an irony in that Blunt was an anti-imperialist), retained the original Arabian characteristics and so, into the twenty first century remain short, wiry, endurance specialists. Throughout that run of years, though, occasional imports of other Arabian stock enriched

[80]Gertrude Bell, p.146

the Australian bloodlines.

One of the most famous of those was Shahzada, a stallion imported from England in the 1920s by the Grace family, of Australian department store fame and fortune. By curious circumstance, a few years ago we acquired several Colonial Arabians, the prize of which was a gentle, rich chestnut stallion descended from Shahzada, named Codex but promptly nicknamed Cody, and who remains a central member of the family. Over a university council dinner one night a few years ago, a Grace family descendant was astonished to learn we had a horse descended from his family's import. He recalled that his grandfather always had two photographs on the desk: his wife, and Shahzada. That was a direct reflection of the Arabian reverence for genealogies of both people and horses. Our Cody descended directly from Shahzada on both sides of his line, so provides a direct link back to what in Blunt's day was still known as Arabia.

Being now in one of the most famous areas of the original Arabia we must, of course, see horses. The Affable reckoned there was a solution to everything in Syria, you just had to find it. In this case it was in the Yellow Pages, the modern successor to word-of-mouth and the grapevine. Several studs are located on the outskirts of Damascus in what were once relatively distant locations, but are now almost outer suburbs as the city devours more and more hills and valleys to build apartments and houses. The studs, market gardens and farms that support the city are good reminders of what it once was like.

The stud turned up by the Yellow Pages was a gem. Located at a "getaway escape" resort that included a swimming pool and restaurant, it turned out later to be well known to several Damascene friends. As soon as we turned into the gate, there on the right was a stable and yard complex. About half of the perimeter was lined with individual stables, and about fifteen horses were there, including foals. Sandi, the expert and enthusiast, immediately spotted three or four really good ones, and the fun began.

The owner was one of those marvellous people who made it so wonderful to be in Syria. He did not know us. He was rung up out of the blue. He immediately appeared and greeted us as if we were old friends, and spent the best part of three hours showing us his horses. They were all first returned to their boxes— and already for Sandi this stable design had become *the* one for a new complex at home. Then they were turned out individually, a couple of the mares accompanied by their foals.

As soon as these horses began to move, we were reminded why they have been revered for so long. Arabs float rather than run, they flow over rather than cover ground. Head up, tail up, no matter how fast they travel, they seem to be in slow motion with vast power in reserve. Even the foals pick it up immediately and no matter how gawky they look, small bodies on impossibly long and spindly legs, they still have the inherent grace that marks them out as special. A couple of these horses were clearly special. One was the offshoot of a Syrian mare and an Iraqi stallion. There was an immediate, if unspoken, understanding that such a breeding option would not again be available for some time, thanks to politics. The other had a French connection, and that had produced a quite different confirmation.

The French connection also opened up another surprising dimension. The stud owner was an engineer whose brother, it emerged, had been based in

Bordeaux for a long time where he, too, bred Arabians, this time for the racing circuit in France and around the world. Some of his horses had won major races including in the all-important centre of Dubai, and he appears in photographs with Sheikh Makhtoum, the famous boss of Dubai and even more famous international thoroughbred owner. The Sheikh's renowned Godolphin Stud in Australia's Hunter Valley is enormous, and has more recently come to include his growing collection of Australian Colonials. The very name of the stud recalls the importance of Arabian horse history. Godolphin was the name of a sire imported to England in 1730, and whose progeny founded the worldwide thoroughbred racing industry as we now know it. For a while in Australia, there were apocryphal stories about the Sheikh or his emissaries turning up unannounced, and offering $A25,000 for Arabian horses that normally traded for twenty percent of that figure, so keen were they to retrieve some of the original breeding characteristics. He never called us.

As we drove away from that stud near Damascus, I reflected that Cody now seemed even more significant, residing in our rural Australian paddock. We had seen something of his family history.

STRAIGHT STREET WEAVER

There were diamonds among the tourist rough of the modern Straight Street, and one of them was the weaver. He had a tiny shop at the bottom of an otherwise anonymous apartment block, just past the Roman Arch heading towards Bab Sharqi, and somehow into that he had fitted an over-two hundred years old loom on which he, his son and some apprentices created silk magic. This was the public face for a factory he had elsewhere containing another twelve looms, this one maintaining the connections to the and turning out timeless art pieces.

He had an ageing but open and welcoming face, greying short hair and an unfailing private charm that, combined with his craft skill, removed the urge to bargain from most clients. Given the amount of skill evident in the work and the sheer experience of being there to watch it being made, any price was a bargain. He would recount his family's history in the trade, work done for the former Shahs of Iran before the advent of the Ayatollah in 1979, and presentations of work by his father to Queen Elizabeth II, as well as to many regional dignities. The name cards he displayed came from ambassadors and politicians, all shown without ostentation while he sipped tea as if there was all the time in the world.

Well, there was, really. He was there almost every day from ten in the morning until ten at night. Walk along the street late almost any night and most all shops would be shut, but not his, he was the constant factor in Straight Street.

Anyone showing any interest got an immediate demonstration of the loom on which only a few metres a day of fine silk could be made, given the elaborate nature of the designs and the large number of colours involved. He or an assistant would willingly get in behind the wooden bar, flick the shuttles back and forth and under and over, before crimping another infinitesimal row of ordered silk into a much bigger picture. The pattern templates feeding down into the loom were all his creations, and on most visits there was something new to be discovered, small though the place was.

He was constantly looking for new ideas or, to use the current jargon, be innovative. One day, that turned out to be a re-arranging of the shop. The loom sat right up front near the window. To one side was the entrance, festooned with scarves, ties and lengths of fabrics in all the rich colours that might be imagined. A step led down between the loom and the wall, a space that could hold one or two average-sized people at most, as they squeezed past yet more products hanging off the wall. Past the loom he had a small glass cabinet sitting parallel to the walls, and behind that a small settee where he sat, designed, or worked on other projects. Now, he turned that glass cabinet perpendicular to the walls, so opening the space up to an additional two or three people. At high tourist time that made a difference because, sometimes, people just kept walking past when they saw the doorway blocked. Those who did not come back missed a marvellous experience, but the weaver was always thinking about how to minimise that loss of custom.

In many ways he was a return to the past, because from this tiny shop and his invisible-to-us factory he carried on a global enterprise. His business partner might currently be in Kuwait. Or the weaver himself might be preparing for another of his visits to Washington—the precious loom is loaded onto a container, and he goes off to ply his trade for two weeks before appreciative audiences. His products go all through the Arab world and beyond. The return of the tourists had, at that point, spread his influence ever more widely, even if one particularly fine scarlet silk hand-made and custom-made waistcoat had not been collected as promised, by its Canadian commissioner. That was two days work, said the weaver, but "no problem, someone will buy it."

There is a curiosity here because the modern world likes to think of itself as having created globalisation and all its problems. Anti-global protestors at G-20 and other meetings, for example, seem apparently to believe they are the first to encounter and confront "globalisation." The same might be said of rock activists like Bono and Geldof. Yet all this activity had gone on for a very long time, as epitomised by this little shop on Straight Street from where a humble and skilled man conducted a global business. Weaving was long a practice in the region, and the French built on that, opening the first spinning factory in 1840. At that point, however, the industry's future was uncertain because of the impact of European goods arriving in wake of the industrial revolution. Because the Christians were prominent, the industry's trials were aggravated by the 1860 massacres that saw large number of Christians killed. Soon after, there were over three thousand working looms in Damascus, and weaving was rebuilt. Towards the end of the century there possibly up to fifteen thousand weavers at work.[81] By 1912, there were almost two hundred factories in and around the Old City. Allied trades like dye-making were also numerous. By that point, however, European goods were back in the markets, at competitive extremely prices, and rising immigration was reducing the ready supply of female labour. The Straight Street weaver will tell you that all his silk now comes from China—while those threads had long been present, it was also around the turn of the twentieth century that they came to dominate.[82] There used to be a local supply but silkworms need trees, and all those had long gone from the areas of Arabia where they once were. Of course, we are reminded immediately of the Silk Road, that legendary ancient and medieval trading route along

---

[81]James A. Reilly, "From Workshops to Sweatshops: Damascus Textiles and the World-Economy in the Last Ottoman Century," *Review*, XVI, 2 (Spring, 1993)

[82]Naval Staff Intelligence, *A Handbook of Syrian (Including Palestine)*, pp.282-7

which the precious fabric and spices moved in the massive caravans.

There is a modern twist, though, in the way the weaver loaded the spindles that fed the silk thread into the loom. He took a roll of thread, attached it to a spindle, then held onto the roll as he attached the spindle—to an electric drill. He then turned on the drill at full speed and the spindle was loaded in no time. That innovation did not come in with the camel caravans.

CAREERS

A walk from the house through the Hamidiyeh to the underpass and on through the "New City" leads, in one direction, to the Tekkiye Sulamaniye that is one of the most beautiful sights and sites in all Damascus. Incongruously, it is sandwiched now between a parking station behind, some nondescript office buildings on one side, the National Museum on the other, the concrete channel that effectively carries what remains of the Barada and, on the other side, the Four Seasons hotel. At that time, the hotel guests' view of the Tekkiye Sulamaniye was due to be blocked by an enormous shopping mall, just the latest monument to Damascus' long trading history.

The complex was created in the mid-sixteenth century to replace an earlier palace wrecked by the latest round of warfare, and it was designed as a pilgrimage centre. Here, those making what was then the long and arduous *haj* to Mecca had a place of rest and contemplation before they set out. With an exquisitely crafted mosque as its focal point, and a series of dome-topped rooms around the central pool and gardens that led off to a *madrasa,* it would have been a calm place before the trials that were to come, because casualty rates on the *haj* were high.

These days it houses the cleverly-conceived craft souk where silversmiths, glassmakers, brass and copper beaters, artists, lute-makers and textile sellers sit side by side providing easy access for busloads of tourists. In one shop, through a very low doorway and under a dome, there was a trove of artefacts and fabrics and glass and curiosities in glass cases, piled up the walls and along the floor. The keeper of these treasures was a genial, articulate man who really knew his trade.

"Where are you from?"

Australia

"You have come a long way to visit Syria."

Well, luckily, I am living here.

"What are you doing?"

I am on a project designed to upgrade the university and higher education system.

"I must give you my other card", he said, retrieving one from under the counter.

He was a French-educated scientist who held a university position as well as running this obviously well-stocked Orientals and antiques shop in the Suleymaniye.

"There is much to do in the universities," he continued

This was a common comment, because many Syrians had a lot to say about the state of their universities. The public universities were huge, and the country's young demographic demographic pipeline meant they would probably grow even more. The planning for this was rudimentary, qualified and experienced staff were at a premium, yet teaching positions were demanding and lowly paid. University management was heavily process rather than strategically oriented. One very competent senior executive, from Aleppo University, had an amusing photograph on his phone that he showed me during a break in a workshop. We were discussing efficiency. The photograph was of an enormous pile of papers and files on a high-backed chair, the mountain reaching to the top of that back. I asked him what it was. He smiled:

"That is my daily consignment of papers to sign."

Daily?

"Yes, the same pile appears every day."

He explained that no matter what he did to try and reduce this, the paper flow continued unabated, as literally the smallest thing needed a forest of signatures to validate any action. This was repeated through all levels of the university, and all the universities were the same. Getting anything done was difficult. On top of that, rising student numbers raised serious infrastructure questions, the supply of good academic staff was lagging, and the numbers of universities were growing. The system had serious capacity restraints, even though the regime considered higher education to be an important lever for social and economic growth.

I thought of him and his chair many times after that, especially after I left Syria and most especially when the later reports came in of demonstrations being broken up at the University of Aleppo.

Because of that general situation, then, thousands of academics like the antique dealer in the Tekkiye Sulemaniye created other lives and incomes for themselves. His conversation centred around that, and around the frustration of not being able to commit fully to his intellectual career which was important to him, not just as a profession but as a way of life. He embodied the continuing Arab love affair with knowledge and thinking. In his case, that was shaped and formed in Paris where he studied, then taught for a while before coming home to pass on his new skills. Being able to do that only partially was an obstacle to Syria's growth, he reckoned, because his experience mirrored that of countless others. The inability of the government to maximise all those skills was holding the country back. Meanwhile, he turned his energy toward his antiques.

Back over on Straight Street, meanwhile, another acquaintance had a much clearer set of plans for himself, by selling carpets.

Straight Street was already running the ever-present tourist site danger of becoming a caricature of itself. The dilemma is always there, of course: because tourists want to come and visit, authorities then promote it, allow souvenirs to overtake craft, do not control development, and very soon the things that made it attractive start disappearing under attack from far more inferior things.

At the Bab Sharqi end of the street lay the main churches. From that end until Bab Touma Street T-junction, a range of "Orientals" shops sold the boxes and brasses that made Damascus famous centuries ago. The theory was that the Christians made the boxes, but that exclusivity really disappeared long ago. Nevertheless, in the side alleys up from the Bab Sharqi end, it was still possible to find small factories making wonderfully distinctive things, each box having a unique character through a mark or a flaw that characterises the true craft piece. Even in that block, though, jewellers and trinkets and fashion designer clothes had started to appear, rendering it more like the main tourist traps in Venice, Rome or anywhere else.

From there up towards the Roman Arch and the up-market Naranj restaurant, there was more residential accommodation, along with a few local craft suppliers mixed in with provisions shops, more Orientals, and a marvellously kitsch souvenir shop purveying all the Bashar al-Assad key rings and fridge magnets anyone would ever need. Pharmacies were strewn through this, with all the modern drugs and no need for a prescription. The chemists were surrounded by bakers, the odd pizza outlet, coffee shops, a few bars, and many liquor shops. From Amin Street up to *Souk* Medhat Pasha there were all the nut shops, metal and wood workers, *nargileh* sellers, general provisions merchants, and the first of the sweets and soaps sellers who marked the beginning of the spice market that led down to the Hamidiyeh.

It was in that section up near *Souk* Medhat Pasha that I found the rug man. He was extremely chatty from the first time I met him, and very fluent in English. While educated in Damascus, he had gone off to the Gulf to make a living as a small time business executive. It had not really worked out for him. First, he did not like Dubai—the Gulf Arabs were different, he thought, and he never felt at home there. This, once more, was a timely reminder of the dangers in stereotyping people just because it seemed they had the same background. Arabs they were, certainly, but with different traditions and ideas. Second, he discovered he was not, as he described it, a "company man". So he returned to Damascus, and tallied his skills: he had good English, liked people, loved to talk, had energy and enthusiasm. That all added up to becoming a shopkeeper, but not a run of the mill one in the *souk,* because he had higher goals.

The carpets came about because he had developed some networks while in Dubai, and because he spotted a gap in the market in Straight Street. His logic was that if there were that many tourists now flocking to Via Recta, then at least a few of them would have an idealised view of the "Orient" and be inclined to replicate Aladdin. He was right. Never mind that Damascus had never really had a great rug tradition, if it was there and sourced from Iran, it was an attraction. In truth, most of his stock was from central Asia or Pakistan, but he kept a good range, and he knew how to sell. His shop was one of the most attractive on the street, and he had put much time and effort into achieving that, figuring that an attractive shop was more likely to attract customers cowed somewhat by the appearance and nature of the other outlets nearby. He was making a fortune.

He had a plan, though—to retire at forty. At this point he might have been thirty, just. Already, he had bought a ten acre property outside Damascus. The house was yet to be built, but the "farm" was already being laid out to gardens, orchards, shrubs, and stock yards. When he decided the time was right to marry, he would then build the house. In the meanwhile, he went to work the property every weekend, investing some of his takings from the rugs. As capital accumulated, he would also buy some properties in the Old Cities because he saw rental rates rising and demand not slowing. Within ten years, he thought, he would be able to retire, enjoy the farm and the family he would have by then, and live on the rental from the Damascus properties as well as the shop sales that would be overseen by a trusted manager.

This was as disciplined an approach to career development as might be found anywhere, and somehow that made him just the latest of a long line of Damascene traders who had thought this way for several generations over hundreds of years. So long as young people like him could flourish, so would the Old City, and Syria. It is to be hoped that his plans have not been dashed too much.

A GENUINE KILIM

He had terrible emphysema, the result of a lifetime's smoking in the Arab tradition.

People in Damascus would offer a cigarette in the expectation that most Europeans would say "no," then would seek permission to smoke themselves. Some would not bother, like the taxi driver late one afternoon who must have been smoking something homemade, because its acridity made Gauloise seem like mild Virginia. It was the evil of two lesser that day: open the window and risk pneumonia, or close it and risk lung cancer by association.

This man, though, smoked on gamely while plying his daily trade in the Hamidiyeh. The shop was narrow fronted like the rest, with a mezzanine reached by a narrow winding set of stairs that required a significant bend at the waist to avoid head-butting the roof. He had the range of goods shared by his neighbouring competitors: silver, pashmina, swords, stones, scarves, damask, Damascene boxes, brass and copper, some Roman coins and, naturally, "special rare" pieces. He also had rare rugs, he said.

So-called Persian rugs have long held a fascination for the West and were really one of the mainstays of the caravan trade towards the end of its most triumphant period. Into the twentieth century, the "silk road" was still really the rug road and Ian Catanach, who inspired my study of Asia at the University of Canterbury, early on recounted a visit to Isfahan and the buying of a rug. By the late twentieth century every major town in the West, it seemed, had a string of "rug special" shops, where "export sales" and "receivers auctions" promised treasures from Iran and elsewhere at ridiculous prices. It was really the "elsewhere" that sourced most of this rather than the genuine centres of Tabriz, Isfahan , Qum and Shiraz, but the mystique remained. The rug became totemic in the West from at least the eighteenth century onwards, if not earlier, perhaps "the " most common signifier of the "Oriental."

The 1979 Iranian revolution put a big dent in the trade, and from then on places like Pakistan, Turkmenistan and similar places in the region began flooding the world with carpets, perfectly good products but nowhere near the handmade masterpieces produced before for hundreds of years. Yet the markets in Damascus continued to be full of shops selling rugs, specialist ones as well as the generalists like my man in the *souk*.

"Do you like rugs?" he coughed.

Yes, I do.

"Well, then, I have very special rugs."

I am sure you do.

"You will see some very special items."

I am sure I will.

By now he was pulling at a pile of rugs in the top attic, amidst the chess sets, coffee tables, boxes, jewellery and crusader helmets.

I will not be buying.

"But you will when you see this particular one, a chance in a lifetime," he spluttered, sipping coffee and drawing on a cigarette simultaneously, a wondrous feat for a man in his condition.

"I will show you some others first."

Out came a ragged-backed monstrosity, clearly knocked up yesterday in some nearby factory.

"This is very good. Iranian."

Oh yes.

"You like it, very good deal."

No, don't like the colour.

"Never mind, I have more, and a very special one."

Over the next few minutes several "Iranian" and "special" carpets appeared, all obviously machine-made recently, with little pile, and self-evidently woollen rather than the silk being claimed.

The "very special" one then appeared.

"You will need to buy this one today."

Why?

"Very rare. I only bought it myself yesterday off a

man from Iran."

What is it?

"It is a genuine Kilim, at least sixty years old and there are no more of them. It will not be in the shop long. You are the first to see it, special price for you because it is Friday."

This rarity looked suspiciously younger than sixty. In fact, its seller looked older. It also looked machine-made, the trim finish a giveaway. It colours were nondescript and, again, it had an unfinished back.

How much do you want for this treasure?

"For you, I have a very special price, 34,000 Syrian pounds [then about $750].

You know, I do not like it that much, and I do not think it worth that money.

"It is a genuine Kilim!"

Even so.

"OK, for you, 24,000."

That's interesting. But I am not buying today, I will go away and think about it.

"It will not last."

That will be my loss.

"18,000."

By departure time, the rug's price was at 12,000 and falling, rather undercutting the veracity of the genuine Kilim claim, and that was where it was left.

A couple of days later, he loomed up out of the *souk* throng again.

"Fortunately for you, the carpet is still here, come and

have a look."

How much?

"10,000, quickly, come and see."

There was time to do that, curiosity overpowering logic.

Up the winding stairs again, banging the head.

Out came the carpet—a different one!

That is not the Kilim.

"Oh yes sir, it is, for you just 9,000, you are very lucky it is still here."

I certainly am.

Over the lengthy course of my subsequent experiment, the Kilim changed guise three more times, and the price bottomed at 5,000.

When I finally left Damascus, the "genuine Kilim" was still in the shop, awaiting anyone interested.

LIVING
WITH/OUT LANGUAGE

He was Palestinian, he said, and had lived in Damascus for twenty six years. Damascus was fine, but "Palestina" was great.

It was late in the day, with winter darkening everything early just before Xmas when he came to a stop in his taxi. "Ah,"he said, on discovering the Australian connection, "you are from Sydney."

Melbourne.

"Sydney. Do you speak Arabiye?"

Now that was an unusual question from a taxi driver.

"You should always speak Arabic. Arabic, Arabic, Arabic."

Unpredictably, he then commenced delivering lessons in Arabic.

We were swinging along past the new and imminent

mall monster on Shukri Al Quatli, before hiving off over Port Said Street and through Marjeh Square before moving up onto Al Beit and Hariqa. The traffic was congested and driving difficult, but the lessons kept coming, along with his excellent rendition of Australia's "thet's noice," and the difference between Australian "yiss" and American "yah."

Where do you get all this?

"I have a lot of people ride in my taxi."

Yes, but you must have an excellent ear.

Along the way, the Arabic lessons transmuted for a period into a discussion about the United Nations— you had to be there to understand how and why. We worked out he thought Kofi Annan had been good enough, but Ban Ki Moon did not rate, mainly because of the apparently frenzied inaction on Palestine. I wonder what he thought of Kofi Annan not all that much later?

As elsewhere in the Arab world, the Palestinian running sore is felt keenly in Syria. All through Medhat Pasha, in particular, but in all the other markets as well, the PLO scarves were ubiquitous, along with Palestinian key rings, fridge magnets, bumper stickers, mugs, plates, clocks and flags. The scarves had evolved: in earlier years they were simple, usually the black and white checked ones with the Palestine colours of black, red, white and green, as worn by Yasser Arafat, in the tassels at the ends. Now, there were a variety of main colours for the checks, and an illustration of the Dome on the Rock, with the words "We Will Return", appearing just above the coloured tassels.

That ambition of return is a brave hope long sustained, particularly in the refugee camps. There are almost a dozen of those all over Syria, springing up first in the immediate aftermath of Israel's creation in 1948, then after each of the successive conflicts. Well over one hundred thousand people live in those official camps, that number matched by the "unofficial" Yarmouk camp alone. It lies in the south-western suburbs of Damascus and has its own hospital, clinic and educational services assisted by the UN. It is very close to the Al Tadamun district, and both figured prominently when the 2011-12 unrest spread into Damascus. By mid-2012 there was fierce fighting through there and both areas, along with the Midan, sustained substantial damage and loss of life. In sympathy with all the inhabitants of all those camps in Syria and elsewhere throughout the Levant, regional news reports had long continued to refer to "Occupied Jerusalem". Ban Ki Moon has his work cut out, and a host of watching critics, like my taxi driver.

"Ride in my taxi more, and you will learn Arabic."

If only it was that easy.

Before 2011-12, Damascus hosted hundreds if not thousands of foreign students learning Arabic, an encouraging sign for the future, because with language comes far better cultural understanding, obviously. That was not always immediately the case, however. One young English student explained to me at length how he and his pals had defended the honour of a female friend, whose honour was besmirched when a local pinched her bum. They chased him through the streets, apprehended him, then frog-marched him to a police station, only to be dismayed by the constabulary's apparent lack of interest in doing anything. The students' social incomprehension on that score was matched only by their blissful ignorance of the high risk factors involved that keep university managers awake at night.

There was an obvious oddity in this rising popularity: the taste for Damascus, as a site for exchange programs and intensive short courses, had developed over roughly the same stage as Syria's evolution into a pariah state, especially in the case of the United States, even though the change from Bush to Obama had allowed for a little more hope of improved interaction. Nevertheless, Damascus and Syria were paradoxes again: the "outside " was still deeply suspicious, yet sent its best and brightest there to learn Arabic. Similar students had been there much earlier. The present boss of the England and Wales Cricket Board took a degree in Arabic studies, then spent a year in Damascus during the 1970s, learning the language in the immediate aftermath of Hafez al-Assad's power grab. This was very close to the Damascus as described by Colin Thubron, and the then-student recalled much later he had few if any foreign colleagues. He did remember that the beer was good, though.

Whatever the inner contradictions here, however, the Antipodean view has to be positive. Being in Damascus yet again reaffirmed the national weaknesses inherent in the continued breeding of essentially monocultural generations, at the very time language skills are increasingly needed. Language teaching in Australia and New Zealand has always struggled, but even more than normal in recent years as a result of cost cutting and budget restraint. Teaching languages is cost intensive, too much so for the new university funding orders. The net result is that Australians increasingly find themselves meeting Europeans who speak three or four languages easily, including English, and in Syria, locals who might speak French, English, Italian, German or anything else. In the face of this, Australia's Department of Foreign Affairs would shortly after say it did not think it important to have a Hindi-speaking High Commissioner in New Delhi. The easy "out" for Australians is to argue that the Syrians have always been on the trade routes and keen to trade, so language was a necessity. Yes, but those Syrians are also in a region and a context where language skill is imperative, so they commit. The general Australian answer is that more and more people speak English, so why bother learning anything else?

It was possible to survive in Damascus and Syria without knowing Arabic, but any small attempt to use the language was met with delight and encouragement. Many locals were also keen to exercise their English—the friend met in the Sarouja barber shop was a case in point.

"My English does not get used, so I am trying to find conversation."

The young man in the bookshop next to the office had exactly the same outlook. Every time I went in there, he would come up and we would spend half an hour in English conversation so that he might practice a little more, and the Arabic-English dictionary was always at hand to clarify a precise meaning.

But in not knowing Arabic there is always the sense of missing out on things, especially when a long slab of Arabic is translated back as just a couple of words. A friend in a shop said:

"we should speak in English more around you, but we need Arabic to say things more fully."

Therein lies a powerful and potent point,

demonstrated almost every day in office debates over the precise meaning of a bland English word, because in Arabic there might be, say, five nuanced variations that could be used for that word in question. The richness of Arabic is surely the key to outsiders understanding more clearly how the place works.

"Lost in translation" became more of an international shorthand in wake of the Bill Murray film, and it did so because of an inherent appreciation of just how important this issue is in resolving differences, and that was precisely the point made by the Palestinian taxi driver: "always speak Arabic, Arabic, Arabic."

HAMMAM BAKRI SPECTACLE

Anywhere in the world, selecting the right spectacle frames is serious business, especially when buying for someone else, namely spouse, even if the model and serial numbers are recorded. The same was true in this shop, in crowded Hammam Bakri Street in the Christian Quarter, just down from the bath house that gives its name to the street but which seemed to have been closed permanently for repairs. While one shop assistant hunted my specified numbers, another assisted a woman there with her daughter, and struggling to choose.

Three models were shortlisted, all narrow-framed and oblong in the latest style, but in different colours. The mirror was consulted frequently, and there was great discussion between salesman and customer before the latter cast out a question.

"What do you think? Nice?"

Me?

She had the typically interesting local face, high cheekbones, etched features, dark haired, in her late forties perhaps, slim, well dressed. The daughter was early twenties, tiny, attractive, and bemused by this turn of events.

"Yes, which ones are nice?"

Try them all on again.

She did.

Those ones are nice.

"These ones?"

Yes.

She took them over to the mirror, put them on and took the clasp out of her hair.

By now the daughter is chuckling, along with me and the shop men.

"Nice?"

Yes.

"I am nice, too? Beautiful?"

Yes.

"You love me?"

The daughter is now hysterical.

My wife would have a lot to say about my answer to that question.

"Ah, perhaps, then, you smile me?"

Yes, I smile you.

"You will buy them for me?"

The banter and the laughter filled the shop, as she and daughter then began bargaining over the cost of the preferred "nice" glasses. Interestingly, they used a method to which most Westerners are reduced—write a figure on a piece of paper, then hand it over. Several numbers were exchanged between customer and salesman, the deal was closing.

"Expensive!"

That was directed at me.

Really?

She handed over the number on a piece of paper.

They are very nice. Is that the number?

"What you think? Perhaps my phone number?"

Yes for glasses, no for phone number.

The daughter looked on, smiling, but now fascinated to watch her mother having fun.

"When are you leaving?"

Any foreigner in a shop must be a tourist, especially in the Christian Quarter near Christmas.

Wednesday morning.

The hair clasp went back in, the smile genuine.

"Are you rich?"

Not enough for you, I think.

More laughter filled the shop as she feigned disappointment.

The deal was done, mother and daughter departed amidst loud chat and laughter in Arabic. Waves and farewells were exchanged through the window and they went off into the throng, leaving the shop, its assistants and remaining customer still laughing.

This human interaction might have taken place anywhere in the world, or become the logline for a Hanks/Ryan remake of *Sleepless in Seattle* (*Dazzled in Damascus,* possibly):" a visiting expert about to leave Damascus has a chance meeting in a spectacle shop with a local woman, then re-finds her on a later mission". However, this was in Damascus, after all, the imagined centre of all sorts of horrors where there would reportedly be no fun, human spark, interaction or challenge. This was not in Macy's or Harrods, but on Hamman Bakri up from St Thomas Gate, five minutes walk from Straight Street, ten from the Umayyad Mosque.

When Said wrote of the "Other", he was commenting on people gone from the West to observe people in the "Middle east" or "Asia". Really, though, that can be turned around easily, so that the "Other" is really the person coming to observe, but being observed. How might this tourist (he must be a tourist) in the optometrist react to some banter? Oh, he is just like normal people, but why would he be buying glasses here? Perhaps he is replacing broken ones, except he seems to be looking for women's frames. Pity he has no Arabic, it would be interesting to learn his story. He likes a laugh, though, that is always nice.

The other reminder here was that gender relations are complex within and across the Damascene communities, but not universally dour. One previous consultant was apparently asked to leave because he was more interested in getting the phone numbers of almost any woman encountered whether scarfed, Christian, Muslim or anything else than he was in the work. Best behaviour was always called for, but here was yet another reminder that some things are universal. Am I interesting? Am I still attractive? Do I still have a life? Who cares what my daughter thinks? This is fun. Let's have a laugh. Back to normal as soon as we leave the shop, same old same old. Wonder how he got here, or what he is doing? He will know now we Damascenes have humour, and are approachable. He will remember that.

She was right, and I hope she enjoyed the glasses.

A ROAD FROM DAMASCUS

A torrent of water was leaving the roof of the main room in the house in volumes not

experienced by the Barada River for many, many years.

The long spell of dry weather broke emphatically one mid-December morning, teeming rain accompanied by massive thunder and impressive lightning. Colleagues come to a seminar from Lattakia and Aleppo confirmed that they had experienced this all the way to Damascus, so the rain was blessing most of Syria. There was great rejoicing because the rain had arrived, as well as spirited but good natured office debate about the cause—the day before had been a special Friday, ending three days of extraordinary prayers inviting divine assistance to deliver rain, such had been the drought. The debate was between the convinced and those less convinced about the efficacy

of that prayer, emphasising that Islam, too, has
adherents with varying levels of faith and conviction.

Meanwhile, mini-rivers flowed through Old City lanes
from Straight Street heights, seeking and finding a
level down somewhere near the Mosque. Those
rivulets were swollen further by water streaming out
of pipes high up on houses, sloshing straight off the
roofs. Two almost impassable lakes blocked laneways
leading to the sweet *souk* (difficult to get supplies that
day, though my supplier was open) while, elsewhere,
my puny umbrella was deluged by waterfalls from
roofs struggling to manage the deluge now being
dumped on them.

This was followed immediately by snow. It began
south of Homs, a cold snap rushing over the quirkily
named Anti-Lebanon Mountains from, yes, Lebanon
and Israel which both experienced violent storms,
thick snow dumped on the lower slopes and onto the
high plains. The road passes up from Damascus to
Homs climb steeply into the hills, so the snow piled
quickly as we edged our way towards an aid donors
update conference in Aleppo. Cars and trucks soon
slid off the road as inexperienced and/or impatient
drivers raced by in the fresh snow outside the traffic
lines, only to find themselves adrift or, worse, slid
down the bank. We were stuck for almost two hours
but, even in the standstill of a huge traffic jam
inundated by snow, the horn blowers continued their
tune. Agatha Christie would have recognised the
refrain. That would get rid of the snow. If not, then it
might relieve the frustration. The storm passed
through eventually, travelling south and dumping
Damascus with one of its most significant snow
blankets for years. Reports had it several centimetres
thick, sitting heavily, disrupting traffic and blocking

thoroughfares. Given Christmas was imminent, it would be picturesque to return to the city where the symbolic trees had already appeared, along with all the other Christian festive season markers.

Returning to Damascus a day later down those heights from Aleppo, passing by Hama and Homs, snow was everywhere evident. Off in the distance, Mount Qassioun looked altogether different, the new stark white colour making it seem even taller and more severe than before. In the nondescript outskirts through which the city must now be approached, massive water pools covered the road as the big melt began and "Car City", a long line of dealers in low lying spots at the side of the road, was up to its hubs in water. Mercedes raced by with impunity and no control. Driving our van, Hammad Ali (yes, named for the former Cassius Clay) expressed frustration with those passing drivers: no brains, he thought. In the Old City, great lumps of snow still graced cars, clogged corners, blocked alleyways and fell off roofs. It was at once bedraggled and distinguished, citizens patiently sidestepping any waterfalls and lakes they encountered.

The steps up to the house had big drifts of snow still lying about, turning to slush but starting to freeze. Snow was even piled up against the door into the entry way, and against the door of the squattie. Even more snow was lying about the courtyard, much of it sliding from the roof up top, and from the one above the kitchen that was piled high beneath the clothesline.

But a background sound of running water complemented the visual change. There were two sources. One was a small hole in the roof above the bed at the other end of the main room. Water from there was cascading onto, humorously enough, the London Fog raincoat I had carefully laid out in preparation for but forgotten to take to Aleppo. The other contributor was a series of leaks along the roof join where the once-separate room had been opened up to join the one in which I worked. The join was faulty. Those two sources ensured that clothes were soaked, the spare bed saturated, and some furniture and coverings dripping. The plasterboard roof near the chandelier bulged ominously, water obviously gathering between it and the upstairs balcony floor. All the floor coverings at that end of the room had given up absorbing moisture and begun dispatching it to low-lying corners. It was vaguely reminiscent of a Venetian *aqua alta.*

Well, I had wanted the full Old Damascus experience. The main problem was the snow still lying on the flat roof of the upstairs bedroom. It was sliding onto the upstairs landing, where the resulting water then found another fault line in the landing tiles. From there it fed into the underlying roof cavity, adding even more pressure to the plasterboard now was in imminent danger of collapse. The only relief was that creek flowing onto the bed and the floor, from where it meandered towards the stepwell and out into the courtyard. This situation needed a solution, or the roof would collapse. The agent called the landlord who soon arrived, huffing and puffing.

Mein Host had been an interesting person from the outset. Neglecting to clean the place before I moved in, he had corrected that with a lot of humphing and other expressions, then pushed off muttering. He was a now-tubby but once strong man, short with an expressive face, the obligatory moustache and swept-back trimmed hair. He rolled into rather than arrived at places, but with enthusiasm and purpose. Having accepted the rent money, he was surprised to learn that also meant he could not come and go as he pleased. That was surprising news for him, it transpired. It also delivered some hilarious phone conversations with the agent, because the landlord's way of dealing with a mobile phone was to hold it as far away as possible, then shout at and/or into it. There were occasions when he could have dispensed with the phone, because at his decibels many recipients were well within earshot. His heart was always in the right place, and his efforts to mime meaning memorable and meritorious, but his alleged practicality was monumentally confusing, and his priorities baffling.

A few days before this great snowfall, the newly-arrived heater had its plug burned out by a faulty socket. The arrangement was that Mein Host would arrive with an electrician and all would be well. He arrived alone. His idea was to replace the heater plug himself, then we would simply shove that into the blackened and melted remains of the wall socket. It was a good idea, he thought. There then followed the usual loud and impassioned speeches with the agent via the phone before he left, to return a few minutes later with a young man who clearly knew what he was doing in matters electrical. The expert set to and solved the problems, albeit with some of his own adaptations, like sticking a screwdriver into the live socket to widen the pinhole so that the heater plug might fit. The already short heater cord ended up being shorter still, but heat was restored. A serious haggle ensued before the sparky departed with SYP 550, about $12, for working in the early evening on a weekend, along with a farewell speech from the owner which doubtlessly emphasised specialist help had not been needed anyway.

Mein Host had his own way of doing things as, let us admit, do we all. Immediately upon arrival at the scene of the Great Snow Dilemma, he proceeded to clear the courtyard, his pride and joy. When reminded there was a waterfall in his main room he seemed little interested, essaying a quick look before returning to more important matters. Then, when alerted that the main problem lay on the bedroom roof upstairs, he promptly proceeded to the bathroom roof on the other side of the landing, and cleared snow that was causing no problem at all. Meanwhile, downstairs, the lake swelled. There was a simple solution to that—he replaced the London Fog with a tarpaulin so as to better hasten the flow of water into the lake. He then decamped, to continue the more important courtyard sweeping.

He did eventually begin to clear the bedroom roof. I knew that, because great chunks of grubby snow suddenly descended from on high with resounding thumps into the courtyard. Huge snow showers resulted, smashing in through the open door of the flooded end of the room where, like Canute, I was waging futile battle with the rising tide. Long streaks of muddy slush careened in, muddying the walls, wardrobe, floor, and me.

By now we were disagreed about the best course of action. That produced another series of loud and animated megaphone discussions with the agent. Somehow, we worked through it all and parted jolly friends, though neither of us had a clue about what the other was thinking, or doing, or why. He probably considered me an odd and unfathomable foreigner, just as I thought him illogical and impulsive. By now it was dark so he left, allegedly to return the next day to clean up. I shifted all my clothes, given the possibility that the dam building in the roof might well bust without Bomber Harris' assistance, but by next day the threat had passed, though the temperature was now cold rather than cool.

Christmas tree numbers had already increased exponentially, underlining yet again just how ecumenical Damascus could be. There was a perfect tableau in one of the main Old City laneways: a lovely Arabic inscription in marble on a wall, above a stall selling Xmas bears and other seasonal things as would occur anywhere throughout the Christian world. From the courtyard at the Orthodox church came sounds of a brass band pounding out a spirited rendition of semi-recognisable carols. Luckily, there were still a few days left for them to practice. The usual signs of Xmas had appeared in all the churches, the Christian Quarter looking like it belonged anywhere in the West. Some churches displayed Christmas lights, as did many buildings and houses along Straight Street. Church bells rang in the special services, and crowds flocked into all the chapels. Christmas shopping with intent could be observed everywhere, especially in the boutique jewellery store I had come to know well, attracted by the quality of design skill and beauty of the finished product. A couple of colleagues bought pieces there to take home as gifts, along with their own memories of Damascus that would not fade.

In the house, the Hammam Minor bathroom was now distinctly cooler in the mornings, so the routine was to get up at first prayer call, speed up the stairs to turn on the Heath Robinson heating affair (because the two hours earlier switch "up" was definitely now needed), then bolt back to bed. The mornings were clear, cool and lovely, when it did not rain, the quiet broken only

by the occasional protesting shout from a child roused
early to prepare for school. The distinctive sound of
the street sweeper's broom and cart betrayed the fact
he was now starting in the dark to give us the clean
streets that made the Old City so attractive. There
were fewer people to greet on the way to the taxi, but
there were still some regulars—like the short, squat,
splay-footed man with the ready smile and the always
committed   greeting,   "*As-Salaam   Aleikum*",
accompanied by the traditional hand to the heart,
surely among the loveliest touches in the Arab and
Islamic way. "*W'aleikum As Salaam*", I would reply,
feeling acknowledged, and as if I really did belong
there.

When they were open, and many now opened a little
later, most shops had their doors drawn, gas burners
blasting away to both prepare coffee and warm the
interior. In that respect, the house was true to its
traditional design principles. Late in the day the main
rooms were cool, until a heater arrived to work for a
few days before burning out that power point. Into
evening, though, the rooms retained the original
temperature because of the thick walls, so to come in
from outside was to feel immediately warmer,
although the allegedly alpaca wool-lined, $15 dark
Bedouin coat was a welcome addition to the
wardrobe. The house was still a marvellous escape. It
was a delight to walk up the steps, open the battered
door and enter the dark but strangely welcoming
passageway, often about the time dusk prayers now
began because it was almost dark by 4.30 p.m.

Writing late into the night, the door to the courtyard
now closed unlike in the warmer weather, I had a
wonderful sense of being separated from but still
welcomed as part of a different world just outside. By

now one of the Brokar Boys had decided I needed to learn some Kurdish, so every time I went for a meal I learned some new words, most of which I never used elsewhere, knowing that the humour of my restaurant friends meant some dubious meanings might be involved. The Bakery Pilot, while Muslim, was concerned to ensure I would be with my family for Xmas. That was the Damascene way. The Antique Dealer made sure that tea was even more available than ever, because of the weather, and because soon I would leave. The Other Bakers still waved, as did all the friends I had come to recognise if not know well. There were a lot of them. I was the fortunate beneficiary of their friendly approaches, warm natures, and open minds. The Aramean still sat in his chair at the head of the *souk*, now rugged up warmly and cap pulled firmly down, ready to chat because tourists were few.

The house and its neighbourhood were now a home, and it would be difficult to leave.

LAST DAY

I woke just before the morning call and went up to switch on the water, then returned to bed listening to the long, lyrical sound of the prayers cut through and echo around the air and the city. I did some final packing, ate breakfast, then braved the bath house for the last time. It was cold, and would be even colder in a month.

It was strange and sad to be leaving a place that had become central to my life. Despite the leaks, peeling walls, odd lights and the coldness, it still had the "something" that had attracted me in the first place, a character. I looked around, walked through the door, down the steps, out into the alley. My splay-footed friend was behind the Azem Palace, walking along and reading the newspaper.

"As-Salaam Aleikum."

"W'aleikum As Salaam."

Hand on heart.

The Other Baker was firing up, and the usual sweet shops were already open. I liberated some money from the ATM, walked past the watchman seated by the jewellery *souk*, and the traffic cops enjoying an easy start to what would be a frantic day. The shopkeepers were brewing their first coffees.

At first I passed up the cab on offer, then thought better of it, luckily. It was battered, but driven by the man who had picked me up a couple of days earlier. I had now been here long enough to know people.

"Jamarik?" he asked.

How wonderful, he knows my destination without asking. I love this place.

"You go everyday there from here?"

Yes, but today is my last day, unfortunately

We took the through-Marjeh Square route, along by the flyover and past the early stalls, under the flyover where the Bedu men sold vegetables having slept there over night, back along then through Marjeh and out onto Shukri Al Quatli, past the "nice old man" traffic cop pointed out to me by an earlier taxi driver.

"You will return to Damascus?"

Oh yes.

We navigated Muwahiyeen Square that was not yet busy, but still involved dodging a truck and a couple of buses intent on their own journeys.

He was puffy faced, slightly balding, warmly and

respectably dressed.

"You leave tomorrow?"

We continued up the hill past the Opera House, then right along to the office.

Yes, sadly.

We pulled up, and I reached for the SYP 100, as I had done for him earlier.

"No, my friend, not today. You are welcome in Syria."

And he would take no money, even though his livelihood depended on it. Making a guest in Syria welcome was a priority, even though he would probably never see me again.

Later that day I left the house finally, circulating the Old City for the final time, farewelling old/new friends at the antique shop, the bakery and the Brokar. The Christmas trees and lights abounded in unlikely places, under a distinctly Arabian sky. It occurred to me that I knew the place both better and less than I imagined. Damascus had become familiar, but still offered much that was unknown and awaited further discovery.

When I left the keys with him, the agent told me the ban on foreigners purchasing property was now lifted, and I should act quickly.

There is a problem now, however: when is it likely that I might get to return?

LACUNA

One report had some of the earliest signs of Damascene discontent emerging in Hariqa, where I walked through every day on my way to and from work. Some police were said to have confronted and insulted a local man whose colleagues and neighbours resisted, and a struggle broke out. The stories then had small fires being lit on local roofs to see who else would light up in shared frustration. Several smoke clouds appeared. The struggle was on.

The fieldwork that informed these essays was barely complete when Syria engaged the so-called "Arab Awakening" of early 2011 that began in Tunisia then flowed into Egypt, Yemen and Libya before arriving in Deraa on Syria's southern border with Jordan, Lattakia on the Mediterranean coast, Homs in the centre, Hama slightly more north, other small country centres like Idlib, and Damascus' outer suburbs like Douma. The expression "cannot be independently verified" prefaced most news reports, as Syria blocked access to foreign journalists who necessarily reported from Beirut, Occupied Jerusalem and elsewhere, eliding Syrian events into those seen first-hand in Libya, particularly. Specialists pointed out that Syria was not Libya, localised conditions and people being quite different, but Syria was predominantly portrayed as another Egypt or Libya, the "push for democracy" an inexorable force among a people held down by allegedly the most repressive regional if not global dictator.

Initially, those non-contexted reports seemed just another example of journalistic license exercised to fill pressing deadlines. There was little or no real understanding conveyed of how Syria got to be as it was, how its system worked (or did not work), the real nature of the contemporary body politic, its complex sociocultural and economic makeup, its linked geographical challenges, or its role in the modern Arab world. In particular, the popular press seemed to have no idea that major world powers did not really want Syrian regime change, unlike their clear ambitions in Iraq, Libya and Egypt. Whatever their public position on and comments about President Bashar al-Assad and his military-backed Baath Party, in private Tel Aviv and Washington and the rest preferred him and the known over change and the unknown, one unspoken fear being that Muslim Brotherhood leadership or old guard Baathist rule might be even worse. A Bashar exit might even further empower Hezbollah and Hamas, turn Iran even more "rogue", embolden the Saudis, and perhaps destabilise Jordan as well as further threaten Israel.

Given that analysis from specialist sources, it seemed at first that the new "Syrian revolt", mirroring the mid-1920s one against French colonial power imposed in the post-World War I carve-up, would pass quickly because no-one really wanted it to continue—not major and regional powers, not the regime itself, and certainly not many of the people encountered over the preceding months. It seemed the regime would not have to become heavy-handed. Yes, there were recent concessions, such as the lifting of subsidy levels on essential elements like cooking oil because people reported times were tough. Friends and acquaintances said life was getting harder because costs were going up for food, energy and other staples. Some linked this to Bashar's attempts to move more towards a more market-oriented economy, itself an attempt to reconnect with the West following the isolation that dated from the millennium's turn and George Bush's placing Syria within the "Axis of Evil." Bashar had succeeded recently in getting France back on side. The project on which I worked was funded by the European Union, which was becoming prominent in Syrian aid and development initiatives. Perhaps oddly, then, it seemed no-one would want prolonged instability and unrest in Syria while some progress was being made.

It was true, however, that around the world human rights bodies and, more significantly, expatriate Syrian organisations pointed consistently to the autocratic nature of rule in the country. A "State of Emergency" had prevailed since 1963 following the turmoil that attended Syria's independence in 1946, the fleeting democratic period, the following rise of the military, the political union then dissolution with Egypt, the rise of the Baath Party then, in 1970, the strong-armed accession of Hafez al-Assad who ruled until 2000 when succeeded by second son Bashar, born two years after the State of Emergency was first initiated. Bashar and his generation knew nothing other than Hafez and the military powers. International watchers and expatriates had long complained about the large numbers of people "disappeared" into jails or worse, the severe restrictions placed upon the populace, and the lack of interaction with the rest of the world by a country and people long part of international trade and travel. Writers like Rafik Schami, especially in his sprawling novel *The Dark Side of Love,* depicted a vibrant yet repressed population that deserved better.

As the West's both imagined and real fear of "terrorism" arose, led by the American neocons, Syria's image darkened even further. The Axis of Evil tag placed it firmly in the "fundamentalist" or "Islamist" sphere, and for the USA that reputation escalated during the Iraq war when Syria certainly supported the insurgency cause, both directly and indirectly. In film and television, Syria was frequently the location of choice for "bad guys" and, so, the target of Special Forces activity. Syria's consequential rapprochement with Iran and the Shia further alienated the West, as did affiliated liaisons with Hassan Nasrallah and Hezbollah, along with Hamas and the rest of the "hardline" brigade arrayed against Israel.

When Bashar acceded to power following his father's 2000 death there was hope in the West, especially amongst liberals inside and outside the United States disturbed by the too-easy labels given Syria by Bush and his colleagues. Liberals, like me, wanted to see Syria as wronged and misunderstood, just another victim of crass American foreign policy of the kind that led to debacles in Vietnam, Grenada, Cuba and other places. That was especially so in the Middle East, where Palestine and its supporters were usually seen by liberals as being on the wrong side of the ledger from Israel and its principal supporter, the USA.

Now Syria might be able to show something different. Bashar was a Western-trained ophthalmologist married into a prominent expatriate family. He was not of the military line, even though he underwent training after his brother's 1994 death, in order to satisfy military bosses about his credentials. Initially, that promise seemed fulfilled as he initiated what became known as the "Damascus Spring," when political debate was encouraged, the press opened up, and more diverse political expression tolerated. That was short lived, the prevailing analysis being that Bashar was dragged back into line by the still-dominant hardliners from his father's generation. For the next few years he became a paradoxical figure for the West—someone who should be liberal, but headed a far from liberal regime, at least in the Western sense. Many observers thought he might not survive politically because he was not tough enough, but by the end of 2010 he appeared to be in control and indeed, reopening ties with the West.

Just a few short months later, however, by April 2011, he was widely portrayed around the world as the dictator of Damascus, the destroyer of democracy, the Syrian slaughterman spearheading an Alawite-led and minority groups'-supported regime that had the army fire on its countrymen, put snipers into buildings to shoot people coming from prayers, made no distinction between men, women and children as victims, and stubbornly ignored what the rest of the world thought was obvious: that Syrians wanted change.[83]

The initial rumblings in Deraa and Lattakia, then Baniyas and Homs led me to think that there were local origins and meanings for the disturbances, rather than a straightforward pro-democracy impetus of the kind seen elsewhere. Deraa had not been notably oppositionist (some said it had done well from the regime), so local issues must be at play, it seemed. Lattakia was as much connected to the Mediterranean as Syria, and had that particular population profile with its strong Alawite presence. Baniyas was the home of a former Vice-President defected to Europe. Homs was long the home to Syrian equivalents of Irish jokes. There were social traits as well: Deraa was a strong tribal centre, Lattakia that mix of Alawites, Sunni and Christians, for example. My interpretation was that this was as much opportunism as ideology, local grievance rather than national movement the driver. The early reports of violence and death were regrettable, but subject both to doubt and the benefit of doubt. There were no direct reports available by which to be guided, so perhaps the regime really was under pressure from the dark forces it mentioned regularly: criminal gangs, outside agencies and all the rest. Even the International Crisis Group and the excellent Peter Harling allowed that. Most informed international observers seemed to hold similar

---

[83]Theo Padnos, "The Cult: the Twisted, Terrifying Last Days of Assad's Syria", *The New Republic,* 4 October 2011 carries something of this line.

reservations, while the press projected boldly in other directions.

For those reasons I happily sent friends and relatives off to Damascus and Syria, telling them it was very safe, that the people were all friendly, that reports about the regime were drawn too starkly, that they would love it. They all went, and came back, and they did love it, though my sister-in-law and her husband reported things seemed quietly tense around the *souk* the Friday they left. There quickly appeared video footage of a noisy demonstration between pro- and anti-regime crowds in the tight confines of the Hamidiyeh, just along from the majestic Umayyad Mosque, and about two hundred metres from my house. My in-laws had left for home that very day.

My doubts, regrets and misgivings increased from that point. The reports might not have been "independently verified" but the plethora of mobile phone footage, blog listings, Facebook, Twitter and You Tube postings all combined to indicate that something bigger was happening. It could not all be fudged, faked, or falsified. That sense heightened as reports of deaths mounted into the hundreds, then into the thousands. There was still doubt about the validity of footage of tanks rolling into town, the apparent shootings, massive troop movements on the roads from Damascus to Homs, Lattakia and Aleppo, but the more of it appeared the more the doubts about that validity evaporated. There was a repressive movement going on, and I had local friends in the middle of it to further heighten my anxiety about what was happening.

The central problem for me lay in trying to understand why it was happening, because it made little if any sense. Bashar had lifted the State of Emergency, later than he might have done but it was at least lifted. That was a key demand from the West, and from those opposing the regime. (The latter would also point out that while the State of Emergency was lifted, strong state of emergency powers were simultaneously given to the Ministry of the Interior).Yet that was followed by more troop incursions, a very tough line in Deraa, shootings across the country and a consequent outburst of demonstrations in more towns, villages and cities countrywide. Lifting the emergency after forty eight years but increasing the repression seemed illogical.

So, too, did the constant effort to block journalistic reporting while the range of unofficial "new technology" and social media versions mushroomed. I was getting minute-by-minute Twitter reports from the scene, yet the regime seemed to think that barring journalists would be productive. Regime spokespersons were unable to provide coherent and/or believable accounts of what was occurring. The Prime Minister and his government were replaced but that seemed scarcely to affect developments, and reports of violence continued to emanate from the country. Some reports had the Iranians aiding and abetting the regime in trying to quell the uprising and that, of course, signalled to the West just how "fundamentalist" this was—Iran was the current bogeyman, any crony guilty by association.

By now the inescapable conclusion was that thousands of people across Syria were willing to assemble on Fridays for prayers, then go out on an anti-regime demonstration knowing they stood a very good chance of being arrested without trial, or even shot. For a very long time, Syrians had known the reputation of the jails, especially those run by the security services, for being brutal and unforgiving. The fears may have eased in recent years but they still lurked, and when the regime now went into full repressive mode, few had any illusions about what might await inside those jail gates. Yet people were still risking their lives. That had to mean something, so maybe this was a powerful grass roots movement from a population that now desired what it saw around the world. I had, after all, met people who, after prolonged introductions and discussion, had quietly suggested that "a little bit more democracy" would be a good thing in Syria. They were not totally cut off from the world, and could see other examples of how a people and a country might live.

By necessity and in its essentials, this was the message being brought by those journalists perched on the borders and trying to peer in: "While the situation in Syria tonight remains unclear, it is certain that pro-democracy forces are defying the repressive regime that is retaliating with brutal force to maintain the control it has held for almost fifty years". Social scientists are trained to repel that sort of blanket assumption and declaration, at least until the mass of evidence has been assembled, analysed and ordered into a coherent story that balances all points of view. If journalists run the risk of generalisation in order to produce a story and a headline, social scientists run another one—they generally grow fond of the places in which they spend time, and of the people with whom they share that time. My central problem here was having to balance the heart and the head. A younger Australian academic specialist on the region told me that he had a "very soft spot" for Syria, and I knew immediately what he meant. For a very, very long time visitors to Syria have fallen in love with the place, and I was just among the latest. In part it is the landscape, but mostly it is the people, and the warmth with which they welcome visitors. That was my experience a few short months, even weeks earlier, now many of those people were on the streets risking their lives and being shot at by fellow countrymen. That made no sense.

Then came the shelling of Homs and the subsequent siege of Bab Amr that saw BBC correspondent Marie Colvin lose her life. Bab Amr lies in the quadrant of the city containing Al Baath University where I spent considerable time working with several senior academics and officials, helping lay out a plan for the institution's future growth. It is a large university with over eighty thousand students and occupies a huge area crammed with modern buildings and equipment. Its leaders were determined to make progress through planning and program reform, and the committee members charged with delivering it were professional, friendly, well informed, and funny. They were a delightful group with which to work. It was a modern campus, as were others in Syria. There were *hijabs* in evidence but outnumbered by designer jeans, and that went for staff as well as students. One committee member had a particularly fine line in self-deprecation, describing on one occasion what she considered to be the mismatch between her jeans and her hip size. That was one of those moments when the blanket assessments of and assumptions about "Islam" were well and truly tested.

Now, though, these fine people were in a city under fire. So were their near neighbours a few kilometres away in Hama. The town of the water wheels will be forever infamous as the site for the single greatest act of repression carried out by Hafez al-Assad, Bashar's father. Up to 20,000 were thought to have perished in

1982 when Hafez sent in the army to crush the Muslim Brotherhood. Yet here it was happening again. These two actions in Bab Amr and Hama were the turning point, and the scenes of later mass deaths in nearby towns like Houla and Tramseh that matched those in Deraa and elsewhere, simply added to the point.

It was from about then, for example, that balanced websites like *Syria Comment* began to see the end of the Assad regime. SC is run by a leading American scholar of Syria, Joshua Landis, and, in general, up until Bab Amr, had maintained a critical and balanced view rather than being a bland relayer of the standard Western position. Some polarised critics thought the balance was actually an apologia for Bashar and the regime that emanated from Landis' marriage to an Alawite. In reality, Joshua Landis was driven by scholarly detachment and excellent information, and the frankness of his views saw the previously open door to the Syrian embassy in Washington D.C. closed to him. From there on in, he began foreseeing the end of the regime.

That proved to be a slow end, though. Every now and then there would be a flurry, such as the Twitter eruption one weekend in mid-2012 when reports had Bashar fled from Syria and his leading advisors all poisoned. Meanwhile, the car bombs began to go off in Damascus, mainly outside some of the dreaded security centres and military barracks. However, even some of the mainstream press now began to pick up some of the more subtle nuances. In a curiously historical moment, for example, the regime army was reported to have shelled Islamists either in or very near Krak des Chevaliers, the great Crusader castle. Those Islamists were said to be from anywhere but

Syria: Saudi, Iraq, even Afghanistan. By now, the UN was accepting the facts as reported by respected agencies such as the International Crisis Group, that this was not a straight black *v* white contest. Rather, it involved several shades of gray *v* each other. That was compounded by divisions within the so-called Syrian National Council, run largely from Paris, within which a bewildering number of factions ran an equally bewildering number of agendas.

Both wiser after Iraq and aware of just how complex this was given Syria's geographic and strategic position, the Americans moved a lot slower than desired by more impatient international commentators anxious for "progress" after the great changes in, say, Egypt, even if the subsequent rise of the Muslim Brotherhood to positions of power there tempered the euphoria. The United Nations' efforts mirrored the enormous difficulties. Special envoy Kofi Annan flew into Damascus briefly, then came away with his plan. That was scuppered by a veto lodged by both Russia and China. The former had a long history in Syria and of backing the Assads. Regionally, Syria was Russia's only remaining ally, really. Its naval base in Tartous and its thousands of citizens married to Syrians reflected that. The Chinese had extensive business interests, including a large share of the Syrian oilfields which though dwindling, were still important. The Annan Plan gave way to Annan Plan Mk II, and then to the Annan Capitulation as he walked away from the role. effectively admitting defeat. There was talk the Russians were no longer adamant Assad had to be a non-negotiable part of any settlement. The Turks continued to press on the northern border, especially after one of their fighter jets was shot down by Syrian forces. In the south the Saudis, without any apparent sense of irony given the state of their own body politic, lectured all in sundry that Syria had to become more democratic.

While I was watching this and despairing several thousand kilometres away, my Syrian friends and colleagues were living through it and all the talk of "Balkanisation" as it appeared different groups would come to control different areas of the county. Those with whom I was able to stay in contact reported confusion, bewilderment, concern, hope and confidence, all at once. Many of them were progressives who I knew would be caught up in developments ("cooking in the kitchen", as one described it euphemistically), and that added to my anxiety. Emails and phone calls were sporadic and necessarily non-informative because, by now, who knew who was listening. All those feelings intensified as the daily conflicts crept closer to Damascus itself. Areas that I knew well were seeing demonstrations, police action and even more serious developments such as unexplained gun fire, explosions and even armed conflict if some reports were to be believed. In one phone call in mid-July 2012, a friend reported helicopter gunships overhead in Shalaan where all the project consultants had lived. This was all unimaginable.

By mid-2012 it seemed that Bashar al-Assad would fall, but when was unforeseeable. In the meantime, the city that I had come to love was changing dramatically. The house in Damascus was still there, I knew (I could see it on Google Earth), but would the city of which it was part ever be the same again?

BIBLIOGRAPHY

This is a selection of works from among the larger numbers of sources I consulted while in Damascus and while writing this book.

A Handbook of Syria (Including Palestine) (London, Naval Intelligence Department, 1919)

Asad, Abukhalil: "Syria and the Shiites: Al-Asad's Policy in Lebanon", *Third World Quarterly*, 12, 2 (1990)

Ajami, Fouad: *The Syrian Rebellion* (Washington DC, Hoover, 2012)

Akkach, Samer: "Leisure Gardens, Secular Habits: the Culture of Recreation in Ottoman Damascus", *Journal of the Faculty of Architecture,* Middle Eastern Technical University, No 1, 2010

Allen, Brooke: *The Other Side of the Mirror: an American Travels Through Syria* (Philadelphia, Paul Dry, 2011)

An Oriental Student [A. A. Paton], *The Modern Syrians* (London, Longman Green, 1844)

Atta, Dale van: "The World's Most Dangerous Leaders", *Readers Digest* (July 2007)

Azad, Khaled: "Residential Architecture in Islamic Civilization", *Journal Islam Today,* No. 25, 2008

Baedeker, Karl: *Palestine and Syria* (Leipzig, Baedeker, 1906)

Bell, Gertrude, *The Desert and the Sown* (London, Virago, 1985 edn)

Birmingham, John: *He Died With a Falafel in His Hand* (Sydney, Duffy & Snellgrove, 1994)

Boggs, Richard: *Hammaming in the Sham: a Journey Through the Turkish Baths of Damascus, Aleppo and Beyond* (London, Garnet, 2012 edn)

Buck, Joan Juliet: "Asma al-Assad: a Rose in the Desert", *Vogue* (March 2011), also at www.seraphicpress.com

Transcript of interview with Joan Juliet Buck on national Public Radio, www.npr.org/2012/4/20/151058724/a-look-into-the-world-of-syria's-first-lady

Burckhardt, John Lewis: *Travels in Syria and the Holy Land* (Cambridge, CUP, 2011 edn)

Burns, Ross: *Damascus: a History* (London, Routledge, 2007)

Chamberlain, Michael: *Knowledge and Social Practice in Medieval Damascus, 1190-1350* (Cambridge, CUP, 1994)

Chandrasekaran, Rajiv: *Little America: the War Within the War for Afghanistan* (New York, Knopf, 2012)

Chandrasekaran, Rajiv: *Imperial Life in the Emerald*

City: Inside Iraq's Green Zone (New York, Knopf, 2006)

Cook, Thomas: *Cook's Tourists' Handbook for Palestine and Syria* (London, Cook, 1876)

Dam, Nikolas van: *The Struggle for Power in Syria: Politics and Society Under Asad and the Baath Party* (London, Tauris, 2011 edn)

Darke, Diana: *Syria.* St Peters, Bradt Travel Guides, 2010 edn

Darley, Tom: *With The Ninth Light Horse in the Great War.* Adelaide, 1926

Debes, Ayman: *Damascus For You.* (Damascus, Trans-Orient, 2009)

Drysdale, Alasdair: "The Syrian Political Elite, 1966-1976: a Spatial and Social Analysis, *Middle Eastern Studies,* 17, 1 (1981)

El-Shorbagy, Abdel-Moniem: "Traditional Islamic-Arab House: Vocabulary and Syntax", *International Journal of Civil and Environmental Engineering,* 10, 4

Finkel, David: *The Good Soldiers* (New York, Farrer Strauss Giroux, 2009)

Follett, Ken: *World Without End* (London, Pan, 2007)

Geertz, Clifford: *Local Knowledge: Further Essays in Interpretive Anthropology* (New York, Basic, 1985)

Gibb, H.A.R.: *The Life of Saladin* (London, Saqi, 2006 edn)

Grant, C.P.: *The Syrian Desert: Caravans, Travel and Exploration* (London, Black, 1937)

Grehan, James: *Everyday Life & Consumer Culture in*

18th-Century Damascus (Seattle, University of Washington Press, 2007)

Harling, Peter: "Beyond the Fall of the Syrian Regime", *Middle East Research and Information Project,* 24 February 2012, www.merip.org/mero/mero022412

Halasa, Malu and Rana Salan: *The Secret Life of Syrian Lingerie* (San Francisco, Chronicle, 2008)

Hooker, Joseph Dalton: *Journal of Excursion to Syria and Palestine, 1860* (Beirut, Kutub, 2009 edn)

Howard, Deborah: "Death in Damascus: Venetians in Syria in the Mid-Fifteenth century", *Muqarnas*, 20 (2003)

Human Rights Watch: *Torture Archipelago* (2012) *"We've Never Seen Such Horrors"* (2011)

Huntington, Samuel P.: *The Clash of Civilizations and the Remaking of World Order* (New York, Simon & Schuster, 1996)

International Crisis Group: "Uncharted Waters: Thinking Through Syria's Dynamics", *Middle East Briefing,* No. 31, 24 November 2011

"Syria's Phase of Radicalisation", *Middle East Briefing,* No. 33, 10 April 2012

Keriaky, Rama Elias (ed.): *Damascus: History and Ruins* (Damascus, Private, 2006)

Khatib, Line: *Islamic Revivalism in Syria: the Rise and Fall of Ba'athist Secularism* (New York, Routledge, 2011)

Khoury, Philip S.: "Syrian Urban Politics in Transition: the Quarters of Damascus During the French Mandate", *International Journal of Middle*

East Studies, 16, 4 (November, 1984)

Kociejowski, Marius: *The Pigeon Wars of Damascus* (Emeryville Ontario, Biblioasis, 2011)

Landis, Joshua: "The Syrian Uprising of 2011: Why the Assad Regime is Likely to Survive to 2013", *Middle East Policy,* XIX, 1 (2012)

Lawrence, T.E.: *Seven Pillars of Wisdom* (London, Cape, 1935)

T.E. Lawrence: *Crusader Castles* (New York, Oxford University Press, 1989 edn)

Lesch, David: *The New Lion of Damascus: Bashar al-Assad and Modern Syria* (London, Yale University Press, 2005)

Lister, W.B.C.: *A Bibliography of Murray's Handbooks for Travellers* (Dereham, Dereham Books, 1993)

Mackintosh, Mrs: *Damascus and its People: Sketches of Modern Life in Syria* (London, Seeley, Jackson, Halliday, 1883)

Maalouf, Amin: *The Crusades Through Arab Eyes* (New York, Schocken, 1987)

Mallowan, Agatha Christie: *Come, Tell Me How You Live* (London, Collins, 1975 edn)

Masterman, E.W.G.: "The Water Supply of Damascus", *The Biblical World*, 21, 2 (February, 1903)

Mathews, Annie-Christine Daskalakis: "A Room of 'Splendour and Generosity' from Ottoman Damascus", *Metropolitan Museum Journal*, 32 (1997)

Melki, James A.: "Syria and State Department, 1927-1947", *Middle Eastern Studies,* 33, 1 (1997)

Moubayed, Sami M.: *The Politics of Damascus, 1920-1946* (Damascus, Tlass, 1999)

Muir, Jim: "Bashar al-Assad's Tightening Grip On Syria Ten Years On", *BBC News,* http://www.bbc.co.uk/news/world-middle-east-10674093

Murray, George: *A Handbook for Traveller's in Syria and Palestine* (London, Murray, 1858) 2 vols

Naval Staff Intelligence: *A Handbook of Syria* (London, HMSO, 1919)

Oxfam: *21st Century Aid: Recognising Success and Tackling Failure.* Oxfam Briefing Paper 137, 28 April 2010. (London, Oxfam, 2010)

Padnos, Theo: "The Cult: the Twisted, Terrifying Last Days of Assad's Syria, *The New Republic,* 4 October 2011

Pickthall, Marmaduke: *Oriental Encounters Palestine and Syria, 1894-6* (New York, Tredition, 2012 edn)

Pope, Hugh: *Dining With Al-Qaeda* (New York, St Martin's, 2010)

Porter, Josias: *Five Years in Damascus* (London, Murray, 1870)

Qalanisi, Ibn Al: *The Damascus Chronicle of the Crusades* trans H.A.R. Gibb (New York, Dover, 2002 edn)

Rabinovich, Itamar: *The View from Damascus: State, Political Community and Foreign relations in Twentieth Century Syria* (London, Vallentine Mitchell, 2008)

Reilly, James A.: "From Workshops to Sweatshops: Damascus Textiles and the World-Economy in the

Last Ottoman Century", *Review*, XVI, 2 (Spring, 1993)

Rice, G.W. (ed.): *Muslims & Mongols: Essays on Medieval Asia by J.J. Saunders* (Christchurch, University of Canterbury, 1977)

Richardson, Robert:*Travels Along the Mediterranean* (London, Cadell Blackwood, 1822), 2 vols

Runciman, Steven: *A History of the Crusades* (Cambridge, Cambridge University Press, 1987 edn), 3 vols

Said, Edward: *Orientalism* (Harmondsworth, Penguin, 1978)

Sakbani, Michael: "The Revolutions of the Arab Spring: are Democracy, Development and Modernity at the Gates?", *Contemporary Arab Affairs,* 4, 2 (2011)

Salvador, Ludwig: *The Caravan Route Between Egypt and Syria* (London, Chatto &Windus, 1881)

Schami, Rafik and Marie Fadel: *Damascus: Taste of a City.* (London, Haus, 2005 edn)

Schami, Rafik: *The Dark Side of Love* (New York, Interlink, 2009)

Seale, Patrick: "Is This the End of the Assad Dynasty?" *Viewpoint,* Online Issue 109, 13 July 2012, www.viewpointonline.net/is-this-the-end-of-the-assad-dynasty-html

Asad: the Struggle for the Middle East (Los Angeles, University of California Press, 1990)

Shaaban, Bouthaina: "The Hidden History of Arab Feminism", *MS Magazine,* (May-June 1993)

Shaery-Eisenlohr, Roschanack: "From Subjects to

Citizens? Civil Society and the Internet in Syria", *Middle East Critique,* 20, 2 (2011)

Shannon, Jonathan Holt: *Among the Jasmine Trees: Music and Modernity in Modern Syria* (Middletown, Wesleyan University Press, 2006)

Sharp, Jeremy: *Unrest in Syria and U.S. Sanctions Against the Asad Regime* (Washington DC, Congressional Research Service, 2011

Sharp, Jeremy: *Syria: Issues for the 112th Congress and Background on U.S. Sanctions* (Washington DC, Congressional Research Service, 2010)

Shoup, John A: *Culture and Customs of Syria* (Westport, Greenwood, 2006)

Simonsen, Jorgen Baek (ed.): *Youth and Culture in the Contemporary Middle East* (Aarhus, Aarhus University Press, 2005)

Smith, Eli: "A Treatise on Arab Musci, Chiefly From a Work by Mikhail Meshakah of Damascus", *Journal of the American Oriental Society*, 1, 3 (1847)

Starr, Stephen: *Revolt in Syria: Eye-Witness to the Uprising* (London, Hurst, 2012)

Sunayama, Sonoko: "Bashar al-Asad's Syria: Will the Son Shine?", *Mediterranean Politics,* 6, 2 (2011)

Tabler, Andrew: *In the Lion's Den: an Eyewitness Account of Washington's Battle With Syria* (New York, Lawrence Hill, 2011)

Teape, Rev. W.M: *In Tents & On Horseback Through The Holy Land* (Stockton, Harrison, nd)

Tergeman, Siham: *Daughter of Damascus* (Austin, University of Texas, 1994)

Thubron, Colin: *Mirror To Damascus.* (London,

Vintage, 1996 edn)

Tobin, Catherine: *Shadows of the East* (London, Longman, 1855)

Twain, Mark: *The Innocents Abroad* (New York, Library of America, 1984 edn)

Vincent, Andrew: "Western Travellers to Southern Syria and the Hawran in the Nineteenth Century: a Changing Perspective", *Asian Affairs,* 24, 2 (1993)

Zisser, Eyal: "Does Bashar al-Assad Rule Syria?", *Middle East Quarterly,* X, 1 (Winter, 2003)

Brian Stoddart is an Emeritus Professor of La Trobe University in Melbourne, Australia where he served as President and Vice-Chancellor. Before that he held Vice-President positions in other Australian universities, as well as posts in Canada, Malaysia and Barbados. Trained as a social historian, he took his first two degrees at the University of Canterbury in New Zealand, and a PhD at the University of Western Australia where he worked on nationalist politics in India. He is an internationally acknowledged authority on sports culture, with his *Saturday Afternoon Fever: Sport in the Australian Culture* still considered one of the definitive accounts. Among his most recent books are *A People's Collector: Arthur Galletti;* and *India and Australia: Bridging Different Worlds.*

In addition to his academic work, Brian Stoddart has been a long-time contributor to the Australian and international media, especially in print and radio. He has extended that contribution into social media, writing regularly now for websites such as *Global Policy Journal, South Asia Masala* and *The Conversation,* as well as his own blog at www.professorbrianstoddart.com

Brian Stoddart now works as an international higher education reform consultant in countries such as Lao PDR, Cambodia, Jordan and Syria. It was during his time in Syria that he was inspired to write this book. He is now also a member of the Syrian Studies Association.

www.ingramcontent.com/pod-product-compliance
Lightning Source LLC
Chambersburg PA
CBHW020148090426
42734CB00008B/739